The Best of the Sligo Weekender

Volume One

The Best of the Sligo Weekender: Volume One

Edited by Peter Henry

Published in 2020 by
Sligo Weekender
Innisfree House
44–45 High Street
Sligo F91 WC79

ISBN 978-1-5272-7784-7

PREFACE

IT IS A PLEASURE TO PRESENT *THE BEST OF THE Sligo Weekender: Volume One*. As the title says, it is a compilation of some of the fantastic writing that has featured in Sligo's local newspaper in recent years. The *Sligo Weekender* always focuses on the people of this county, and consequently most of the chapters in this book are about the remarkable men and women who make the North West such a special place.

The most difficult thing about putting together this book was choosing what to include. Many wonderful pieces of writing have been published in the *Sligo Weekender* since its foundation in 1983, and of course only a few could be included. However, I have subtitled this book *Volume One*, and so look forward to further publications containing even more great content from Sligo's local newspaper.

Credit must go to all those who made this volume possible: the *Sligo Weekender*'s director Dorothy Crean; staff members Aoife McGowan, Daniel Battle, Kathryn Doherty, Jonathan Costello, Una Brennan, John Bromley, Liam Maloney, Alan Finn and Gerry Kilgannon; our contributors, especially Gerry McLaughlin, Michael McGurrin and Brian McHugh; our stockists and advertisers; and everyone interviewed in this book.

We are delighted to make a contribution from the proceeds of this book to the important suicide prevention work of North West STOP.

PETER HENRY, EDITOR
NOVEMBER 2020

CONTENTS

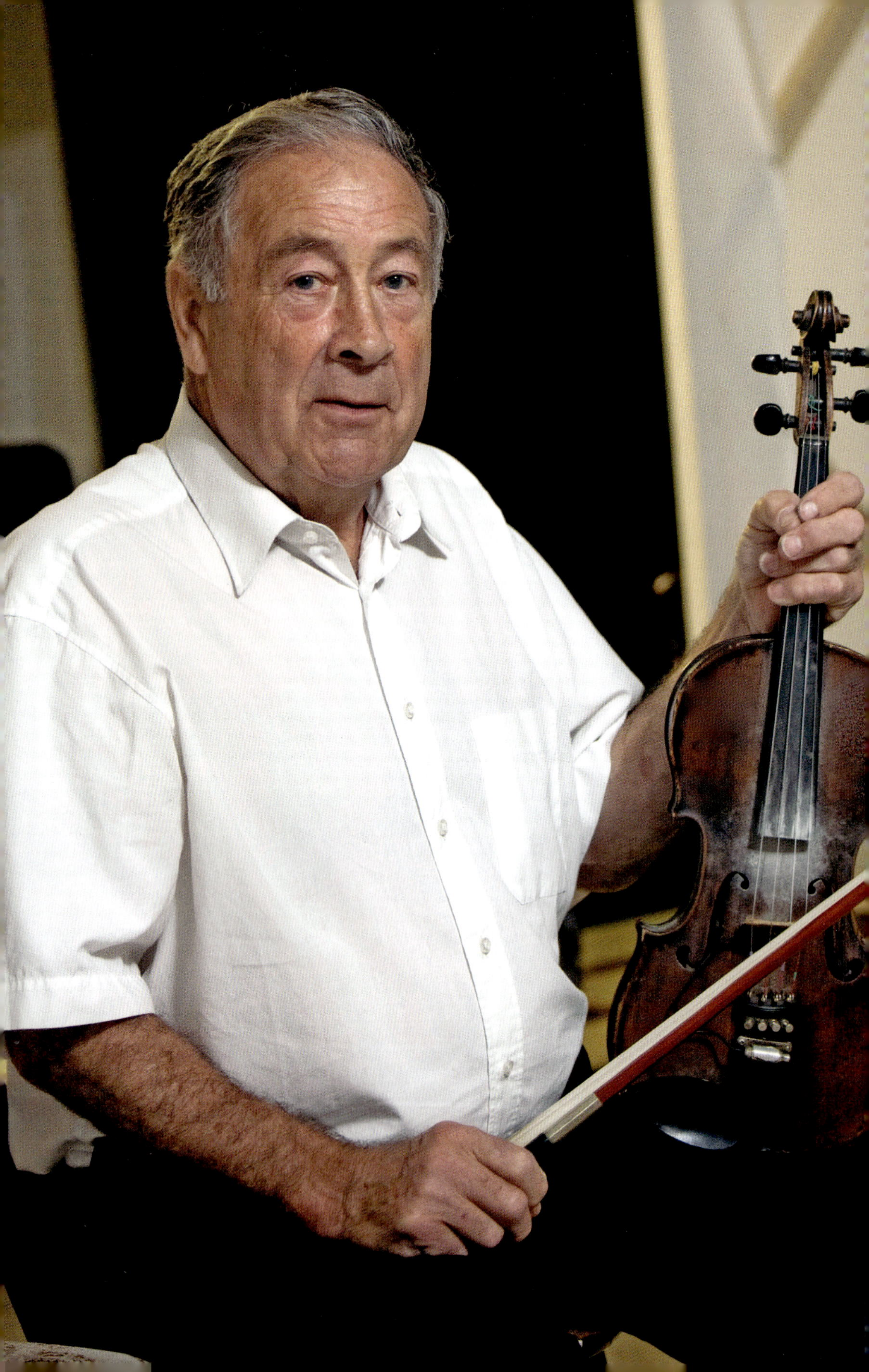

GERRY DONAGHER

Gerry McLaughlin spoke to ex-Easkey Vocational School principal Gerry Donagher, 84, about the great passions of his varied and fascinating life

PUBLISHED ON APRIL 16, 2020

'TEACH YOUR CHILDREN'. CROSBY, Stills, Nash and Young sang that paean to all those truly great teachers in the 1970s.

And 84-year-old Gerry Donagher, genial ex-principal of Easkey Vocational School, was certainly one of those for around 40 years in those flat green fields of west Sligo on the edge of the broad Atlantic.

Gerry cherished and nurtured all of his children equally, and he fed them on his dreams of all that is right and kind and good, with a smile and a quip to make them feel happy, wanted and valued. He made them feel that they had something to offer to make this world a better place.

As Gerry told this former teacher: "Education is great for imparting knowledge and helping people to become better in

LEFT: GERRY DONAGHER WITH HIS FIDDLE

various ways, but children may not remember much of what you taught them. "But they will remember how you made them feel at a particular time and they will remember especially how you made them feel about themselves."

Speaking to some of his many grateful past pupils it is clear that Gerry excelled at making them feel good about themselves, and that is a rare gift indeed. Gerry was also very determined to make sure that every child in his school reached his or her potential. He very quickly identified different talents in different children and encouraged them to reach their goals.

The Latin word for teaching is *educo*, which means to foster or to draw out, and Gerry has done that for decades – a renaissance man, a duine ildánach as the ancient Irish would say, and a man who uses both sides of the brain.

Gerry has been gifted with a sunny spirit, a kind heart, a forensic memory and a love for music. He was also a builder, a plumber, a mechanic, a botanist, a historian and a bit of a stand-up comedian, a man who loves to entertain his fellow man and woman, and a man who loves to be entertained, with a great zest for new things.

Apart from teaching he was a sage community leader, getting involved in the Civil Defence, compiling a book about the schools in and around Easkey, helping to stop the demolition of Easkey Castle in the 1980s, planting trees in an area that was not known for much botany, playing the harmonica (for which he won an All-Ireland medal) and the fiddle with his wife Bridie

Kilcullen, son Kenny and daughter Aileen in and around Easkey and lovingly restoring a Model T Ford that was used in a bank raid during the War of Independence.

Gerry, his wife Bridie, Aileen and Kenneth brought out a tape of Irish tunes in 1990 along with some friends.

The family also played in concerts and in pubs around the area . Gerry was a founder member of the Easkey branch of Comhaltas Ceoltóirí Éireann in the mid-1970s and he and his wife Bridie promoted traditional Irish music over the next decade and helped to bring three fleadhs to Easkey.

His versatility and natural social graces meant that he was able to bring many different types of personalities with him, a vital quality in any leader, but there was not an egotistical or domineering bone in his body.

He also had and has the ability to defuse a tense situation in a heartbeat, and he takes neither himself or his many talents too seriously.

And his eloquent and energetic spirit lives on his children, John, Kenneth and the indefatigable Aileen, who is principal of the Owenbeg National School and the accurate keeper of the Donagher family history.

Gerry was born in Kilmactranny in November 1935 on the Sligo-Roscommon border and he went to school there for a while before switching to Highwood.

Gerry also remembers some of the effect of the Second World War on his early youth.

He said: "I remember when they announced the start of the Second World War as we went to a neigbbour's house, the Martins', to listen to the news. That was in 1939 and I was only four.

"And I remember the planes flying high over Kilmactranny and I remember the ration books which everyone had in those days."

It was there he came under the influence of the wonderful Betty Hughes, grandmother of current Sligo Senior Gaelic football star Pat Hughes from Geevagh. Betty is still alive today at the great age of 94 and lives in her own home.

Betty put Gerry in for a scholarship to go to Summerhill College in Sligo, and he was accepted. Gerry went as a boarder and was there from 1949 to 1954, when he met "some wonderful people".

And Gerry had great admiration for a teacher called Fr Tom Foy, who used to write poetry and got Gerry playing the harmonica. Fr Tom was a big influence on his life.

And he was one of the organisers with Louis MacSharry and Andy McGloin of a school reunion in 2004 for their 45th anniversary.

Gerry went to agricultural college in Monaghan for a year in 1955, and spent two years in UCC studying science before coming to his first teaching post in Easkey in 1957. He stayed there until 1997, spending many years as principal in a job he said he "truly loved".

Gerry said: "I taught rural science and I was big into botany and planting things, but they were not into planting much around there so they got into a bit of a gunk when they saw me planting trees."

In Gerry's early years, he and two young gardaí, Cyril McGovern and the late John McNamara, stayed in digs with a Mrs Sweeney in Easkey.

"It was great craic. I remember coming home from Ballina around 3am. We spied these two asses and we got up on them and were riding them around the road.

"I also used to read tea leaves and I told John McNamara that he would be carrying a woman out of the dance tonight. John said, I will be carrying no woman out of the dance tonight? Sure amn't I on duty tonight?

"But the dance was in the Seafield Hotel and didn't a woman collapse at the dance and John was on duty and he ended up carrying her outside."

Gerry met the love of his life, Bridie Kilcullen, through her sister Kay Kilcullen, who is now Kay Treacy, who was teaching in Easkey.

"Kay brought me up to Bridie's house in Seaview outside Enniscrone. They owned the Seaweed Baths in Enniscrone and she was very musical, which also helped."

Gerry and Bridie were married on April 1, 1964. He became school principal at Easkey Vocational School in the early 1970s.

His eloquent daughter Aileen, who was born in 1966, has fond memories of her days at school with her father Gerry and his forward thinking ways.

Aileen said: "I was nearly reared in that school and I remember Leaving Certs playing with us and chatting with us and it was lovely.

"If there was a school concert the bigger ones used to be minding us. It was very much part of our lives and we were always there, and I started as a pupil in 1978. I remember that all of the teachers had a real love of their subjects a real passion and they also were very keen for us to succeed.

There was a great atmosphere at the school and dad believed in a mixed education and he was well ahead of his time.

"He believed in multiple intelligence. Intelligence cannot be measured by being a good reader or a good at numeracy. If you measure different people there are people who have high intelligence in sports, music and the traditional system would only have people who were good at reading or literacy or numeracy.

"That system tended to look down on these other very valid forms of intelligence. Dad believed that both sides of your brain needed to be developed so both the practical and the intellectual should be developed side by side.

"I had a great mix of practical and academic subjects and it was very educational in the true sense of the word."

Gerry was also involved in bringing a factory to Easkey in the early 1980s, Easkey Fashions, and it created employment.

He was instrumental in blocking a nuclear power plant in Easkey, which took a bit of courage as much of the public opinion was that this would bring big employment to the area. Gerry said: "Most of the people thought it was the best thing since the sliced pan and there were not many objectors and we were not popular.

"Within weeks it was switched to Carnsore Point in Wexford. It was rejected there too, which in hindsight was a good thing."

As a teacher he was very concerned that children should be happy at school and no "child should ever leave the school feeling like nothing".

Gerry said: "As a teacher you should seek their strengths, help them to recognise and realise those strengths and make sure they are respected and valued for their strengths and never patronise them.

"That is the most important thing, that a person feels worthwhile and respected and valued. We are valuable in this life."

Gerry retired in 1997 after 40 years, eight years after his beloved wife Bridie passed away in 1989. "I had intended retiring early so Bridie and I could go traveling around the world but sadly she died and that did not happen. I stayed on and I retired in 1997," he said.

Gerry got involved in the Civil Defence in the 1990s to give him an interest after his wife passed away.

He said: "I did that for quite a few years and my children used to say I was in Dad's Army. It was a great outlet and I met some interesting people from different walks of life."

Elsewhere, Gerry brought out a book about the history of the schools in the area in the mid-2000s called 'From Slate To Mouse'.

Aileen did the typing and Gerry compiled it.

He said: "I covered seven schools – they were Easkey, Rathlee, Clooneenmore, Owenbeg, Killeenduff, Fortland and Easkey Vocational. That was an interesting project to be involved in."

Musically, Gerry was an All-Ireland champion in the harmonica on two occasions and he brought out a CD in 2010 of various tunes.

He said: "It was a double CD as I played some traditional airs and some more classical airs on the harmonica.

"It was pretty varied, and we have traditional stuff and some Stephen Foster-type stuff."

Gerry was always a great man for the underdog or the disadvantaged and nothing gave him greater pleasure than seeing them doing well and getting successful careers.

Gerry said: "If I spotted a pupil who was good at something I would try and get them on the path that would lead them to being what they were capable of.

"This was very important if the child was not being encouraged at home or there was no great tradition of learning or *meas* for learning in that house. Sometimes there was little or no history of education in the homes and there was no aspiration to go on beyond school.

"Some pupils became teachers because of my encouragement, and that is very satisfying. Others became great tradesmen and others great farmers and one or two botanists – and it all depended on what they were good at.

"It was a question of building their confidence. Some of those pupils come back to see me. Some pupils lacked confidence and did not see any worth even in the things they were good at and it was my job and joy to make sure they realised their talents. The feeling that gives you as a teacher and a person is priceless.

"I loved teaching and I did not give too much homework. For example, in maths, I would show them how to do two questions in class and that would be their homework and if they did that correctly that was grand.

"I knew I had taught it well and it made the pupils feel great, which was very important, and I never believed in piling on homework that occupied a pupil for two hours. Homework had to have a purpose.I also believed in life skills designed to help with self-worth".

Gerry also had a great interest in history, reads avidly and recorded some of the stories he got from the older people around Easkey when he came there first in the late 1950s.

"They are all on bits of paper if I could find them, and they are in a folder somewhere. I also wrote some pieces on the Easkey Castle."

For good measure, Gerry was also involved in a successful campaign to save the historic monument, which was built for the O'Dowd chieftains of Tireragh, from destruction in the early 1980s.

ABOVE: KENNY, GERRY, JOHN, BRIDIE AND AILEEN DONAGHER

"There was an article in the Sligo Champion saying that the county council planned to knock down the castle because it was an environmental and health hazard.

"People got energised and we started a Save the Castle committee and we had fundraisers and music sessions in different pubs to collect money for the campaign.

"We collected money at the time, and we got the castle pointed to save it. It was saved from crumbling and it was a great community effort.

"I thought it would be made into a lovely visitor centre but when it was checked in the Deeds Office in Dublin, we found it was owned by commonage, which proved to be too complicated and we had to give up on that."

Gerry also has a famous Model T Ford which was originally used in a bank raid in Sligo by republicans during the War of Independence, which he acquired outside Enniscrone in the 1960s.

He said: "It was all falling apart, and I managed to get the engine together, but the body was not great. I used to have the children sitting on bags of hay on the back. It took a lot of work, but it was worth it in the end and I painted it a nice green colour."

Gerry went for drives in the car and took a number of guests for a spin in this lovely vehicle, including this correspondent back in 2002.

Gerry said: "It was a real labour of love for me over many years and was always interested in mechanics as well. I was friendly with the late Eugene Gillespie in Sligo, who was a great vintage car enthusiast."

Today the Model T is in a yard owned by Gerry's energetic son-in-law and well-known undertaker David McGowan.

Gerry has also had a powerful interest in plants.

He said: "I was told by quite a few people back in the early 1960s that I was wasting my time and that no trees grew in Easkey. I loved plants and I planted the type of plants that can survive the worst of the winter winds. I planted them, and they are all around the house today. I brought seeds from all over the world from my travels and I even grew grapes."

His daughter Aileen says the family are very proud of their eclectic father. Aileen said: "He is a great man and a man of deep vision and ahead of his time.

"Another of his hobbies was photography and he had a unique way of developing photographs. He used to go into the wardrobe to use it as a dark room for developing the negatives.

"We were told not to go near the wardrobe as daddy was in the wardrobe. Back then it was black and white and then you could pigment them.

"After that it was videoing and he was always ahead of his time but sadly the laptops and computers did not have the same effect on him.

"He also built an extension to the family home. When researching insulation for the floor we went around collecting bottes from the pubs because they were good for insulation – they trapped pockets of air.

"There was a wedge put into the rafters to make sure there was a slope on the roof and I remember us all hammering nails into it. And he did all the plumbing in the house and he fixed anything that needed fixing."

Meanwhile, Gerry was also fond of travelling. He said: "I went to Australia in the late 1990s. Fiji too.

"I wanted to see the world and I read a lot of history and looked up different people and I have a lot of stuff written down, their history and their memories. It is very educational and really opens your eyes."

Gerry likes nothing better than telling a joke about life in the school.

He said: "There was these two hardy big young lads and I caught them flaking into each other behind the school. I took them into the office and gradually got them to shake hands as they were not saying too much.

"It was a slow process, a few inches at a time, and eventually there was a handshake.

"It must have been a bit traumatic for them as I heard one say to the other as they went down the corridor: 'I'll tell you one thing, after that it will be a while before you and I box again!'"

And that is Gerry Donagher – a smile and a quip never far from his lips as he pondered life's little ironies. A great teacher, a Renaissance man and a man for all seasons.

PETER HENRY

Former councillor and publican Peter Henry tells Gerry McLaughlin about life at the pub he ran with his late wife Mollsie – and recalls the development of the part of town the pub served

PUBLISHED ON JULY 16, 2020

THE FIRST THING YOU NOTICE ABOUT the one and only Peter Henry is that soft south Sligo lilt with a just a hint of Mayo in a voice that is very much west of Ireland. It lingers even though he has been living in Sligo town since the late 1950s.

And the second thing is that he radiates a crackling, electric energy that totally belies his 81 years.

This is a man who has lived life to the full, given it his very best shot, a formidable figure who has always been ambitious, eloquent, a dealing man, willing to take a chance, a hard-working man, an extremely intelligent man and a kind man to the less fortunate.

But most of all he is a courageous man

LEFT: PETER AND MOLLSIE BEHIND THE BAR IN THE BLUE LAGOON, AND PETER WITH HIS FRIEND THE LATE BRENDAN GRACE

who managed to convince the Allied Irish Bank to loan him a considerable sum of money so he could buy his beloved, legendary Blue Lagoon bar, lounge and nightclub in 1961 for just over £4,000.

His life philosophy is best summed up in his own phrase: "I never stood back from anything."

And he did not baulk either in 1980 when he paid nearly £50,000 for his lovely, distinctive flat-roofed home called Orient on the Pearse Road, a fine spacious house of which he is righty proud.

This unique house won architect of the year for the man who designed it in 1955, according to Peter.

Peter tells the *Sligo Weekender* that he had been looking at it for quite a while and then decided he was going to buy – and that is Peter, a thinker and a doer, a man of action and a man of vision.

He ran the Blue Lagoon with his equally gifted late wife Mollsie (née McGrath, from Ballymote) for 46 years and turned it into one of the leading venues in the North West.

The Henrys had all the top bands in their famous cabaret in the 1960s and 1970s. The brilliant Christy Moore is a close friend of Peter, as was the great Brendan Grace.

The Blue Lagoon also hosted Pat McGeegan (father of Barry McGuigan), who came second when singing for Ireland in the Eurovision and played there a few days afterwards.

The Pattersons, Mary Black, Mary Coughlan and Dolores Keane have also performed in cabaret.

U2, the Boomtown Rats and Patrick O'Hagan also featured as well as Sligo's own Maisie McDaniel and Fintan Stanley.

In other spheres, great dart throwers like John Lowe and Eric Bristow gave exhibitions on the banks of the Garavogue.

It was also a great venue for birthdays and anniversaries and wedding receptions.

Before Peter took over the Blue Lagoon in 1961 he ran the Dooney Bar in Temple Street, and prior to that he had a travelling shop which traversed large parts of Sligo. It was then that his social skills with the public were honed and he loved every minute of it.

Peter has many other passions, not least politics. He was a Fine Gael member on Sligo County Council from 1985 to 1999.

And he is a great supporter of Sligo Rovers. He was a Management Committee member and has also been a great fundraiser for the Bit O'Red. He is still annoyed at the fact that Ian Baraclough was sacked after Rovers' stellar success in 2012.

Peter Henry was born in Cloonacool on May 31, 1939.

He said: "I am the only one of our family that did not emigrate and there were six of us. Times were tough and two of my brothers died.

"I remember Mayo winning the All-Ireland in 1951 and there was not a cloud in the sky. We were all around a battery radio. And they have not won an All-Ireland since."

Peter went to school in Cloonacool and then he cycled in and out to Tubbercurry Technical College.

He said: "I got a job at 10 shillings a week on a travelling shop – they were very important in the 1940s and 1950s. On a Friday morning I would start at Ballydrehid and go down around Kellystown, Strandhill and back up around Pearse Road.

"I was working for a man called O'Rourke. It was a great way to get to know the country and the people were fabulous. They were always offering me tea.

"Women had eggs and at the time we would take eggs from them to pay for part of their groceries.

"I took over the travelling shop and in less than two years I trebled the turnover. We sold everything. I enjoyed it very much and it was great training for later life."

Peter spent four very happy years at the traveling shop.

"Then the Blue Lagoon was for sale. I was afraid that I might not get the licence from District Court judge Jack Barry as I was only 20 – but I got it. On March 3, 1961, we took over the Blue Lagoon.

"Seán Ford in the AIB gave me the money and he put five of us in business that month, including the butcher Tom Fox, Frankie Mooney, who left Lipton's and went out on his own, and Kieran Horan of Horan's menswear.

"There were seven people before me who were trying to buy the Blue Lagoon, but they were turned down and I got it.

"It cost £4,750 and that was a lot of money. I told my parents, and my mother arrived in on the bus the following day saying she could not sleep and that we would all end up in jail.

"When I bought it, the turnover was £80 per week. I spent millions down there, but I enjoyed it.

Peter and Mollsie began to renovate it. He said: "Between the pub and the house there were four thatched houses and on the gaol wall there were two other derelict cottages. The contractor Josie Maye took it all away for me for £200. I once came across people who were born there – some of them were Dunbars.

"In the front of the gaol was a garden and the prisoners used to grow the vegetables and the townspeople used to buy those vegetables. That happened before my time.

"There was a poor man who was given three months for making poteen.

"But he was very friendly with the governor and the gaol was known back in the day as 'the Lough Gill Hotel' – and he used to come down to the pub for a few bottles of stout."

Peter met his wife Mollsie McGrath in Ballisodare. She had two uncles that owned a pub in Ballymote – they were Keenans.

Mollsie, who was a very witty and vivacious character, worked with Peter initially in O'Rourke's after she had worked in O'Connor's of Ballisodare.

Peter said: "We built a lounge on the town side and we had music at the weekend and Renee Laurence played the piano and Joe Gunning sang with Pat O'Hara's band.

"For the first extension we did I got £28,000 from the AIB. That was a lot of money in the 1960s. It was in three stages.

"Joe Taaffe and the Taaffe brothers and Jim Willis did the building and they were very good. They did all my work until I came up to Pearse Road and they did the work here for me as well. I never asked them for a price for a job because I knew they wouldn't rob me."

He added: "My first cover charge in the Blue Lagoon was for Pat McGeegan who came second in the Eurovision Song Contest in the mid-1960s. We charged half a crown in and that was the first cover charge in the west of Ireland. We had the Pattersons from Donegal and they had a programme on UTV every week. And we had U2, and we had the Boomtown Rats, The Bogey Boys and Stagalee.

"We opened the doors at 9.30pm and the queues were over to the end of the gaol row and they came from all over. I still have two of the contracts from the U2 gigs. We also had Christy Moore who is a personal friend of ours. Christy Moore is a genuine man, he loves his music and he likes people to appreciate what he is doing.

"And Brendan Grace was also very good to us and to our son Ivan, who passed away at 12 years from a brain tumour."

"On Thursdays we had a band in. Marie and the Wild Life played with us for almost 30 years."

Peter continued: "We also had the Dubliners. They lived the high life and they drove big cars and stayed in the Great Southern Hotel.

"They played in our place on a Saturday night once, and on the Sunday they decided they wanted to go up Lough Gill.

"They wanted a crate of beer and they sang all the way up and all the way down, and they could be heard all over the place as their voices carried on the water. They were something else.

"Luke Kelly was a great singer and character and he would only take a few pints in the corner from the late Paddy McDonald.

"And then Luke went upstairs to rest for a while and then he came down fresh and he was a wonderful character, but the Dubliners led a hard life on the drink.

"I also had Mary Black, Dolores Keane and Mary Coughlan. She used to drink black rum but she has given up the drink now. In later years we stopped serving drink to the entertainers.

"The Jazz Lads played with us for years as well, and I was in the tech in

Tubbercurry with Pauric Potter. His father was a sergeant in Tubbercurry, and they are very well known all over Sligo.

"They queued up to see Maisie McDaniel whenever she played in the Blue Lagoon.

"We had Sandy Kelly in later years, and we had traditional nights in the lounge area, the Tudor, on Monday nights for the tourists in the summer.

"John Fallon, father of Seán Fallon of Sligo Rovers and Glasgow Celtic fame, did the opening of the Tudor for us and there was a great crowd and it was in the 1960s.

"At that time people came out to their local pub for entertainment – and if they came on a Saturday night, they came every Saturday night. People spent more money then, even though they had a lot less money at the time."

Peter was a founding member of the Vintners' Federation of Ireland. He said: "I was also vice-president and I put a lot of work into it."

Peter and Mollsie were almost 47 years in the Blue Lagoon and Lough Gill was a very useful amenity on its doorstep.

He said: "Lough Gill, The Drowse and the Liffey were the three first salmon fishing rivers to be opened in Ireland.

"I got involved with a travel agency in Germany and they were sending over fishermen. The Sligo Park Hotel was not yet built, and I put the fishermen up in Ballincar. They hired a car from Dublin and I organised the boat and the ghillie and it was going great from 1965. At that time I had 16 boats. But the Troubles began and that ended that – and only a very small number continued to come. They looked at the map and saw how close Sligo was to the border".

At the Blue Lagoon's peak, Peter employed a staff of 18 and had a lot of part-timers.

He said: "Paddy McDonald was with me over 40 years and Christy Monteith, who was from Ballybofey, was there for 28 years. Gladys Sheridan was there for 24 years.

"My son-in-law Aidan Meehan, who is married to my daughter Imelda, has been there for 42 years and he and Imelda now own the Blue Lagoon."

"Una Connolly was there for 17 years and Séamus Mullaney was there for 11 years."

His daughter Imelda, who successfully followed in Peter's career in politics, explained that the Blue Lagoon was sold in 2005-2006.

Imelda said: "My husband Aidan now owns the Blue Lagoon after it was sold to another party after dad retired. Aidan bought it back and we now run the business. We are living there now."

And then the ever-informative Peter gives a potted social history of the immediate hinterland of the Blue Lagoon.

Peter said: "Doorly Park was a nice part of Sligo. You had 100 houses there – 50 houses in Martin Savage Terrace and 136 in Garavogue, 40 in Abbeyville and 89 in St Anne's.

"And they were all good customers and we had some good people from Cranmore.

"A priest called Fr Niall McDermott spoke out against the building of so many houses in Cranmore without proper facilities as he had seen the ensuing difficulties in other parts of the country.

PETER WITH HIS DAUGHTERS MARTINA, MAJELLA, IMELDA AND OLIVIA

"But then he got transferred, and Cranmore has suffered as a result of the inadequate infrastructure.

"Doorly Park is named after the late Bishop Doorly. Sligo Corporation bought the estate around there which included the racecourse and the gate lodge which was formerly owned by the Wood-Martins.

"The council bought it all in 1945 for £300. In 1955-56 they built 100 houses in Doorly Park and they put on deferential rent, which meant you had to have a certain income to qualify for a house.

"You had the ESB, the post office, and mental hospital attendants who all had good income. They moved into Doorly Park and were charged 18 shillings and sixpence a week.

"And the houses in Garavogue were five shillings and sixpence a week.

"What do you think of that? If you started deferential rent now you would be slaughtered.

"There were great people in Doorly Park, Garavogue, St Anne's, Martin Savage Terrace and Abbeyville, and we got great support from them all."

When asked why and how he got involved in politics he said, in typical fashion: "You see, I didn't go back from anything."

Peter was first elected to Sligo County Council in 1985 and never lost an election, retiring in 1999.

"All my people, the Henrys, were Fine Gael. Mattie Brennan, the ex-Fianna Fáil TD, his mother was Henry and the Henrys were Fine Gael. And then all the Fine Gael people in Mattie's area voted Fianna Fáil and Mattie was 20 years in the Dail. I was persuaded to run by some local Fine Gael people, and it was busy as I would be dealing with people on a Monday and a Tuesday who had needs."

It was Peter's own punters that played a strong part in his election.

"I suppose I got 100 votes in Doorly Park alone and I had another 100 up here where I live on Pearse Road. I would have got votes in Cranmore as well as I knew them all – and all politics is local."

Peter spent 14 years on the council and did three terms.

"It was the people of the area that elected me. I did my very best to represent them and I did my very best for them and that was my philosophy.

"I enjoyed it to a certain extent, but it is very different from running a business."

But Peter's skills in that sphere were useful when a consensus was needed, and he has a natural instinct for closing a deal.

The main issues during Peter's term of office were infrastructure, water, roads and balancing the books.

Imelda said: "Dad was a great worker for his constituents and got a lot of different things done for people around their homes."

"I did not go into the council straight after dad. Fine Gael asked me to run in 2004 and I did seven years on the council and then I was elected to the Seanad from 2011 to 2016."

When asked if she would be tempted to go back to the politics, she said: "No, but I did a lot of work for the Vintners for the last five years and even though I got my interest in politics from my dad, it was my mother who talked me into running. I enjoyed the council more than anything."

Peter said: "You have some very good people in Sligo County Council who get through a lot of work for the town and the county."

Even though he retired officially in 2005, Peter is still working and has been involved in successful ventures, including Strand Campus in Strandhill.

His restless mind will always ensure that he will constantly be involved in some venture or other.

In another guise, Peter has been a life-long, active supporter of Sligo Rovers and has been a major fundraiser and is a keen fisherman.

Peter was very much involved with setting up the Sligo Rovers 400 Club, which is now the 500 Club.

He said: "It is €20 a month – €240 a year – and we have 508 members. We give the club a cheque for €10,000 every month and we also have a monthly draw for €1,250. I started it.

"I go to all of the matches and my grandchildren are going now as well.

"Sligo Rovers won three trophies between 2012 and 2014 and it was disgraceful the way the manager Ian Baraclough was sacked [in June of 2014].

"He was a great fellow and now he is managing Northern Ireland. It has been all downhill since that. My son-in-law won two FAI Cup medals with Rovers – Martin McDonnell, who is married to my daughter Majella. He started at 17 and finished up at 34.

"Sligo Rovers means a lot to me. Ian Baraclough came to my wife Mollsie's funeral and I have great time for him."

But after detailing his practical contribution to the Bit O'Red, he pays tribute to the late Jack Charlton and his love of the Irish soccer team.

Peter said: "Poor Jack Charlton is dead. I went to all of the Irish team's matches abroad.

"At that time I went with the late Tommy Mullen and Joe Hanley and Jack Charlton's wife was in our group.

"Then there was the row between Jack and Eamon Dunphy, and she left us and had to go as peacemaker."

Peter is a director of the Sligo Tourism Development Association. It was founded in 1951 and Peter joined it in 1974 and is still on the board.

He said: "I was also five years on the board of directors at University College, Galway, when I was a county councillor.

"There was a lot of money from Europe at that time and the modern development started in my time. I enjoyed that and the amount of funding from Europe at that time was unreal.

"I bought my house in 1980 – it was owned by Meldrum of Sligo and it cost me £49,000."

But he always returns to his happy days in the Blue Lagoon. "We ran a good show there," says Peter, and Imelda, who began working in the pub when she was 12, says: "It was like a little family there."

Imelda said: "We did up the pub and we have a beer garden. We cater for parties at the weekend and we don't do food. We open at 4pm in the afternoon and it is run very well."

So, what does Peter think Sligo needs to do to develop?

He said: "The disappointing thing about Sligo is that the population has not increased that much in the town. Business is tough and is very competitive. We have a lot to offer tourism-wise and WB Yeats is our greatest draw, along with Lough Gill, Knocknarea and other sights."

"I have good energy, I don't drink and have good health. I still get a buzz from doing a deal.

"Sligo means everything to me, and its people were very good to me and I especially found it in and around the Blue Lagoon. They were all our friends."

Imelda said: "There used to be a committee in the area years ago and if somebody died and they did not have the money, they would have a night in the Blue Lagoon to raise funds.

"The late Willie Hudson and the late Margo Dunbar and dad were on that committee, and dad helped to pay for a number of funerals."

Peter said: "One family did not have a bob to bury their mother and we had fundraisers for that family and we also put up a headstone.

"People were great, but we had a great committee. We had Frankie Langan, the late Jimmy Callaghan and myself on the committee."

Imelda said: "The Blue Lagoon always was and still is very much part of the community. People that would have been going into the pub in dad's time, their children are coming in now.

"You would often see families gathering to meet up even though they might be living in different parts of Sligo.

"I started working in the Blue Lagoon when I was 12. I think it is an unbelievable learning curve for any person to work in a pub because you meet all types of people from all walks of life. I had a love for the pub from an early age and I followed in dad's footsteps in a lot of ways, and I am also involved in charity work, too. It was always very well run by Mam and Dad and now my husband Aidan. It is a very happy, friendly place, and everyone looks out for each other. We were ringing up the older people to see how they were during the pandemic."

One thing is certain. Peter and Mollsie Henry ran a place that will always be part of the rich social history of Sligo and holds magical memories of the way things were.

And Peter certainly never stood back from anything.

MICHAEL COSGROVE

M Cosgrove and Son, one of Sligo's oldest businesses, first opened in 1898. The delicatessen has stood the test of time and survived many changes to the town. Michael Cosgrove spoke to Alan Finn about the shop's history, staying ahead of trends, and his concerns about Market Street's future if parking restrictions are implemented

PUBLISHED ON FEBRUARY 27, 2020

IN AN EVER-CHANGING SLIGO TOWN, there are very few premises that can claim to have had a constant presence that spans three centuries.

Some businesses have earned a reputation of immortality and have managed to thrive while retaining a sense of time standing still.

Among these businesses is the 122-year-old delicatessen M Cosgrove and Son. The shop has been present at 32 Market Street

LEFT: MICHAEL COSGROVE OUTSIDE HIS MARKET STREET SHOP

since the day the keys were handed down to Michael Cosgrove, the grandfather of the current owner, who is also named Michael Cosgrove.

Michael said: "My grandfather first got this shop in 1898. It was previously owned by a woman called Mrs Harte. He married her niece and shortly after that he took over the running of the shop."

As times change, the shop has largely stayed the very same, with perhaps the only major change coming when the shop was converted from shop and café into simply being a shop.

"The shop only came as far as the near side of the deli counter – the rest was a café. It was called the Lady Erin Restaurant and Shop.

"My father, Kevin, decided to get rid of the café side because he had wanted to expand the shop. I then expanded the shop further again by opening up as far back as the shop goes now."

Combined shops and cafés were not uncommon in the late 19th and early 20th century. In fact, the ability to offer a dinner was a very lucrative business for just about anyone with the resources to cook meals.

Michael said: "Back then, cafés were called eating houses. Sligo was full of them. Having the shop and café together on the premises would have been very common for years, and lots of private houses were even eating houses. People were coming into town looking for a dinner for five shillings. You wouldn't get a huge selection, but at any eating house you went to you would most likely get roast beef, roast chicken or roast pork."

Cosgrove's selection of produce is unlike anything else you will find in Sligo today, but its array of niche, exotic and otherwise hard-to-find foods is a necessary practice which dates back much further than many people may think.

"My father changed it that way because he saw the writing was on the wall for small shops when the supermarkets started arriving in the 1960s," said Michael.

"Small shops were disappearing. We decided we needed to get into something different and thankfully we are still here today because of that."

As a result of this, Cosgrove's has found itself keeping up with the latest diet trends for the best part of almost 60 years, with the sale of traditional products beside specialist brands that have an established market in Sligo.

"You have to keep up with the trends and, more importantly, be a step ahead of the trends if you can.

"You have to be there first in the market, and by the time the supermarkets get this stuff in you have established it and are ready to move on to the next diet fad, because there is always something new."

While the traditional products don't sell like they used to, Michael is still pleased with the variety of items sold every week which justify their impressively varied stock, while the lack of packaging has also proven to be a big hit with customers.

"We used to sell a tonne of potatoes every week. Now we might be lucky to sell one potato let alone a tonne of them.

"Cooking habits have changed a lot. We sell an awful amount of cheese. The stuff we make ourselves like cooked ham and salads are still popular. People also like that you can pick up loose items from cereals and mueslis to nuts and fruit, so we don't have as much packaging as most places."

M Cosgrove and Son has also become a pilgrimage destination of sorts for many tourists, who include it on their itineraries. The interest in the shop doesn't surprise Michael, who said that the loss of small shops like this isn't a problem exclusive to Ireland.

He said: "They don't see shops like this any more – they are all gone. The feeling of stepping back in time is part of the charm and I intend to keep it that way.

"I am proud to keep an old shop like this thriving when you have people coming into the shop and thinking to themselves, 'wow', because they are seeing a place like this maybe for the first time in their lives."

For at least 70 years of its existence, M Cosgrove and Son was situated in Sligo's busiest street. Market Street and neighbouring High Street have since suffered hardship, which Michael feels has had a lasting impact on what should be a bustling part of town.

"Market Street was full of small shops back in the 1960s and '70s. Now they are all gone.

"When I was growing up on Market Street there were around 100 people living here. Now there is only one. That's an amazing statistic.

"Market Street and High Street were once the busiest streets in Sligo. You had loads of families living in flats and apartments and behind the shops, but the town has changed so much."

He went on to say that he is concerned by proposed plans to remove parking spaces on Market Street. He feels the car parks can lead prospective customers away, taking business away from an area which has worked hard to regain a sense of vibrancy.

He said: "There is a new plan for the area where there will be virtually no parking on this street and that will be hugely detrimental to us as rates have doubled.

"And if we don't have parking and people coming into the street then Market Street is in real trouble.

"There are reasons why Market Street and High Street dropped off the way they did. This particular area is thankfully quite active with Taheny's Electrical, Cait & I, Paddy Power, Shoot the Crows and the Woollen Market, to name a few, but if parking is restricted any more than it already is then it spells bad news for this end of this street."

Also proposed recently was the re-introduction of the Living Above The Shop scheme, which was earmarked for Market Street and High Street. Michael feels this won't solve the problem to the extent that is necessary and feels more needs to be done to give business owners an incentive for opening a business on the streets.

"I think the scheme would help to a degree, but it will never be like the way it used to be. People don't want to live over shops, they want their own space, they want suburbia and that's their choice.

"There is an awful lot more could be done in relation to rates, parking, tax rebates and tax breaks for people opening up small shops in slightly run-down areas."

MICHAEL COSGROVE

Michael Cosgrove has worked in the shop for 43 years now and says his enthusiasm for it now is the same as the day he started, and has no plans of kicking back and putting his feet up any time soon.

He said: "I can't see myself doing that, to be quite honest. I enjoy working here. I would get bored stiff sitting at home doing nothing.

"There is a great social aspect to it too. I know most of my customers well and they know me a long time. You can talk away to them about anything in here. There is always a chat to be had."

He owes the continued success of M Cosgrove and Son to a combination of factors, and he believes they will all be necessary as long as the shop has a place on Market Street.

He said: "Service, hard work, the range of products, our customers and maybe a little bit of good luck have all gone a long way over the years and the shop always brings challenges that I like to take on."

While a lot of great work is taking place to modernise Sligo town, there will still always be room for a sense of old-school familiarities, and M Cosgrove and Son will hopefully continue to be a nugget of authentic history nestled among new and bold businesses of the 21st century.

TONY FAGAN

'Fago' played 590 times for Sligo Rovers, scoring 47 goals. Gerry McLaughlin spoke to Sligo soccer legend Tony Fagan about his lengthy career on the field and his view of the game today

PUBLISHED ON AUGUST 27, 2020

A LOCAL AND A WORKING-CLASS hero is something to be. The great Sligo Rovers icon Tony Fagan was and is both, and will always be the 'People's Champion' of Sligo Rovers.

In this bastion of the beautiful game, there is only one Fago.

When he was young and wore the invincible and bright armour of youth, Fago had flowing locks and a beard, prompting the late great sportswriter Con Houlihan to liken him to Christ.

And there were a few hard nuts who tried to crucify him in the unforgiving cauldron of League of Ireland football from 1967 – but

LEFT: TONY FAGAN RECEIVING THE HALL OF FAME AWARD FROM JOHNNY GILES AT THE *SLIGO WEEKENDER* SLIGO SPORTS AWARDS IN FEBRUARY 2010

they failed, for Fago was as lean and hard as whipcord, kept himself in superb shape and never stayed on the canvas.

True warriors are often wounded but never show the pain.

He was a combination of the best qualities of Liverpool's Tommy Smith, Leed's Billy Bremner and Chelsea's Ron Harris, but without their venom.

More importantly, Fago was the heart and soul of the club he loves more than life itself for 20 years, played for them 590 times and scored 47 goals – from midfield.

Fago was also a key figure in Sligo Rovers taking the League of Ireland title in 1977, their first one in 40 years under the great Billy Sinclair.

And he has the distinction of captaining Sligo Rovers to their first ever FAI Cup victory in 1983, a magical day that he treasures even more as he supped sorrow from the rusty spoon of defeat in the finals of 1970, 1978 and 1981.

But all changed utterly in 1983 when Harry McLoughlin's divine chip over the Bohs goalkeeper's head put the whole town in paradise for weeks, and Tony and his comrades suitably celebrated the occasion.

Tony was the oil in the engine, the spark that lit the flame of hunger and desire in his comrades, the man who never backed down no matter how big the challenge, the man who made the tackle at the right time, the man whose ferocious will to win on the field was inspiring but was tempered by modesty and humility outside the arena of battle.

Fago was the ultimate warrior for the Bit O'Red, the one who played with and against some of the greatest footballers to ever grace the League of Ireland.

But he commanded their utmost respect for his ability, his honesty, his desire, his commitment and his utter determination not to be beaten.

He inspired countless Sligo Rovers players over a few generations and was part of great teams that included David Pugh, Gerry Mitchell, Tony Stenson, Paul McGee, Gary Hulmes, Johnny Cook, Johnny Brookes, Chris Rutherford, Jimmy Burnside and Harry McLoughlin (one of the most gifted of them all).

Fago has seen countless players come and go to Rovers from Dublin, Northern Ireland and from cross channel.

And here is the thing. Despite his outstanding qualities he never wanted to play for anyone else, his heart was always in his home town, this eternal boy from St Brigid's Place.

All good things come to an end and Tony parted company with the club in 1987 in his 38th year when he was captain and played his final year for Finn Harps, where he was equally inspirational but broke his ankle.

Ever the gentleman, he does not comment on the background to his departure, but it must have been a long and lonely walk away from what had been his home for two decades.

But one of Fago's greatest qualities was loyalty and he showed that in spades by coming back in 1992 to manage the reserves along with Willie McStay.

He is still a big fan at The Showgrounds. This modest, humble and witty man who knows who he is, knows where he is from and holds his home dear to his great heart.

It was a proud moment for Tony when he was inducted into the FAI Hall of Fame at the FAI Cup final in 2010. This was an honour for one of the finest and longest serving League of Ireland players of them all.

Tony was born in St Brigid's Place, MCR territory, in 1949, two doors from Caheny's pub.

"There was not much money around and we had nothing only playing football in the streets. There were no distractions like mobile phones or computers, and it was a happy upbringing.

He added: "Only for Charlie Devaney and his family there would have been no underage football in MCR. They set up the under-12s and from there I went to the Boys' Club and I stayed there until I signed for Rovers and we won a lot of cups for that side of the town with Charlie.

'The Boys' Club was up as far as 18 and it was in O'Connell Street and the group of boys that were in it were from mixed areas so we put a team together and we played in the FAI Youth Cup around Ireland and one year we went to the quarter-finals.

"But lack of experience cost us and only for the Boys' Club we would never have known what Dublin teams were like at U-18 level.

"I had four or five years with both clubs, and they set me on the road. Johnny Armstrong was a big local hero of ours playing for Sligo Rovers and there were a lot of players brought down from Dublin all through the years. Every year there were new players coming in but the likes of David Pugh, the late Gerry Mitchell and Jimmy Burnside were all great local talents. And I was lucky enough when I joined Rovers in 1967 that these men were still playing. It was a great help to have these local lads and they helped me to settle in."

In his youth Tony and a "gang of young fellows from the street" used to go the matches in the 1950s and "we used to spend most of the time running around The Showgrounds".

He said: "If you got a good result, you came home, got a ball up on the street and you were trying to re-create what happened and that you were Sligo Rovers playing into the gates.

"Louis Dykes and Wilie Bradley were before my time and were great servants to the club."

And while Tony was never the biggest player, at 5ft 8ins, he never shirked a challenge.

"Yes, I am the same person I was then as I am now, and I often wonder how I developed into a midfielder as I used to play as a right winger.

"I was light, and football has changed a lot and it much more defensive now. It can be very negative at times but there is an awful lot of this coaching and getting young players to play to a particular system. Sometimes when you see young lads training or playing a match you might see two or three coaches shouting out instructions. They are taking away their natural talent, I mean let's see what they can do firstly and then put them into a system. Too often they are trying to fit square pegs in round holes. Creativity is stifled."

Tony's young talents were not confined to soccer as he played Gaelic with Muire Naofa and county Minor football with Sligo in 1967.

And the following year, 1968, Sligo reached an All-Ireland final.

Tony said: "Muire Naofa started up and they got all the soccer players from around the streets. You weren't supposed to be playing soccer, the foreign game, but we managed and I enjoyed the Gaelic, but I had to make a choice and I chose soccer.

"Jimmy Kilgallon and Aidan Richardson went on to play senior for Sligo GAA team. I was too light to play Gaelic."

Tony joined Rovers in 1967 and it was a very different world then, in many respects. It was the era of flower power, really long hair and shirts and ties to match, and Tony was well up with the fashion too.

"There was no real coaching at all and no facilities. There were no lights in The Showgrounds, and it was in darkness. Everything has changed so much for the better.

"There was an old track in front of the main stand and that is where we used to do our sprints on cinders they got from some coal yard and were just thrown on the track. You could not run around the pitch and sometimes the club used other facilities like the rugby club.

"It was easy for me for the first year as the then manager Tony Bartley signed quite a few full-timers who were training with the likes of David Pugh, Gerry Mitchell (RIP) and my neighbours Dessie Gallagher and Tod Burns, who have also sadly passed away."

Tony had a dream debut against the mighty Shamrock Rovers, who had a team of talent like Liam Tuohy, Johnny Fullam, Bobby Gilbert, Frank O'Neill, Tony O'Connell, Mick Smyth and the teak-tough Pat Courtney. He scored in that 1967 match, as did his friend the late Dessie Gallagher.

Tony said: "Dessie and myself came from the same area and were only 10 or 15 houses apart and he was there before I signed, and he used to play on the left wing.

"It was a great feeling, the two of us going out to The Showgrounds that day, and it was a great honour for two local lads like us.

"We were two young lads from the Boys' Club and you can imagine the feeling the two of us had when we were coming back down MCR way again. It was a dream come true."

The following decade was tough for Rovers. They lost to Longford Town and then Ken Turner took over as team manager and took Rovers to the FAI Cup final in 1970.

That was a three-game epic against Bohs and was a real heartbreaker for Tony and his comrades. There was huge support from Sligo for all three matches.

Tony said: "We had massive support. It was hard to get money in those days to follow us and not only did they go up to Dublin on the Sunday, but they also went up on the Wednesday night. We had enough chances to win it and took an early lead and it was just not meant to be."

Rovers also competed in the Blaxnit Cup, an All-Ireland competition where the top four teams in the whole of Ireland took part.

"We played and we beat Ballymena United in The Showgrounds and we beat Derry City at the Brandywell in the semi-final.

"We beat Coleraine 1-0 in Windsor Park but they beat us something like 4-0 in Dalymount in the second leg."

The period from 1970 to 1977 was lean. The club went into full-time systems at various times, but just did not have the resources to keep it up.

Tony said: "They went back to part time and then you were bringing fellows from Dublin and Derry and the locals and you had about three or four camps.

"We never really trained together or had a chance to try any tactics. You were just told to go out and play in a certain position.

"That all changed when Billy Sinclair came in as manager in 1976. He was very good and brought back tactics and they went back full-time.

"Billy was a great tactician and he let a lot of part-timers go and he brough in a good few young lads from England.

"Billy was a great trainer too and he sorted us out and he tried to change the club and he introduced golden goals to try and make money and was very interesting and committed."

The 1977 team was pretty strong with Fago, Tony Stenson, Alan Patterson, Paul Fielding, Chris Rutherford, Graham Fox, Michael Betts, Paul McGee, Gary Hulmes, Mick Leonard and Pauric McManus.

Tony said: "They were all young and keen and their aim was to come over here for a season or two, play well and maybe get a move back to England. When we did win the title in 1977, it was the end of a 40-year famine.

"We had to beat Shamrock Rovers in the last game, and they had Johnny Giles, Eamon Dunphy and Ray Treacy. But we got the vital goals from Gary Hulmes, Chris Rutherford and Paul McGee, who later joined QPR and played with Stan Bowles.

"It was hard-won and there were great celebrations. It was great to be on the team that won it and that night we were in Dublin but when we got home, we celebrated for two or three months and it was just great going to the Town Hall and the Mayor's Parlour.

"They were good lads and we got to the FAI Cup final in 1978 again. But Paul McGee was signed by QPR in November 1977 and players started to drift away.

THE SLIGO ROVERS 1969-70 TEAM. BACK: KEVIN FALLON, JOHNNY BROOKS, DAVID PUGH, TOM LALLY, GERRY MITCHELL AND PAT MCCLUSKEY. FRONT: KEN TURNER, JOEY WILSON, TONY FAGAN, JOHNNY COOKE, DESSIE GALLAGHER AND TONY 'TOD' BURNS

"If you come from a big city in England it is hard to come to a town in the west of Ireland, which is much quieter. Billy brought in more players and we lost it on a controversial penalty kick."

Rovers were also in the FAI Cup final in 1981 with Patsy McGowan as manager.

Tony said: "After Billy Sinclair departed, the club could not afford a full-time system and they went back part-time and they brought Patsy in and he brought lads like Paddy Sheridan and a few lads that had played for him at Finn Harps."

McGowan had also guided a Jim Sheridan-inspired Finn Harps to their only FAI Cup title in 1974.

"Patsy was a great character and a great motivator. You could understand why Finn Harps had done so well under him. He could not see you losing a match and never worry about the opposition it is all in your own hands.

"Patsy would have you walking on air and he was the only man that tipped us to win our first ever FAI Cup in 1983 when he said his heart said Sligo Rovers could win it. I always had great respect for Patsy."

Paul Fielding was player-manager in 1983 and Sligo went back to part timers. Tony said: "We were not going well in the league but were going well in the cup."

Tony was captain of that team and Johnny Skeffington was also in that squad. Sligo Rovers wrote their name proudly in the history books by beating Bohs 2-1 in the final.

They went a goal down early on, but Tony Stenson equalised and Harry McLoughlin's wonderful lob à la Pelé sparked manic celebrations in the town, and this highly gifted but very modest winger will be forever remembered for that wonderful sorcery. But Rovers were well prepared for this final after a four-match epic with Cobh Ramblers and they came back from 2-0 down in the semi-final to win 3-2.

"That match was in Dalymount. I was captain and it was just great. The spectators had a brilliant night and you could not even get a pint in comfort as they were all congratulating you, but it was just wonderful.

"Of course, we had plenty of good nights later."

Tony was 34 that time but always "trained very hard" .

"You don't always get out what you put in and I finished at 39 and had a very long and enjoyable career."

Tony's indomitable spirit shone through in that career.

"No matter how hard I was hit, I would never let the other fellow see that I was down, and I was a competitor all my life."

Tony last played for Rovers in 1986-87, when he was captain again, and then moved on to Finn Harps for a year at age 38.

He said: "We went to the semi-final of the FAI Cup and played Shamrock Rovers three times before losing out and we were the last club to play Shamrock Rovers in Milltown.

"They beat us 1-0 in the 93rd minute in The Showgrounds. There were a lot of Dublin lads in our team, including Fred Davis and Dom Kearney. I was there for 20 years and fellows would come in for one or two years and then they were gone. I played with hundreds of fellows over the years and many of them remembered me even if I might forget them.

"For example, Johnny Cooke was on the books of Man United and he was released to Rovers and scored a goal for us in the 1970 final. That was a huge change and he ended up as a scout for Man United in later years.

"He had been away for almost 50 years and then he came over on a scouting mission and I met up with him. He was glad that we were still alive. I was after getting my ankle done and he asked me on the phone how will I know you after all these years, and I told him I have a grey head and I will be the fellow on crutches.

"I went to The Showgrounds to meet him, and David Pugh and Tony Stenson also turned up and we had a great time reminiscing with Paddy Gilmartin, who was the ex-chairman of Sligo Rovers.

"You can make great friends in sport and there are some younger people who have died, and we are just lucky to be above the ground and remember.

"We also had a great goal scorer in the mid-1960s called Johnny Brookes, who was there the year before I signed.

"He went off to the US with David Pugh and they played with Tampa Bay against Santos and Pelé.

"David Pugh was a very good player and was probably ahead of his time."

Tony finished his career with Harps when Chris Rutherford was manager and Harps were second or third in the table when sadly Tony broke his ankle when he was 39.

"It was better that it happened at that time than when you were 17. It was sad because I thought Harps were good enough to get promoted. There are not too many players who go on to 38 or 39 so I suppose I was a bit of an exception."

But the game has changed utterly according to Tony as players tend to fall like flies at the slightest contact.

"Some people kid me that I would not last five minutes in the modern game. Even going for 50-50 ball they would be roaring and crying even before you put in the tackle. The ball is awful lightweight these days and so are the boots. But the first touch has improved a lot and the pitches are great, which is good to see."

Tony came back to Rovers in 1992 and managed the reserves along with Willie McStay.

Tony said: "Lawrie Sanchez and Steve Cotterill and Jimmy Mullen wanted to start up a reserve team and they asked me if I wanted to go back and I agreed. Willie came and he won the treble with Sligo Rovers in 1994 and we also won a Reserve League and Cup and that was a mighty year. Many of the reserves were Sligo players and the first team were full-time professionals.

"It would be a good experience for young players to get playing with full-time first team players. Willlie McStay went back home to Scotland and he joined Celtic."

Tony was there for three to four years.

But there has always been a difficulty for young local Sligo players to break into the first team.

Tony said: "You see, Sligo people think that if you are from Dublin or somewhere else you get a better chance than a local. It is only in the latter years with the under-19s that young fellows can train to the same system as the first teamers. That brings them on more and local lads are getting a better chance."

Was it frustrating for Tony that many of his talented young Sligo Reserves did not get the chance to play first team football?

He said: "I said to Lawrie Sanchez one day that I had a full-back that was going well and that he could play full-back for the first team for a few games.

"I said to him, your full-time players could look after one young fellow on the team by giving him the right passes and talk him through the game and let him see why they are full-timers.

"He replied, 'Fago, I am only here for a short time and I can't experiment as I am here to win something.'

"Now Lawrie Sanchez went on to manage Fulham and Northern Ireland and did very well and Steve Cotterill too.

"Laurie's tactics were very good, and you could see why he had done so well with Wimbledon."

Swinging forward, Tony was a happy man when Sligo Rovers won the FAI Cup in 2010, 2011 and 2013 and were in the final in 2009. "Those were great teams," he said.

Paul Cooke and Gerry Carr took over and built up a great team.

Tony said: "Paul Cooke did very well, and he got offers to go back and he left the team with Ian Baraclough and the same players were there. Success brings success."

Tony still goes to all the Rovers matches with his son-in-law and his four grandchildren, all boys.

"We have six seats together and I don't get quite as excited as I used to and keep my comments to myself.

"I do hear people giving out but I keep my thoughts to myself."

He added: "If the Sligo people see that you are trying your best and that you are committed, they will support you to the hilt.

"God loves a trier and people will see that, but if you have talent and don't do it people will see that too."

The club does get great support from the ordinary people of Sligo.

"They are very good and here are always collections. Other clubs do not have the same fundraising, which can be up to €70,000 or €80,000, but that does not last too long when you go full-time and you have a big wage bill.

"They are all full-time in Sligo Rovers these days and I don't know how they are doing it. It must be a colossal bill, especially when you have no huge sponsor locally.

"And if you are not doing well some people tend not to come."

Fago was given a well-deserved *Sligo Weekender* Sligo Sports Awards Hall Of Fame award in 2010, but in typical deadpan fashion he downplays its undeniable significance as well as a Hall of Fame award by the FAI.

"It [the FAI award] was presented at the FAI Cup final, a great year as Rovers also won the cup that year."

He added: "Whenever you get to the FAI Cup final, they honour a player from the club and there are three or four past players who have got this award. The more times you get to a FAI Cup final the better chance you have of getting an award."

Tony was delighted and honoured to get the award and he is still the longest serving Sligo Rovers player.

"Yes, I don't go in for records, but they have so many stats that they could tell you how many times you went to the toilet in those days! I wasn't brought up on that I just loved playing and did so as long as I could."

Outside of Sligo, Tony has deep admiration for Johnny Fullam of Shamrock Rovers and Finn Harps scoring machine Brendan Bradley.

"I am glad that his scoring record has never been beaten."

Tony had some great battles with Finn Harps and has many friends in the Donegal club, and also fondly recalls Jim Sheridan and Con McLaughlin.

And, although so many players came and went from Rovers, Tony and the likes of Harry McLoughlin were happy and quietly proud to only play for their own club.

And even though he is "old and grey", Fago is still recognised all over the country.

He said: "It is great, and it is nice that they remember me for the service I gave to my home club for 20 years.

"Sligo is a great soccer town and it is nice to see everything running so well at The Showgrounds even though it is always hard to gather money.

"They have a full-time manager and a lot of full-time players."

When asked for his greatest single memory of those terrific 20 years, he does not hesitate.

"I suppose winning the FAI Cup for the first time ever after so many disappointing defeats, being a local on that team and captaining that team too was really special. And if they are asked who was the first man to lift the cup, they will say: Fago was!

"I am hoping that Rovers can continue to be successful and it has been a few years since we won anything. If you are challenging for honours it gives people hope and they will come out.

"Sligo needs an average attendance of 3,000 per match to keep going and you can see the likes of Cork and it can break up easily. It is very hard to get up there and when you are up there it is very hard to stay there."

So what does Sligo Rovers mean to Fago?

He said: "When I was young it meant everything to me. I never realised I would play in so many important matches. If you had told me back then that I would play in four FAI Cup finals, in two League Cup finals, in a Blaxnit All-Ireland final, I won the league and captained Rovers to the first ever FAI Cup title and played quite a few league games along the way, I would have pulled your arm off."

Yes indeed, but the pleasure was all ours, Fago – the eternal legend who gave his heart and soul to his own club for 20 years. In a different class – and definitely the People's Champion.

Ü. SLIGO CREDIT UNION

Great loans for a great Sligo life.

Talk to us about an affordable, tailored loan.

*Where **u** come first*

ESCAPE FROM SLIGO GAOL

A hundred years ago, IRA batallion leader Frank Carty was broken out of Sligo Gaol. Alan Finn looks back on the escape – which set the bar for a daring rescue attempt from a more notorious prison less than a year later

PUBLISHED ON JULY 16, 2020

WHETHER IT WAS ESCAPING FROM the authorities, escaping prison or escaping death, 100 years ago Frank Carty was not one for being contained.

The one-time leader of the IRA's Tubbercurry Battalion is listed among Sligo Gaol's most notable prisoners, but with the help of a few friends he ensured he would be more famous for absconding.

Carty was arrested in February 1920 for his suspected involvement in a raid on

IN THIS CHAPTER: SLIGO GAOL IN A PHOTO FROM THE 1950s

the home of Colonel Alexander Perceval at Temple House, an act which yielded a number of weapons.

He was identified by Colonel Perceval's wife as being the apparent ringleader and was placed behind bars.

This was based on her memory of being tied to a chair by him during the raid, but it would later transpire that he was not responsible for this.

Carty's story at this stage appeared destined to end behind bars as well, but Michael Farry's 'Sligo 1914-1921 A Chronicle of Conflict' indicates that he was "rescued from the gallows" in June of that year.

Being rescued from the gallows was not enough for those on the outside, however, as Billy Pilkington, the commanding officer of the Sligo Brigade, concocted a plan to break his south Sligo contemporary out. Depending on who you asked, this could have been considered brave or foolish in what was a heavily garrisoned town.

Pilkington used Carty's south Sligo links to his advantage and assembled a group from the area who were unknown to the local Royal Irish Constabulary. Pilkington opted to post all local men outside the walls while all the men inside the jail were unlikely to be recognised and could fly comfortably under the radar assuming they got away.

In all, 53 men were involved in the operation to get Frank Carty out of Sligo Gaol – 20 men served as lookouts, another 20 were stationed outside the walls with weapons, 13 men climbed over the wall and the remaining few were tasked with cutting the telephone wires.

No chances were taken lest the alarm be raised before they had even started – a cautious approach which extended to the men not even being allowed to smoke outside the gaol walls.

Keeping the men on the outside and inside connected was Alex McCabe, a Sinn Fein MP, who up to this point had been keeping a low profile in refuge at Summerhill College following his return to Sligo after a spell in Mountjoy prison.

The rescue attempt proved to be efficient and quiet – Carty was quickly located without any need for gunfire, but time was of the essence and the men quickly realised that they risked being foiled if they all had to scale the makeshift ladders they used to get in. The outside team quickly pulled down the main gate before any prison guards could raise the alarm.

Pilkington had already ensured chief warder Hooke could not foil the mission with one flick of the wrist when he was isolated and held at gunpoint before being bound, gagged and relieved of the keys which would remove the barrier standing between Frank Carty and freedom.

The Governor of Sligo Gaol, William Reid, was sound asleep in his house, located just a stone's throw away from the prison itself. Harry Conry, who would operate as an intelligence officer for Michael Collins just a short time after this event, ordered another man to quickly scarper across to Governor Reid's quarters.

Carty was out, all 53 men retreated to relative safety and the escapee would continue to not only be a nuisance for British authorities, but an elusive one to boot.

Following the rescue, Carty commanded a flying column until November of the same year when authorities caught up with him in Moylough.

Carty and 13 other men were being pursued for an attack on a RIC lorry in Chaffpool near Tubbercurry, which had resulted in two casualties.

Prior to apprehending Carty, the RIC and the Black and Tans responded by torching several south Sligo businesses. After being traced to a house where he was hiding and following a struggle, Carty was overpowered and hauled off to Derry Gaol.

The prison of 1920 was notorious if you were held there – in 94 years, nobody had ever escaped and it was considered 'escape proof'.

You would be forgiven for thinking Carty's escape from Sligo Gaol was only possible because it happened in his native county and one of Ireland's most wanted men could not possibly escape a maximum security facility on this occasion.

Nobody could get out, but information could get in, despite the gaol's reputation, thanks to some covert IRA sympathisers.

Word of Carty's imprisonment reached Charlie McGuinness, a noted Irish adventurer. Getting the Sligoman out of prison suddenly consumed his life, but his first attempt could have proved costly. McGuinness

instructed Carty to force a transfer to the hospital unit by any means necessary. McGuinness had identified this section of the prison as a weak point.

Carty was moved after complaining of severe back pain. McGuinness got the wheels in motion when word reached him, but his plan of escaping by roof unravelled, somewhat literally, when the hook gave way as he attempted to climb.

Somewhat miraculously, McGuinness's foiled plot went completely unnoticed, providing an unlikely second chance to break Carty out.

Three days later, a ball of twine was smuggled into the prison specifically for Carty who was instructed to throw it over the wall where it would be attached to a rope ladder which would pull him to freedom.

This plan proved to be successful, with Carty subsequently being moved from safehouse to safehouse in Derry before sailing to Scotland where he would spend time training IRA men based in Glasgow.

Once again, within mere months, Carty was subdued. His luck finally ran out as members of the IRA failed to intercept his transport to the city's prison and found himself incarcerated in a facility with an even tougher reputation than Derry Gaol.

Carty was sentenced to 10 years in jail and transferred back to prison to serve his time in Mountjoy. Although not an escape as such, he would not spend long behind those walls either as he found himself a free man within just months – just in time for the beginning of the Civil War.

With his latest spell of freedom, Carty dedicated his time and effort to seizing control of Collooney which was under the control of Free State soldiers.

Following the first attack, a divisional meeting was held to decide on how the IRA would respond to an attack on the Four Courts. Carty proposed that another attack in Collooney would send out the right message.

Opinions differed and the members from this meeting decided to seek advice from leaders of Flying Columns in Mayo. Nearly all the members at least.

While they headed west, Carty and Mayo native Tom Carney stayed behind and lead an independent assault on Collooney which proved successful and provided them with the freedom to operate from there for a brief period.

Carty's orchestrated attacks on Free State soldiers continued for a number of years in the region before once again, for a final time, being apprehended by the Royal Ulster Constabulary in 1925. He subsequently spent time in Crumlin Road Jail in Belfast.

All the while, Carty was an elected TD since 1921 but, being opposed to the Anglo-Irish Treaty, he refused to enter Leinster House despite his multiple re-elections. He would only take his seat for the first time in 1927 when he entered the house as a founding member of Fianna Fáil.

Carty also represented the Tubbercurry area on Sligo County Council. He first took his seat in 1928 and served Sligo until his sudden passing in 1942 at the age of 45, just a month after his latest successful re-election.

All information was verified using Michael Farry's Sligo 1914-1921: A Chronicle of Conflict *and* The Aftermath of Revolution: Sligo 1921–23, *and Bill Kelly's* The Complete Book of IRA Jailbreaks 1918–1921

PREVIOUS PAGE: FRANK CARTY

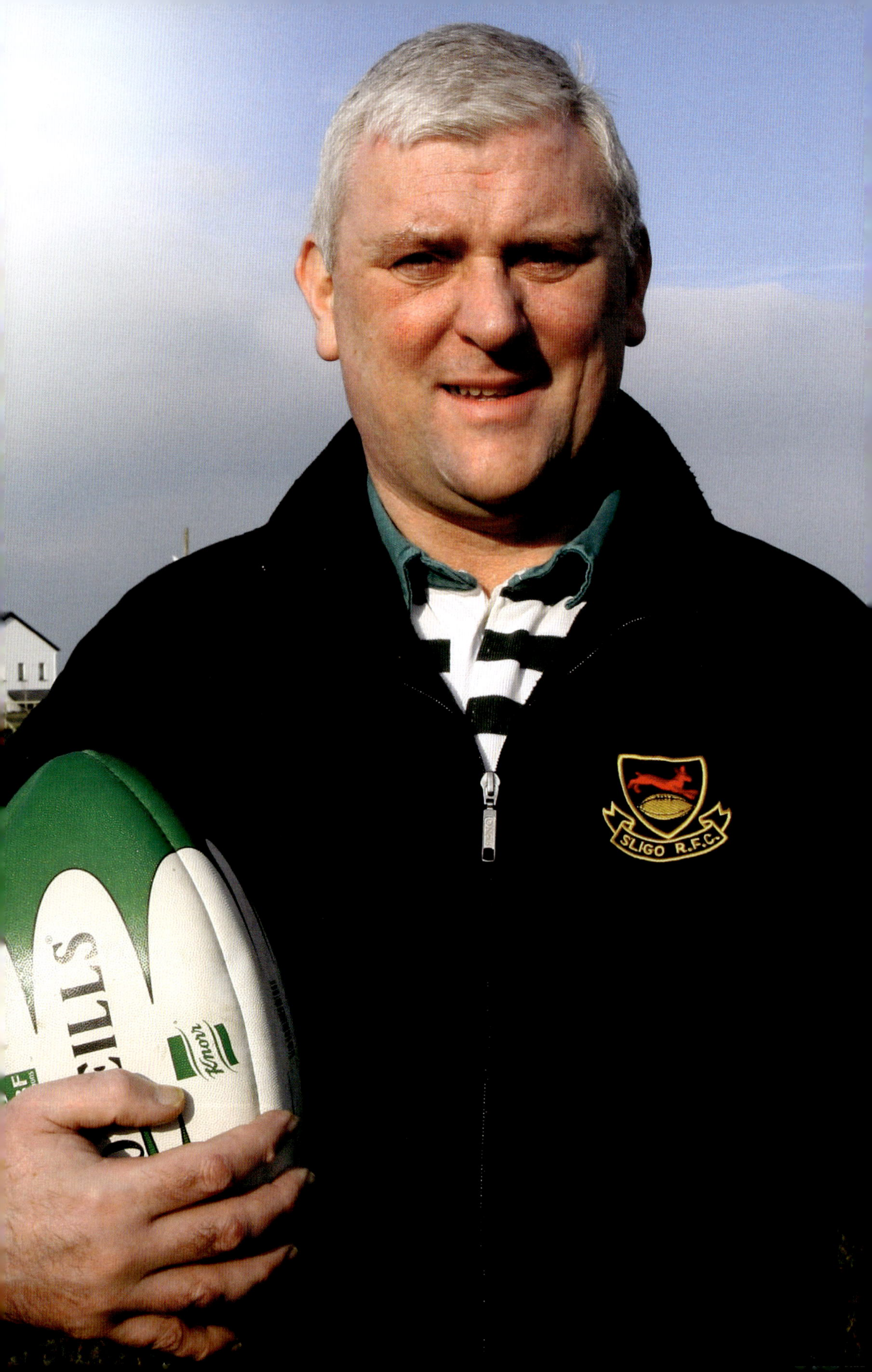
SLIGO R.F.C.

PAT CURRAN

Pat Curran has been involved with Sligo Rugby Club since he was a teenager. Gerry McLaughlin spoke to the player, coach, manager and mentor about his dedication to sport

PUBLISHED ON OCTOBER 8, 2020

THIS IS THE STORY OF HOW RUGBY won the heart of a Strandhill man when he was a teenager around 1970, and 50 years on, Pat Curran is still in love with the game of William Webb Ellis.

For most of those 50 years, Pat has given much of his time and talents to Sligo Rugby Club and has watched with quiet pride how it has developed into a formidable force in Connacht.

In his prime he played with distinction for the club as outhalf and fullback, and his Gaelic football kicking skills were invaluable

LEFT: PAT CURRAN

in rugby. And he also had the physique to deal in a calm but decisive way with physical challenges.

Pat has worn all the jerseys for the club as a player, coach, manager, mentor and general counsellor to a few generations of rugby players from in and around the town.

He has always been a positive force for the good of the game and the club he loves so well. And it gives him great pleasure to see that the club has been hitting the heights in the past few years.

Like many of his generation, Pat grew up watching Irish rugby legends like Willie John McBride, Tom Kiernan, Mike Gibson, Barry McGann, Fergus Slattery, Johnny Moloney, Syd Millar, Ray McLoughlin, Tom Grace, Barry Bresnihan, Willie Duggan and Moss Keane.

They were the shining stars on the black and white screen who strode around the compact old Lansdowne Road stadium like green gladiators.

He grew to know the Lansdowne roar on the silver screen and presiding over all was the golden voice of Fred Cogley, a unique voice who had few equals in conveying mounting excitement as Mike Gibson magically evaded tackles to get a wonder try.

Or when big Willie John McBride went through the English white shirts like a German Panzer tank on tour and carrying at least four of his comrades with him. And even though their voices were very different, Cogley was the Micheál O'Hehir of that generation.

But Pat also had and has a great love for the GAA, with his father a devotee and his mother a proud Kerry woman.

He also served Coolera-Strandhill GAA Club for many years, winning a Sligo Intermediate Football Championship title in 1989.

His love for the GAA is equal to that of rugby and he was at many of Sligo's great GAA triumphs, including that wonderful day in Castlebar when the mighty Mickey Kearins led his county to a Connacht title by beating Mayo after a replay in their own backyard in Castlebar in the hot summer of 1975.

Pat was also there on that fantastic journey in 2002 when Sligo came within a whisker of beating the eventual All-Ireland winners Armagh.

And he was at Hyde Park when a wonder goal from the great Eamonn O'Hara gave the Yeats County their second Connacht title in 2007.

On the rugby front he has savoured quite a few Triple Crowns and Five Nations triumphs as Ireland grew into a mighty international force in the past 15 years.

But there were earlier triumphs too in 1982 under Kieran Fitzgerald and in 1985 when Michael Kiernan kicked a great dropped goal to clinch another Triple Crown.

However, as a proud Connacht man, he has treasured his province's emergence as a major force and has great memories of playing against those two great Galway rugby clubs, Galwegians and Corinthians. He has a special regard for the sublime talents of out half Eric Elwood who played rugby for Connacht and Gaelic football for Galway Senior footballers.

But there are hundreds of rugby players who also play Gaelic football all over the country.

Pat has some golden memories of both codes as he reflects on his dual life in the GAA and then mostly in rugby.

When the *Sligo Weekender* called, Pat had come back from a an Energia Community Series match where Sligo had beaten Galwegians by 25-15, which is a good result on any day.

He said: "That was a good win and we have been able to beat them [Galwegians] over the past few years. The game was in Strandhill, our home pitch.

"It is very weird at matches as we have a small stand, which is a shed really, and nobody could fit into it and people had to stay apart.

"Then a big walloper of a shower came at the end of the game, and you can't go into the clubhouse. But we still won and that is always good."

Pat was born in 1956 and he grew up in Strandhill and went to national school there from 1960 to 1968. He lived in a country area called Mannionstown.

GAA was a very big presence in the Curran home.

He said: "My mother was a Kerry woman and my father always had a great interest in the GAA.

"There were two GAA clubs in the area at the time, Coolera and Strandhill. My father played a bit with Strandhill, but he was a carpenter and most of his work was away from home and he was in Dublin, where he played with Clanna Gael.

"He was Jimmy Curran and my mother was Joan Kerrisk from Firies in Kerry, between Tralee and Killarney – they were part of the East Kerry team that won the county championship and my relations down there would know Jack Sherwood, a Kerry county footballer."

There was no Gaelic football at national school for Pat.

He said: "To my regret all they did at break time was play soccer. But there was a great interest in Gaelic games in our house. Kerry were a great team from 1975 to 1986 and it was just wonderful to be able to follow them and also to have a family connection with the county.

"But we always followed Sligo as well and my earliest memory is of a county Junior final between Coolera and Keash in 1961 and Coolera lost.

"One of the Coolera players was a temporary teacher of ours in Strandhill called Paddy Carty. I remember him coming off the pitch in his red jersey."

Although Pat had a great grá for GAA, he "did not get stuck into football until about 1967 or 1968".

Pat said: "I played with Coolera under-14s for the first time when I was about 12 and it was such an honour for me to play and I was just so happy to get a game. Pete Cooney was a great man in Coolera at that time and he gave us great encouragement. The chance to play my favourite sport made me very happy."

Pat did not win any county titles at underage level, but he did win a county Intermediate championship in 1989 with Coolera-Strandhill. "We won an Intermediate League title that year too," he said.

Pat, who does not have many GAA honours, said: "My best position was wing-back, but I used to play in the forward line as well."

In those years Brian Devaney, Johnny Kivlehan, Francie Finan, Liam Flannery, Justin Scanlon and Benny Scanlon were all prominent for the senior team.

"We won the North Division Junior Championship in 1991 by beating Maugherow in the final and that was my first Divisional medal."

But that Intermediate win in 1989 was the pinnacle of his Gaelic achievements.

"It was great and we had Brendan McCauley and John McPartland Snr as management. We had a good squad of players with Mickey Scanlon being very prominent, Damian Gilligan, Francie Finan, who had made a return during the championship, and Kieran O'Keefe, who was living in Strandhill, was playing with St Mary's but transferred to Strandhill.

"We beat St Farnan's by 1-9 to 0-6 and I got a point from right-half forward, but got injured, but winning that title was really special. That was the first victory since we took a Junior title back in 1971. We had played

PAT AND VIRGINIA CURRAN WITH KEN DOHERTY AT THE *SLIGO WEEKENDER* SLIGO SPORTS AWARDS IN 2009. PAT WAS THE HALL OF FAME RECIPIENT AT THE AWARDS

Senior as well and I played against St Mary's in a Sligo Senior League final in Ballymote in 1978-79.

"They were a great team with some wonderful footballers, and it was always going to be very hard to beat them. I think we lost by six or seven points.

"Reading your article about John Kent in the *Sligo Weekender* brought all those famous names back to me and I remember them all very well.

"I remember being in Markievicz Park when they won their first Connacht title in 1977, cheering for them and they beat Corofin in the final. That was a mighty victory and it was as if the Sligo team were after winning it. There was a big crowd at that game."

But in a parallel universe, Pat developed a deep passion for rugby, the sport that took up most of his life.

"In rugby it was 1970 when Sligo Rugby Club moved to Strandhill. They started training there and they had a second team and I used to go over there when the weather was bright and be kicking a ball back.

"I started getting very interested and then they built a clubhouse and they had an official opening and four Irish internationals were playing. Willie John McBride, Tom Kiernan and Noel Murphy played for Sligo against a Connacht selection that included Barry McGann, who was a great out half. It was wonderful for us at that age to see these guys in action and some of them wearing the Sligo jersey in 1970."

And in those years the great commentator Fred Cogley inspired a whole generation to take an interest in the game with his unique voice.

"I can still remember his commentaries and he was a great commentator and he had a good knowledge of the game, too."

The early 1970s was a golden era for Irish rugby and many believed they would have taken the Triple Crown only for Scotland and Wales refusing to travel to play in Ireland because of the Troubles in Northern Ireland.

By then, Pat was in his 16th year and had started to play rugby.

"I was going over to every match they played, and it was similar to Gaelic in that you caught a ball. The goalposts looked the same."

Others who joined up at that time and the rugby club managed to put an under-16 team together in 1972.

"A lot of the team were from Strandhill, a few lads came out from town, maybe their friends had asked them. We played Sligo Grammar School in a few friendly fixtures and I started out playing outhalf and finished up at full-back."

Pat's Gaelic football kicking skills came in handy in those positions.

"I loved playing outhalf but as time went on, I tore ligaments in my shoulder. I struggled with it thereafter as every time you tackled someone or even any quick movement, you were in pain. You had to rest after every match. Eventually I made sure that if anyone was coming at me, I would try and get them on my left shoulder, and I was constantly keeping my right shoulder away from them."

Pat hit penalties for Sligo Seniors and played for 15 years. His first match was against Old Crescent down in Rathbane in Limerick when he was 19.

"We lost by 25-10 and I was full-back and we had an under-19 team that played in the Connacht League as well, so I was drifting from one team to the other. Then in 1978-79 we got a very good team together and we went very well in the Connacht Senior League that year and we rose to be third.

"We also beat Shannon's Senior team, and they were one of the top teams in the country at that time. That was October 1978, down in Limerick, the same year that Munster beat the All Blacks. Brendan Foley, who played for Ireland, was playing for Shannon.

"In those times you did not have any All-Ireland League, it was just a Connacht Senior League. There were only six or seven teams in Connacht at Senior level so he rest of the time you played friendly fixtures. So to beat Shannon at the time was mighty."

Sligo were backboned in those year by Charlie Culhane, "a great prop forward".

Pat said: "Also on that team was Dessie Butler, John Seaward, who had played with UCC and was working in Sligo, and Brendan Keating from UCG. We had a very good pack of forwards, with the likes of Seán Cryan, who was the captain, Morgan Walsh and Alan McMeekin. We had a good team but did not win anything."

Sligo got to the Connacht Senior Cup final in 1982 and they lost 8-6 to Corinthians of Galway and Pat missed a drop at goal with two minutes left – something that he will never forget.

"They were our biggest rivals and we had great support down at that match and it would have been great if we had won it. Sligo people came from all over the place to support us, from GAA and soccer backgrounds as well."

Pat played with the club from 1972 to 1992, an action-packed 20 years.

"I fractured my hip playing against Westport and I had to stop playing." One suspects that the great-hearted Pat would have soldiered on for much longer otherwise.

But he had the honour of playing for his province Connacht at Junior level from 1984-1986.

"We beat Munster in the Galway Sportsground and that brought great joy to us and I played full-back. From the club we had Noel Fairbanks, Barry McConkey, the hurler Ronan Watters and Eric Brett."

Sligo were in another Connacht Senior Cup final in 1992 and lost to Ballinasloe 10-6. Injury meant that Pat was a "disappointed" spectator.

But he had a very active life and played GAA for Coolera-Strandhill in the summer and rugby in the winter.

"What I found was that as soon as the rugby season was finished, Gaelic was starting and in one GAA match after playing a rugby match the week before I remember going out and was absolutely useless. It takes a while for your body to adjust, and it took a few training sessions and matches to get back into the Gaelic."

Brian Devaney, Brian Harte, Tommy Bree and George Lindsay were also dual players along with Pat for a while.

The rugby club was helped by a lot of people coming to work in the town for many years, but this "has changed dramatically in recent years".

"There are a lot of local players and Summerhill College are playing rugby now and they have some pretty good teams. Sligo Grammar School always had a great tradition of rugby and our Senior team today would be made up of a mix of those two schools. That is a sign of real progress."

After Pat retired, he and John O'Connor began coaching the club's second XV. Then the club got an ex-Greystones coach called Pierce Power who asked Pat to get involved with him at the helm of the Senior team.

"I coached the Senior team for a bit in 1998 but we were relegated out of the All-Ireland League. I coached the Connacht Junior team for two seasons, but at the same time he was back with Sligo and they won the Connacht Junior Cup in 1999.

"I was coach, John O'Connor was manager and Gavin Foley was the captain. Peter Mullan and Kenny O'Neill (a brother of GAA star Karol O'Neill) were our heroes in the final as we won 19-15 against Connemara. Kenny scored 14 points with two dropped goals from out near the middle of the field. That was a big win for us and then I stood back from it for a while."

The club kept playing Junior rugby until they got promoted in 2010 and were back in the All-Ireland League.

Pat took a break in 2001 but he was an assistant coach and manager with Connacht Juniors. He never took office in the club, but he did captain them in 1985.

Pat said: "I did groundsman a few times too. I spent almost 30 years pretty much non-stop to 2001 and then I came back in 2010 and was assistant manager with Connacht Juniors and we won our first ever inter-provincial title.

There were five Sligo lads on that team including Mata Fifita, Wesley Maxwell, Paddy Pearson, Aaron Spring and Jamie Bowes.

"That was a great boost as we beat all the other provinces and the same year Sligo had won the Connacht Junior League and Junior Cup. So we were headed into the All-Ireland League."

That was a big step up for Sligo.

"We were worried but they have done very well and we won Division 2C of the All-Ireland League in 2017-18 and that was great and we went up to Division 2B.

"We also won the Connacht Senior Cup in that time and we won the Connacht Senior Cup and Connacht Senior League last year. So we are having good times really.

"Mata Fifita is a great player and is still playing and it is a well-balanced team. Aaron Spring was very good, and he went away to Australia.

"The current coach is Paddy Pearson. Fellas like Jack Keegan and Ryan Feehily also played GAA with St Mary's and Ryan is a very good hurler for Naomh Eoin.

"Until Covid-19 struck, we were playing in the All-Ireland League in Division 2B."

These days the club has expanded rapidly with many successful underage teams, with a women's section as well.

Pat said: "We would easily have 300 to 400 players and they come from all over the county, from Easkey in west Sligo, from Tubbercurry and Ballymote and from north Sligo. "Tommy Carroll of St Mary's played with us and Gerry Monaghan trained with us, but he was also a very committed basketball player. It would be very hard for senior county players to commit to rugby as there are so many demands."

The club is in a good place at the minute and Pat hopes that this progress will continue.

He said: "We have a good relationship with the local press and Liam Maloney at the *Sligo Weekender* gives us great coverage. I became friendly with his late father Willie, who was always on the gate at the Easkey GAA pitch. He was a most pleasant and witty man."

For Pat, the great thing about rugby and GAA is the friendships made over many years.

"That is the great thing about all sports and rugby always had a great social aspect to it. The more sports you play, the better understanding you have."

But Pat is also a very keen Sligo Rovers fan and has particularly happy memories of the Bit O'Red winning the FAI Cup for the first time in 1983 when they were captained by Tony Fagan. Harry McLoughlin scored a magical goal and Tony Stenson cracked in "a bullet of a goal earlier on in the match".

"That and Sligo GAA team winning the Connacht title in 1975 and I will never forget the final whistle and it was such a warm day. Mickey Kearins was brilliant and any time he got the ball he scored and from anywhere. And he got pushed, shoved, dragged around the place and tackled late but he was still able to score with the left foot."

Pat goes to as many Sligo senior GAA matches as he can, and he has special memories of 2002 when Sligo almost qualified for the All-Ireland semi-final.

"We beat Tyrone in Croke Park and we could have beaten Armagh in both matches and it was a fantastic time and we were on a great journey. I remember thinking in early August that there were only five teams left in the All-Ireland Senior Championship and Sligo was one of them. That was wonderful."

And winning another Connacht title in 2007 is another cherished memory for Pat in Hyde Park.

"I will never forget Eamonn O'Hara's goal that day. I have it on YouTube and I look at it from time to time and Michael McNamara hit a great pass upfield and David Kelly gave Eamonn a perfect pass. He was on the run and he had to go on his left foot and by God did he bury it. Eamonn is a great ambassador and I know him very well and he lives here in Strandhill."

Although Pat has an interest in all sports, rugby naturally holds a very special place in his heart.

These days Sligo Rugby Club has a Senior team and a Senior Development team and a third team as well. Pat has not been involved so much in recent years, but he sometimes helps with the place kicking with some of the youth players.

"I am still a big fan and there are a good few of us older lads and we travel by bus or by train to away matches to give the lads as much support as possible. It's called the 'magic bus' and we would have around 10 to 15 on board and we have a good sing song on the way back."

Rugby has always been a great leveller and a great cross-community game as well.

"It is great that you play on an All-Ireland League basis. It is all about the one country and you meet people from all over the country which is an education in itself. We have a regional competition going on now until Christmas with Sligo, Corinthians, Galwegians and Ballina involved."

Pat also goes to international matches whenever he can get a ticket.

The game of rugby has changed beyond all recognition even in the last decade and has gone very professional. So is there a two-tier system?

Pat said: "Yes, there is a big gap and it is a full-time job for the professional players. I often wonder, do any of them get fed up of it? But Gaelic footballers train maybe just as hard but do not get paid."

So is the professional game inspiring young players to take up the game?

"Yes it is, and youngsters can now meet all the top stars from the provinces at all the matches. Rugby has a glamour it did not have before and the laws of the game have improved. Line-outs are much better and penalties at rucks have improved."

When asked to pick the Sligo RFC players who have impressed him greatly over the years he mentioned the likes of Mata Fifita, Paddy Pearson, Ken O'Neill, Ryan Feehily, Charlie Culhane, Stephen Kerins, Gavin Foley, Aaron Spring and Kuba Wojtkowicz.

Pat is glad to see Sligo doing well nationally and beating Blackrock College last year was a big boost.

Rugby always had a great social side. He said: "That always has been there, you train hard, it is a tough physical game and in our day, you met the other team after the match and you had a chat over something to eat or something to drink.

"Anything that happened stayed on the pitch and many new friendships were forged after matches. The home club would always provide food."

There is now much more respect for the officials than is the case in Gaelic football and soccer.

"That has been in it for years. We were told when we were young that under no circumstances were we to talk to referees or talk back to them. If you wanted to call the referee, just say 'sir'. "One of our coaches, Damian Heaslip, was very firm on this and we were to respect referees at all times. They are out there, and they were doing their best and as well as that you would meet them in the bar afterwards. And you could ask them a question if you needed to without making it too difficult for them in a social setting. That is in all levels."

So what are Pat's hopes for the club for the future?

He said: "I would like to see Sligo win Division 2B and just to go up as far as we can. Rugby has been good to me and it made my years very enjoyable. It is a sport I love, and I have made many good friends from it."

After listening to Pat for around 50 minutes, it is not difficult to see why he has made so many friends over the years.

He's one of the good guys.

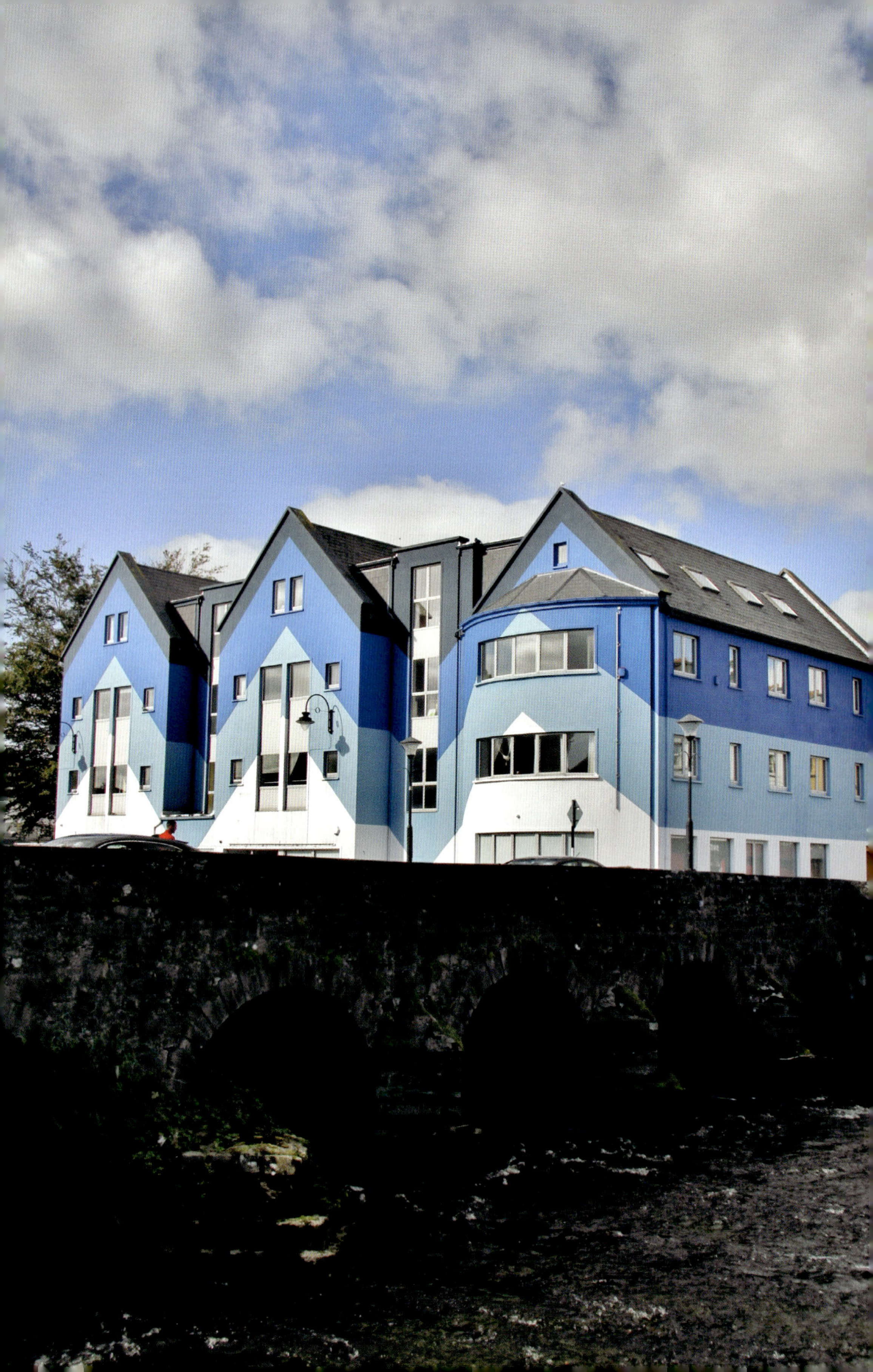

THE BUILDING BLOCK

Remote working is bigger than ever. The Building Block by the Garavogue river is well ahead of the curve, promoting it since 2016. Alan Finn chatted to its owner Martin Doran and several people who work there about the benefits of this shared space

PUBLISHED ON JULY 23, 2020

HEADLINES BEFORE THE COVID-19 pandemic were often dominated by the cost of rent and house prices in big cities, so it is not too surprising that remote working was already been explored by many people who moved to further their careers.

The Building Block's arrival in Sligo was geared towards members of the workforce keen to strike a better work-life balance from the comfort of their own hometown.

With the prevalence of remote working increasing this year,

LEFT: THE BUILDING BLOCK.
RIGHT: MARTIN DORAN

little has changed in that regard for the co-working space as demand for such working environments is only likely to grow.

Building owner Martin Doran, originally from Sligo, opened the premises in 2016, seeing it as a beacon of hope for the future rather than a negative reminder of the Celtic Tiger era.

He said: "It started off in an exciting manner when we decided to open the space. The building was largely vacant for 10 years, with the HSE being the only tenants on the top floor. We wanted to enliven the town centre and to allow businesses to grow in Sligo town and this seemed like a prime building to do that."

The lifestyle of Sligo has huge appeal to many people in big cities who yearn for life in a town with a more relaxed, easygoing attitude.

"Sligo has one of the best lifestyles that I know of in Ireland. There is plenty to do with the lakes, beaches, mountains and other outdoor activities, the nightlife is quite vibrant and the town is large enough to really hold its own. This is a lifestyle that you don't really get to enjoy in Dublin. The commutes are very different and the environment just isn't as easily accessible. The question always was 'can we create co-working and remote working spaces?' like we have done in Sligo and it is clear to see there is a drive for people to move and work in places like Sligo," continued.

"In Dublin, people have to use large public transport which isn't as convenient an option as it was and then you walking into a large office in a high density situation. Places like the Building Block offer an alternative to that to allow you to live and work in a less dense population and still be connected with a work environment."

The former Summerhill College student is familiar with the business landscape of Dublin and says the change in attitude among very traditional companies has been seismic, with some making what were considered highly unlikely moves to allow their staff to work four-day weeks.

"I work closely with a number of other industries and we have seen a groundswell change in policy. They want their staff working less in the office directly and there is a massive change in the acceptance to work efficiently from home.

"Some very traditional firms expect their staff to work four-day weeks. That was unheard of years ago when staff were often working crazy hours, so there has been a substantial shift. The next step has to be doing the same job from Sligo and leaving triple the rent behind in Dublin."

As well as being positive for the employee, Martin said that the Building Block also puts employers' minds at rest who still have their qualms about employees working from home.

"You might wonder are they working at their computer, are they doing a bit of DIY around the house or lying on the couch watching TV. I think employers will be happier to have staff in an environment like this."

"And a company can only pay you X amount for the role, but the employee has costs like rent and travel. The cost of employing people in Dublin is extremely high. If they can employ people in Sligo where the quality of life for the employee is much better, it is a win-win scenario," he added.

Martin is very optimistic about the future of Sligo but feels a lot more could and should be done to manifest the image everyone has of the town, stating that something as simple as planting trees rather than placing them in pots can make a big different to the environment people are expecting in Sligo.

"As a town, we have to brand ourselves better. We are more than a gateway city. I think we should be trying to brand ourselves as a green city. Plant more trees throughout in the ground rather than in pots, for example. You will attract more people if you can sell that image of Sligo – the surfing community did a very good job of that.

"Sligo has a lot more to offer, but you have to put your money where your mouth is to change the look and feel of Sligo," he added.

KEITH PATTERSON

International companies offering their employees a chance to work from their hometown is something we may see a lot more of in the future.

The discussion around remote working was not a hot topic pre-pandemic, but some employers had already been utilising this option. One such company is Salutem Insights, with whom Keith Patterson works. The

Rathcormac native was offered the chance to work from Ireland. While working from home did not appeal to him, working from the Building Block provided an ideal alternative.

"I came in here in February after working in England for a few years. I moved back to take up a job as an analyst with Solutem Insights, they offered me the option of working remotely anywhere I wanted in Ireland and being from Sligo originally it just made sense to come back. I also have a friend who previously worked out of the Building Block and he recommended it to me after I just couldn't settle working from home."

Transitioning from the traditional office to a collaborative working space has proven to be smooth for Keith, who has enjoyed the sharing an office with a variety of different workers ranging from fellow remote workers for international companies to the self-employed.

"It has never really been an issue for me that my colleagues here are all working for different companies or their own companies and I know my colleagues in the agency are only a zoom or phone call away. It is obviously a bit different to be in this working space with people who aren't working in the same company as you, but the social aspects of it are the exact same as a normal office which is good."

Remote working being embraced on a large scale may take time, but Keith is hopeful that Sligo is on the cusp of benefitting greatly by this model which will allow many like him to stay close to home rather than feeling they have to move for work

"Before the pandemic there was a great buzz around the town, there was talk of Sligo becoming the new Galway. We are still at a point where most major companies are not thinking of opening their head office in a place like this, you'd still have to go and do these jobs in the major cities, but having something like the Building Block in Sligo is a great asset in being able to do this remote work comfortably."

LEFT: CLOCKWISE FROM TOP LEFT: KEITH PATTERSON, TOM O'SULLIVAN, TREVOR FINNEGAN AND NIALL HEALY

Solutem Insights has chosen to make the most of remote working and Keith feels environments like the Building Block will appeal greatly expats currently plying their trade elsewhere.

"It depends on the company but in Solutem there is already another couple of people working in similar environments around Ireland. My company are very happy to have me working here, I am happy to be working here and I think it is something that will appeal to a lot more people working abroad and in other parts of the country."

TOM O'SULLIVAN

The growing transition from the traditional office setting to remote working is a discussion which has grown with great prevalence throughout the Covid-19 pandemic.

Much of Ireland's workforce made the sudden switch from their normal work surroundings in March to the environments they call home.

Remote working is seen as the inevitable future, but operating from home is not considered a viable long-term option for many.

This idea is not exclusive to the home, however, as co-operative working areas like the Building Block provide a perfect alternative for those who still want to separate work and life.

Tom O'Sullivan, an actors' agent and ambassador for the Building Block, moved to Sligo from Dublin in 2017 and quickly set up in the premises.

While the nature of the building is geared towards optimising individual work, Tom highlighted the beneficial social aspects of the Building Block.

"The advantage of a collaborative working space is that rather than having to work from home, this space encourages people to come into a working environment.

"Even though we are individuals with individual companies, we can avail of the social aspect of working out of here and not dealing with various distractions which present themselves when you are working at home.

"We have a great reservoir of talent here too, if you are having a problem with some aspect of your company you can run it by a colleague here who has probably experienced the same difficulty at some stage so there is an invaluable resource to dip into here for problem-solving."

The Building Block never fully shut down throughout lockdown, offering workers the chance to continue working in their space which ultimately suited some as social distancing was far from an issue.

Members are slowly returning to the building, which has been safeguarded in adherence with public health guidelines, and Tom said there has also been an increase in enquiries from prospective new members in recent weeks.

"We were affected by the lockdown, but we did stay open. We gave our members an option to terminate their membership and give them the break of paying the monthly member fee and we have seen a lot of those members coming back and pick up from where they left off.

"We have capacity for new members who find themselves working from home as opposed to their office in Sligo, Dublin or Galway."

Working from home can be good for productivity, but often comes at a price for many, according to Tom, who spent several years doing just that before seeking out a remote working location.

He said: "I worked from my kitchen table for the first three years and there is a lot of pros and cons to working from your own home, but over time you do see it as being more cons than pros. You are never really switch off, you might feel more productive but at the cost of burning yourself out quicker.

"We are hopeful now that as things are opening again, more people will view the Building Block as a great area for remote workers at a cost of only €217 a month, which gives them 24/7 fob access and that's unbeatable when we see this as the way working is moving forward."

There is increased interest in moving from the big city to towns such as Sligo in order to strike a better work-life balance, but Tom feels the environment of remote working will also appeal greatly to locals who have moved elsewhere to work but harbour a long-term desire to be based in here.

"I think the pandemic has shown that people do not have to uproot themselves just to work at the office of their company. If you can do it from home, you can do it from a collaborative space like the Building Block.

"I feel interest will continue to grow in wanting to work here and working in these environments will be ingrained in the work culture of Ireland. This can be good for both your employer and your own work-life balance because you are cutting down on the amount of commuting, you are back home within minutes rather than hours and you can still wind down and enjoy the remainder of the day in comfort."

TREVOR FINNEGAN

Decentralisation has long been an idea pursued in the interest of Sligo. In recent years, workers in Dublin have increasingly sought a move west for a better work-life balance. The Covid-19 pandemic has propelled this way of thinking forward for many who want to swap the hustle and bustle for a quiet and peaceful lifestyle.

Trevor Finnegan is among those people to have made the switch to Sligo with his young family. Trevor, who works with revertdesign.net, did not choose Sligo at random however. He is no stranger to the county, having come back to the town every year to visit and work for his grandparents in Café Cairo.

"I spent all my summers in Sligo and worked here every summer through my teens and would have had plenty of visits to places like Strandhill and Rosses Point as well.

"My wife and I both lived and worked in Dublin for around 15 years and when we had our first child we knew the time was right to move out of there and settle down in the west and Sligo was always our first choice so it was great that everything worked out that way.

"The Building Block was a big bonus in moving here," he said. "I spoke to people who worked here who just made it sound all the more appealing when they told me what it was like to work here. I found out very quickly there was people involved in similar businesses here too so it helps even more to have people who you can collaborate with in the same field."

Trevor has been based in the Building Block for the last 18 months after a number of years working in an office in Dublin.

He said: "It's a good place to work. It has been ideal because when we moved down to Sligo two years ago, I had been working in an office in Dublin up until then but this was just the perfect space that I was looking for to work when we decided we wanted to move here. I've gotten to know a lot of the people in here and they were all very helpful to me when I was settling in first."

Business still takes Trevor back to Dublin on occasion, but 99 per cent of his work takes place in Sligo and he sees this model of relocating to regional towns, or a return home many big city workers, as the future.

He said: "We still have an office in Dublin and I would go up and down now and again, but so far it has worked out really well for me to be based here and this is something I definitely see as being the way forward for many people.

"The major cities are overpopulated and people are realising there is more to life than sitting in traffic for an hour to work and go home, so this pandemic has been a big wake-up call for both employees and employers."

"Some towns experienced mass emigration so this would be a great way for local authorities to regrow the population and this would allow smaller shops to open up again and local producers to thrive."

NIALL HEALY

The advent of the Building Block has offered a new incentive for self-employed Sligonians to return home. Niall Healy, a self-employed software consultant, uprooted from Carlow with his family in favour of re-establishing the life they knew in Ballincar. There are many factors to be considered when moving and jobs naturally play a big role in this. For

Niall, the Building Block offered the ideal location for him to conduct business.

"I am from Sligo originally. We had been living in Carlow and we decided after some deliberation we had to come back and from that point of view I was lucky my profession lends itself to remote working so it was a perfect fit.

"We had always thought about coming back and as the kids got older we decided it was a case of now or never, so we came back and we were delighted we made that decision."

When the Covid-19 pandemic became very real in Ireland, Niall decided to work from home in order to allow his wife, a nurse at the North West Hospice, to work on the frontline.

Despite having a home office, Niall feels there is an inherent need to have a separate place of work that is removed from family life in order to strike the ideal work-life balance.

"I am delighted to be back working in here. Home working is excellent but can be constrained by circumstance and suitability.

"I was lucky to have a standalone office but even with that, it was still a big improvement work wise to get back to an environment like this."

Niall is a strong advocate for the future prevalence of remote working in Ireland. He feels the advantages it presents are numerous and can enable people to be more productive than ever before if they operate from a shared working space.

"I think there is a whole reconfiguration and perspective on remote working. It will be much more prevalent going forward and what has been enlightening for me is the extent to which remote working can be more efficient than it was in an office environment.

"Tools like Microsoft Teams and Zoom are very efficient for collaborating as a team and I think myself and my colleagues who work in this area have been a lot more productive like this than when we would all sit down in person in one place."

2020 could be seen as the beginning of the era of collaborative working spaces. Contrary to what people think when they hear the term 'remote working', Niall believes the future of this is in shared spaces rather than at home work as not every home will be suitable or adaptable for this.

"For shared, co-working spaces, this is their time and they offer advantages across the whole spectrum of how you would assess working from home to working in an office, it really offers you the best of all worlds. There's no circumstance in which you could make a case that working from home offers you more of an advantage than working in a collaborative environment and it presents a lot of opportunity to interact with people who you can really learn from."

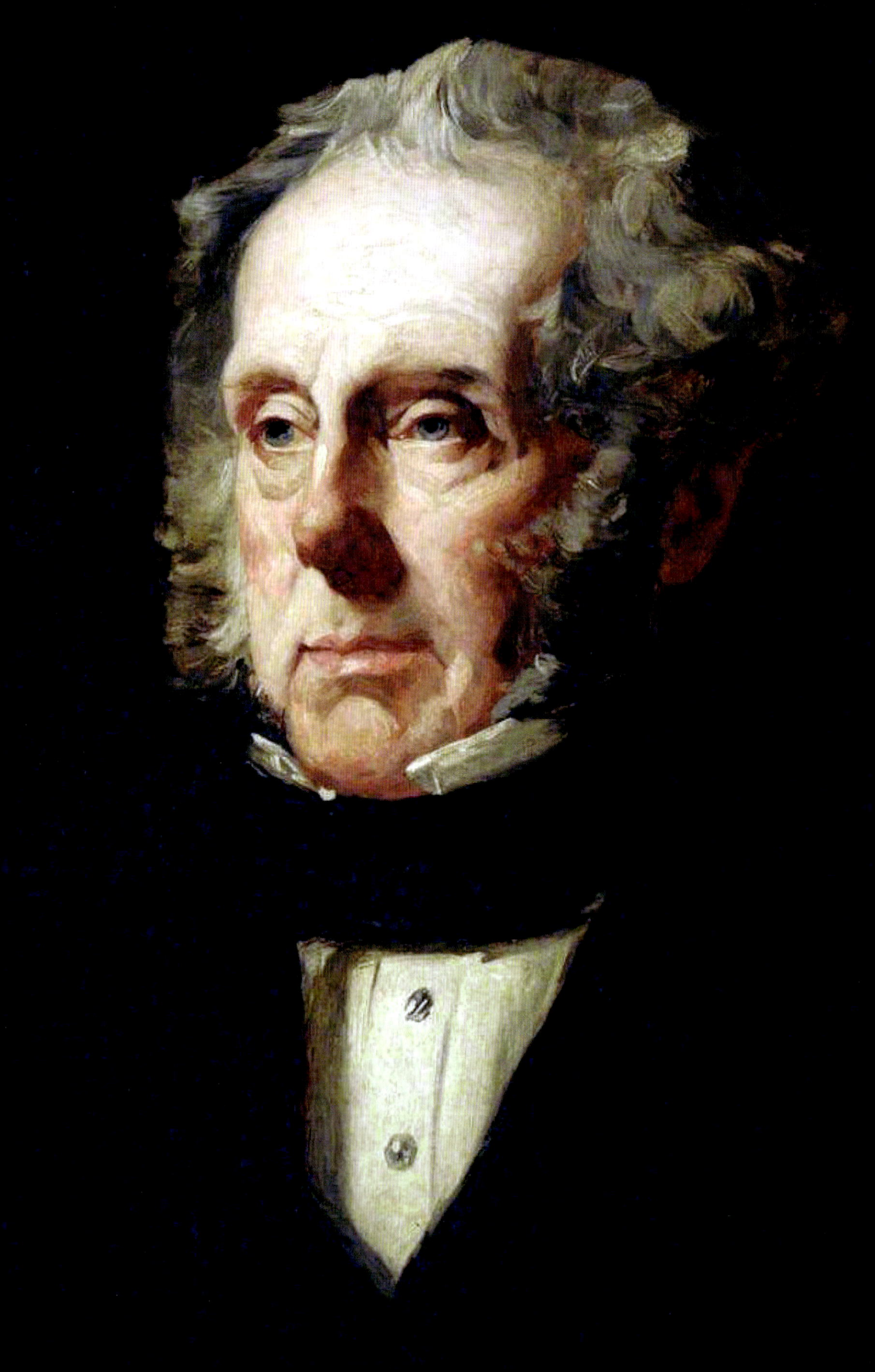

PALMERSTON AND CATHOLIC RIGHTS

Lord Palmerston's Sligo tenants suffered terribly in the Famine, leaving him with a reputation for cruelty. But he was also an advocate for the rights of Irish Catholics. Peter Henry met author John McKeon to learn about his research into the infamous landlord

PUBLISHED ON MAY 30, 2019

HENRY JOHN TEMPLE, 3RD VISCOUNT Palmerston, is remembered as the absentee landlord who oversaw the horrors of the Famine on his vast estates in Sligo. A book written last year by historian John McKeon gives a detailed picture of those awful years under Lord Palmerston. But he was also an outspoken advocate in London for Irish Catholics' rights, and a recently discovered speech emphasises this seemingly unlikely aspect of the man. I called out to Mullaghmore, part of the former estate of

LEFT: LORD PALMERSTON BY FREDERICK CRUICKSHANK

Lord Palmerston, to meet John McKeon and find out what he learned while researching his book.

While Palmerston, who lived from 1784 to 1865, is known here as the tyrant of his Sligo tenants during the Famine, in England his legacy is that of a politician, having served several times as prime minister and foreign secretary.

John told me about this powerful man and his activity in Sligo. He said:

"Palmerston inherited the place in 1802. There was unrest around that time after the 1798 rebellion and the Act of Union. But in 1808 he visited for the first time, and he wrote a letter at that stage that outlined what he considered the main issues on the estate. These, he said, were overpopulation and landlessness.

"To try to solve these issues he looked to get rid of the middlemen, those who generated profit from rents and kept some land for themselves.

"Another of his prime objectives was to build proper schools. He wanted to build these schools, and there was tremendous opposition here to them as they were seen as a trick. Palmerston and the Bishop of Elphin, Patrick Burke, signed an agreement allowing him to go ahead with them. He set up two in Ballymote, two in Sligo town and several in north Sligo. Some of the current primary schools are the successors to those he set up.

"The other thing he wanted to do was to build roads. So this tremendous network of roads that we have now in the Mullaghmore and Cliffoney area were started very soon after his arrival.

"Palmerston also helped to build St Molaise Church in Cliffoney and he built a house there for the Catholic priest.

"He made a lot of investments like these. Some of the area's other landlords objected to this type of investment, saying that they should be the function of the state. It was also putting pressure on them to do the same."

Another legacy of Palmerston is the harbour in Mullaghmore, about which John has also written. It was built in two stages by the engineers Alexander Nimmo and Robert Stevenson. I asked John if these improvements to his estates – which were located in north Sligo and Ballymote – were for the good of the people or for his own good.

"Both," said John. "He was quite clear about that. He expected to make more money and also felt it was necessary for the people and that it would be a win-win. As it turned out, it wasn't a win for him – he ended up losing money. The harbour, for example, might benefit us now, but it didn't help his bottom line at the time."

John's research for his book revealed that painting Palmerston as an irredeemable tyrant would fail to take into account the facts. He said: "He is accused of raising rents during the Famine. That didn't happen. He is accused of being anti-Catholic. But he stood for their rights to vote 20 years before Catholic Emancipation.

"Now he did have self-interested motivation – that was certainly the case. But he wanted to both improve the people's situation and his own bottom line."

Palmerston's major project was carrying out "land squaring".

John said: "Sir Robert Gore Booth at Lissadell had been implementing land squaring since the 1820s. Squaring involves the consolidation of smaller holdings. Palmerston saw it as highly controversial and was afraid it would lead to social unrest.

"But he did begin implementing it in 1837. The situation was that a tenant with three acres might have those three acres in 20 different plots. You can imagine the difficulty of farming that. So squaring gave you the land, assigned by lottery, in a single plot.

"Getting rid of the middlemen hadn't been a panacea. So squaring was an attempt to go further. It continued right through Famine times."

Squaring directly affected those who rented land. But nearly half of those on the north Sligo estate, John told me, had no land. They were labourers, or cottiers, and it was these who were hit badly when the Famine arrived. They were in a desperate situation.

John said: "Between July and September 1846, the Famine hit the estate badly. And the ongoing squaring contributed greatly to the people's concerns. The following year, despite employment and soup kitchens, it was estimated that 4,000 to 5,000 people were in danger of death. Assistance to leave was considered one way of helping people."

Assisted emigration is one of the legacies of Lord Palmerston most deplored when we look back at his time. John told me that the motivation during the Famine was both to save lives and to improve the financial situation of the estate. Assisted emigration had not been introduced in response to the Famine. Rather, it had been offered before then as part of the squaring project, though take-up had been low.

I wondered about how people felt getting on these boats. Were they all reluctant and in fear, or did some even welcome it?

John said: "The newspaper cuttings from the time indicate that many people were hopeless and just wanted to get out. There were some who had money, but a lot of them were the landless labourers who had nothing."

Palmerston was a busy man elsewhere, managing estates in Dublin and England, and attending to his political duties. Did he really have much input into what was going on in Sligo, I wondered, or was it all delegated to agents?

John said: "His involvement was close and he visited regularly. Even later in 1863 when still prime minister he was dictating the size of the garden in what is now the convent in Mullaghmore, which was built at the time as a guesthouse.

"Resident landlords accused him of being an absentee landlord. But he accused them of being 'absent from the minds and hearts of their tenants'. He said they lived walled away from them.

"Classiebawn was after his time. When he was in Sligo he stayed in the pub in Cliffoney, a village he built. The pub is now O'Donnell's."

The O'Donnell's pub website says: "It is said the ghost of Palmerston still haunts the pub, but we would say it is a very friendly presence."

I asked John about an 1829 speech by Palmerston made in the House of Commons "on the Catholic question". He had not been aware of this document while writing his book. A *Sligo Weekender* reader kindly sent me a copy of this remarkable defence of Irish Catholics earlier this year, and it doesn't appear to be the product of a mind consumed with hatred for the people of Ireland or their religion.

John said: "His speech makes three or four major points. It's very much for the Catholic right to vote. That's consistent with what he had said before. His second point is the lack of capital being invested in Ireland.

"The third point is new. He is ridiculing to some degree his colleagues' arguments against Catholic votes and the alternatives they were proposing.

"The fourth point is that Catholics were allowed to serve in the military, very important to a country, but MPs wouldn't allow them to serve in the House of Commons or allow them to vote."

I looked up the passages to which John was referring, and they are forceful. Palmerston says: "A Catholic may lead the fleet of England into fight. In that perilous hour we are content to commit our fortunes to the Catholic, confident in his patriotism, his honour and his faith. But when the question is as to a seat in this house, we tremble at the dangers that would befall the state."

Palmerston even refers to "Protestants of the north", who, he says, are "corrupted by the possession of undue and inordinate ascendancy" and "brought up from their earliest infancy to hate the great majority of their countrymen".

On absenteeism, perhaps with himself in mind, he told the Commons that "Catholic Emancipation is its only cure".

John said: "It's a good read. There's a capable and intelligent mind behind it. Palmerston was in communication with Daniel O'Connell. The ideas in the speech can be found elsewhere."

I asked John about how Palmerston has been perceived in Sligo since his time. He said: "His bad legacy comes primarily from the Famine and the assisted emigration, which was interpreted as dumping people off the land without concern for their welfare and in the interest of the estate's profitability. It became and remains the prominent narrative. It's certainly not fully true. But there was a Famine and there was a lot of misery associated with assisted emigration.

"Compare him with Lord Lansdowne in Kerry. He said that he wouldn't incur the expenses that Palmerston did during the Famine. And fewer people died on Palmerston's ships than did on others.'"

These facts don't, of course, exonerate Lord Palmerston from responsibility, but they surely show that his reputation as an arch-tyrant is perhaps not completely deserved.

I asked what the man was like personally. John said: "People liked him. He was a hit with the women. I think he was a workaholic in England. He was a very active man, physically and mentally.

"The parish priest in Cliffoney, Malachy Brennan, was a friend of his, and they shared many dinners together.

"It's all part of the story of the area. And that was mainly my motivation in learning and writing about him."

John told me how as part of his research he helped to track down descendants of those who survived the wreck of the Carrick, the major shipping disaster of the Famine. The Carrick had been used for assisted emigration from Palmerston's estate to Quebec. John was able to show one family exactly which house in north Sligo their ancestors had left during the Famine.

The Famine brought great hardship to Ireland, and Sligo was one of the worst-hit places. The annual commemorations in Stephen Street car park show that we haven't forgotten this tragedy. In Sligo, Lord Palmerston will always be remembered as the absentee landlord who oversaw years of human suffering on his estates. John's research has shown the complexities behind this legacy.

Other historians will rightly emphasise different aspects of this powerful man's life, but John is to be thanked for his contribution to the recording of this difficult time in Sligo's history.

John McKeon, Lord Palmerston: An Absentee Irish Landlord, *is available in bookshops in Sligo town.* Speech of Viscount Palmerston on the Catholic Question *is available on Google Books*

EUGENE MACHALE

Cliffoney-based charity worker, Gaelic footballer, referee and Sligo Weekender *columnist Eugene MacHale tells Gerry McLaughlin about his life as a garda, a GAA man – and a no-holds-barred writer*

PUBLISHED ON JULY 2, 2020

ONLY THE GREATEST COLUMNISTS tell it as they see it. This has become the age of anodyne, ghosted, pallid and awful offerings from the majority of pundits, where some ex-players sit so tightly and are scared stiff of offending anyone.

But that is a complaint that the true legend that is former Garda Eugene MacHale, will never suffer from.

For, a columnist without an opinion is about as useful as a promise from a dodgy politician. A columnist must never be afraid to express that opinion, something MacHale excels at.

The globetrotting Eugene, who has raised over €100,000 for charities in several

LEFT: EUGENE MACHALE AS A MANAGER WITH BALLYMOTE GAA CLUB IN 2010

countries, has written a sports column for the *Sligo Weekender* since the mid-2000s, which makes him one of the longest serving scribes in the land, in sunshine and in shadow.

His well-written, entertaining columns have enlightened, educated and sometimes enraged readers in almost equal measure.

One thing is certain, he would never want to be described as a safe pair of hands when it was necessary to put the boot in.

The Cliffoney-based community activist, charity worker, Gaelic footballer, team manager and referee isn't afraid to call it as he sees it, with his views often aimed at the GAA hierarchy.

Eugene is also well known for hard-hitting comments in the national media about Sligo GAA and his native Mayo and his direct hits have ruffled loads of pretty plumage for which he cares not a jot.

But he has an innate sense of justice and fair play and has put his heart and soul into the GAA over many decades.

In 2020 he swam against the tide yet again by telling the press that club players were "being used as guinea pigs" when club action resumed.

A few years ago, he publicly called for the Mayo players to apologise for their alleged stance in the departure of their joint-managers Noel Conneely and Pat Holmes.

If there is something to be said, Eugene will spit it out and back up his argument with passionate examples and like the rest of us he does not always get it right, but he generally says what he thinks.

"If I think something is wrong, I will speak out and I am very grateful to have a forum in which to do this in the column.

"Too many people are afraid of causing offence, but you can't have utopia and wrongs are committed and these should be highlighted," said the Knockmore native.

And the colourful, charismatic and controversial Eugene could never be accused of telling you what you want to hear. But then he comes from a large family, many of whom are GAA leaders, so he has great training in arguing his point.

He has always been a champion for the 'little guy', for the wounded, the bruised and the broken. He writes as he speaks, from the heart.

His sentences are short, pithy and to the point and have infuriated many of those "amateur politicians" who populate the GAA, the organization that he loves with a savage and undimmed passion.

But that does not mean he condones its perceived faults and he left Sligo and made history by becoming the first referee in the history of the GAA to get an inter-county transfer and he is now the oldest referee in Donegal at the age of 62.

Eugene left in protest at the way proposed suspensions from the Sligo GAA Competitions Control Committee were being slashed by the county's Hearings Committee some years ago.

In one instance a fellow referee who verbally abused him at a match had a six-month ban reduced to two months.

In another case a well-known Sligo county player had a red card given to him by Eugene rescinded.

And even though he has a great love for the GAA in Sligo, Eugene saw these two decisions as an insult to all referees, so he walked.

But the GAA is not the only part of Eugene's varied career.

As a member of An Garda Síochána for decades, he was present at some harrowing scenes, including the grim discovery of the murdered remains of Margaret Perry from Northern Ireland in Mullaghmore in 1992.

Eugene was a star Gaelic footballer with Knockmore in his native county Mayo, winning five county championships in 1980, 1983 (as team captain), 1984, 1989 and 1992, five SFL titles and a Connacht Club title.

He represented Mayo with distinction, featuring from 1978 to 1986. He starred in two All-Ireland semi-finals, in 1981 and 1985, netting a wonder goal against Kerry in the 1981 semi-final.

When in Sligo, Eugene played with Grange-Cliffoney (which later became St Molaise Gaels) and scored six points in winning a county Junior title with the north Sligo outfit in the 1990s when in his mid-40s. He was also player-manager for a term.

He managed Easkey (their first ever outside manager), Aodh Ruadh, Ballyshannon, Drumkeeran, Omagh-St Enda's and coached IT Sligo.

He once famously said he "would play Billy Wright"(a notorious Loyalist killer who was killed by Republicans) if it ensured victory.

A fitness fanatic, he has also walked in many places in the world raising thousands for charity in far flung places like Tanzania, Kenya, Cuba, New Zealand, Vietnam, Glasgow and India. He has also taken part in a number of 100-mile walks in Ireland, mostly for the Irish Heart Foundation.

But he is perhaps most widely known as a very good community garda in north Sligo, a place he has served in since 1980.

Like many other officers Eugene has seen his fair share of tragedies in his work, horrific road accidents, murders, suicides and has seen a growing disrespect for the uniform in a changing society.

As an officer he was a strong believer in common sense in settling some problems rather than racking up ego points through the issuing of summonses.

The law must be applied, but sometimes the law is an ass and Eugene was always able to know the difference.

He was a quintessential community garda who knew his patch and more importantly knew his people, and some have told this writer of his kindness and great empathy in times of deep sorrow.

Eugene was born into a great sporting family of 10 in Knockmore, County Mayo on December 12, 1957.

He is the seventh of 10 siblings. His brothers and sisters are Sean, Raymond, Noel (RIP), Philip (RIP), Eddie, Ann, Mary, Aidan and Irene. His parents were the late Sean and Brigie MacHale.

"I have some great memories and also of great triumphs with Knockmore, our local GAA club that meant everything to me and still does. I always looked up to my older brothers and they were my heroes and I could not wait to get on the team. And even though I went on to play county football, to the day I die I will always look up to the club men."

His older brother Eddie played county football with Mayo, Sligo and Leitrim.

Eugene joined An Garda Síochána on June 21, 1978, and his first posting was to Ballymun in Dublin. But he got a transfer to Kinlough in 1980 and was in that north Leitrim and Sligo area until he retired from the force in 2009.

He said: "It was a quiet village similar to where I came from, but the Troubles in Northern Ireland were at their height and there were quite a few men in the barracks. We were lucky enough that there were no roads from Kinlough leading into the North as they were all cratered.

"I often felt sorry for people that lived along the border on both sides at the inconvenience of the cratered roads. When I look back on it, it was wrong that ordinary people were victimised like that and they were.

"But even though we were policing very close to a war situation, we always had a great relationship with the people and that never changed despite what was happening.

"I can remember the Hunger Strike in 1981 which was a very emotional time but, again, the people and the gardai still had a great bond. There were huge demonstrations all over the place and it was a terrible time in our history.

"On reflection, British prime minister Margaret Thatcher was wrong not to accede to the Republican prisoners' requests. There are always mistakes made, there were mistakes made in 1916 and I think she was wrong in her unflinching stances and I am not advocating for the prisoners.

"And when you make martyrs of people, well the next generation will look up to them and it was the same in 1916 and there is not much real difference between how the 1916 leaders were treated and the way the hunger strikers were treated."

Eugene also saw at first hand the aftermath of the tragic murder of Northern Ireland woman Margaret Perry. She was murdered and subsequently buried in a shallow grave in Mullaghmore in 1992.

"We were in the station in Kinlough, when we got the call to go to Mullaghmore. I remember reading about her disappearance in the Sunday papers the week before and they were pointing fingers at who did it and who didn't do it.

"Little did I think that a week later that I would be standing at the shallow grave that she was buried in". We were told there was a body found and I never thought it would be Margaret Perry. She was buried in a shallow grave and we took her fully clothed body out of the grave.

"It was very sad, and you always think of death in terms of your own and every single human being has a mother and father, and most have brothers and sisters. A death like that is horrible and you could only imagine what her family was going through.

"The body was transferred to Sligo General Hospital and it shocked me as I was living in the area and I could see where she was buried from the back of my home in Cliffoney.

"It was hard to believe that such and act was carried out in such a beautiful place and I had a young family of my own after marrying Claire in 1987. That brought it home to me even more and it is just so difficult for any parent to lose a child."

But tragedy was no stranger to Eugene as he was present at a number of fatal road crashes in the area which have left a mark on him.

"There were a number of fatal road traffic accidents that I had to investigate and it is much different than nowadays. Back then you would investigate it on your own even though it was a fatal accident.

"Every single one of them brought their own pain, sorrow and heartbreak. But the death of 15-year-old Marie Rooney who went to school with some of my own daughters was a very sad case to investigate.

"It is a person that you know, and it was terribly tough. It was absolutely heart-breaking and I knew her family very well. We brought her body to Sligo General Hospital and I stayed with her until her family arrived and that was just so sad."

Closer to home, Eugene and north Sligo were stunned by the death of Kevin Fowley in a tragic accident in Bundoran in 2004.

Eugene said: "He was living next door and he grew up with us and it was just heartbreaking, unbelievable and so sad for his family. I still keep in touch with all families that have been bereaved".

On a happier note, Eugene says he could not serve in a nicer area than north Sligo.

"The people are decent, honest, hard-working and friendly. We had our own courthouse in Grange and it was sad to see it closed. The same thing happened to the station in Cliffoney and so many small garda stations throughout the country were shut down and this just so wrong on so many levels. It was totally wrong and there is less of a garda presence in the area. But without the support of the people, no police force can survive and if you haven't the support of the people then you have no law and order because really it is the people who police themselves.

"The more contact a police officer has with the community, the more he or she knows. I don't agree with garda stations being closed. When a garda goes to work in an area he builds up a trust with the people.

EUGENE PLAYING FOR KNOCKMORE IN 1983

"That does not happen overnight and then they will confide in you and tell you what you should know, they might not tell you everything and that is all you want to know.

"If something happens in an area where there is no local garda and outside police come in, the locals are reluctant to trust them or talk to them."

He said: "Sadly, that is happening all over the country and the local garda was always vital. And when you are dealing with the public, treat them with respect and like the way you and yours would want to be treated.

"I tried to treat them all in the same way that I would like my own family to be treated and hopefully that was a great help." And when in court you would always try to speak up for defendants. There is good in everybody and everyone deserves at least one chance. If we were all brought up the same way that certain people were brought up, we would all be in court."

Meanwhile, Eugene became heavily involved in his local club, Grange-Cliffoney (later to become St Molaise Gaels) he was also manager of the club's Intermediate team.

"In 1992 I played my last year with Knockmore and I joined up with Grange-Cliffoney in the late 1990s. I always kept myself in good shape and I don't drink or smoke. I felt very much part of the community with the club as were my daughters, who were growing up.

'The GAA is wonderful at this and I was made very welcome and really felt at home and we had wonderful times and we beat a very good Eastern Harps team in a county Junior final.

"Andrew Lang was the real manager of the Intermediate team. Tommy McGowan was manager of the Junior team and he was a great character. He was a wonderful passionate man for football. He loved the club and he loved to win, and he instilled that in us and always got the very best out of players. And you look at managers nowadays and they are coming with degrees in this and that.

"But the one thing that is important for any manager is the ability to get on with the players and to get the best out of them and Tommy McGowan certainly did that."

Eugene continued to play Gaelic football until he was just short of 50.

"Nothing beats playing and I was so lucky to have been born at the same time as a great crop of players that came through in Knockmore. My club meant everything to me. I will always remember 1983 when I was team captain of Knockmore. I arrived back at our house with the cup and to greet my mother after winning the county title was very special."

Elsewhere, Eugene is very well known for his walks all over the world for various charities, but most notably the Irish Heart Foundation.

"The first walk was in 2000 and that was a walk in the Holy Land. It was the late Frances McAndrew who was doing Trojan work for the Irish Heart Foundation here in Sligo and asked me would I do a walk, and this was the start of many overseas walks.

"We flew out to Jerusalem and there was trouble at the time and we could see shelling in the distance. It was a 100-mile walk and you did between eight and 10 miles a day. And you had this inner feeling that you were in a very special place, to think that Jesus walked some of these roads. I am a person of deep faith and I had that great feeling of great spirituality.

"We did not go near the tourist places and we stayed in ordinary places for if you are trying to raise money you need to keep all costs down. I was the only man from Sligo but I met a man called Peter McHugh from Hollymount in Mayo and we became friends and did many walks together later. I was there for about 10 days."

The next walk was in 2002. This time it was from Dublin to Grange. Eugene left for Dublin on a Sunday. His garda colleague, Sergeant Pat Neary, was the driver of a camper van which was their accommodation, again to try and make as much as possible for the charity.

"I left on Sunday and arrived in Grange on the following Saturday evening. It was a tough walk and I got badly blistered, but it felt great and when you have the health and fitness to walk it is not really a big problem.

"I think the people who should be really complimented are the people who go out and help you on the walk, I always had great back-up. "And the people who give the money deserves the highest praise and I find the Irish are an amazing people at how charitable we are."

Also in 2002 he had one of the "greatest experiences" of his life when he went to the Missions in Nairobi, Kenya with Fr James O'Kane from Cliffoney.

"That was an amazing experience, there was serious poverty but there was a happiness and joy about the people that was very moving to see. It was such an eye opener and we went around visiting with priests and I could not imagine that there were people in the world as poor as they were and yet they still were happy with so little.

"I remember one Sunday at Mass and it flew by. It was one hour and 50 minutes and could you imagine a Mass like that in Ireland. It was an experience I will never forget. If I was a single man I would have stayed out there and that is the way I felt about it. I would have worked as a missionary.

"It was so rewarding. We were going around meeting people and helping them to get water supplies and for those people it was like winning the Lotto where they did not have to walk miles and miles for their water. To see the joy on their faces was something to behold".

Then in 2004, Eugene walked from Ballymote to Parkhead to raise money for a statue to Brother Walfrid from Ballymote, who founded Glasgow Celtic to help the poor in Glasgow.

Former Sligo Chief Superintendent Jim Sheridan went with Eugene and they travelled in a camper van to Paradise.

"I am a Celtic follower and we were coming back from a match one day and someone said we should put up a statue and I suggested that I would do a walk from Ballymote to Parkhead.

"Seán Cunningham, who used to have Shenanigans in Sligo, travelled with me to many Celtic matches and former Finn Harps and Sligo Rovers star Jim Sheridan was also on board.

"Jim Sheridan walked with me and Paudge Quinn from Ballygawley in Tyrone was very good to us and we stayed outside his place and he gave us food and money. When we reached Scotland Sean Cunningham was driving the bus for us."

"We were invited to the late Sean Fallon's house in Glasgow, a great Sligo Rovers and Glasgow Celtic legend, and he was a personal friend of Seán Cunningham. That was a great experience to be with such a famous man like Seán Fallon, who was so down to earth and so welcoming, and that was a highlight.

"Celtic knew we had done the walk and we did a lap of honour around the pitch at half-time in their match and we were interviewed by Celtic TV and the crowd sang 'You'll Never Walk Alone' as we walked around the pitch. That was a wonderful experience and the statue was put up".

The following year Eugene went on another walk for the Irish Heart Foundation to Cuba.

"It was a beautiful country with all the old big cars there and my wife Claire was with me. It was like going back in time and was another great experience. We were walking in a forest and we came upon a building which was a school. The children there were orphans but they had computers and great health facilities. We did a 100-mile walk and Havana was a special place for cigars and old buildings and a great sense of history."

In 2006 he walked from Ballina to Croke Park for the Mayo-Roscommon Hospice and it was the week before the All-Ireland final between Mayo and Kerry.

He said: "That was a very emotional walk and one that was well supported too. I had a camper van this time as well and I had different drivers and my good friend David Warren drove the last leg for me. I landed in Dublin on the day before the All-Ireland final but it was a tough walk, too."

That same year he went to Tanzania, the "hottest country I ever walked in". He said: "That was for the Friends of St Luke's and it was a real eye opener. The Maasai tribe were there and they were very athletic and wore very colourful red shawls around them and they loved their cattle. And if any of their animals were killed, they would follow the animal that did it and they would keep after it until they killed it. But it was a country ravaged by poverty and Aids and that was really educational, too."

In 2007 Eugene was off on his travels again to India for the Irish Heart Foundation in September. He went to Kerala on the south-western coast of India, immortalised in that great Makem and Clancy ballad.

Eugene said: "The people were lovely and it was densely populated. Drivers have a habit in India of never stopping, just blowing the horn and it took some getting used to.

"Cricket was played on every spare patch of ground and it was very warm, and the people were very friendly".

Then in 2008 Eugene went to Wellington in New Zealand, but did not get to finish that walk, as he rushed home to be with his mother Brigie who was very ill. This was for the Friends of St Luke's in Dublin and he was only three days on the walk, and he decided to come home to see his ill mother.

"I came home, and it was a long journey and I was with her on the Monday and she passed away on the Monday night. I was very close to my mother and something told me that I should go back home. It was the best decision I ever made".

And in 2009 he went on one of the most remarkable walks of them all to Vietnam which was "an amazing country".

"The people who were brutalized by war with the French and the Americans were unbelievably gentle and friendly and industrious. They would do anything for you, and they were a great people. We could see when we went into little villages how they had so many industries, little carpentry shops and barbers and all sorts of enterprises.

"You could see there why they would never be beaten in war because they had so much resilience, bravery and pride in their native place and they had real steel. They would survive where most of us would perish and I was there for a fortnight and that trip was for the Irish Heart Foundation.

So over a decade Eugene walked over 5,000 miles for charities and that did not include the hundreds of miles of training he had to do for those epic feats and raised in excess of 150,000 euro for various charities, a remarkable achievement by any standards.

"I was just glad I had the health and strength to do it. I am going to do another walk."

Meanwhile, closer to home he is a very well-known columnist with the *Sligo Weekender*.

He said: "I went to manage Easkey and I was friendly with sports editor Liam Maloney and his dad Willie, and Liam asked me to do a column and I am still doing it all these years later.

"At the end of the day, it is only my opinion, and everyone is entitled to their opinion. I am lucky enough in that I can get my opinion into a newspaper that a fair amount of people will read. Others have opinions, but don't have that chance, so I feel privileged. It would be a very dull world if we were all the same.

"Throughout my life anything I would see as wrong I would speak out, no matter it was. Of course, I make mistakes like everyone, but my views have always been genuinely held and I have the height of respect for the views of others. If you believe in something and you think that something is wrong, you give your opinion.

"People might say I am controversial. I never want to be controversial, but I will always give my opinion and argue it and maybe in hindsight I might say maybe I wasn't right there.

"But that is not the point, the point is you must have a view especially if you feel strongly about something and you need a thick skin at times. too, but hey, that's life. Some people don't want to give their opinion or are afraid to speak out or think it might not be to their advantage if they want to 'get on' in life or sport.

"But I will tell you what I think, not what I think you might like to hear, and that is how I have been all my life and I am not about to change now. I would never try to be personal I would try to be fair commenting on a match, a sending off and I give my honest opinion."

Eugene has commented on so many local, national and international events, but one thing that frustrates him is how club players are treated in the GAA.

"The club was everything to me and I never want to see club players being paid as it is an amateur sport. But I think that club players are being treated like second-class citizens and it is totally wrong. Don't forget that 97 per cent of players are club players and three per cent are county players. The three per cent have a recognized body, the Gaelic Players Association, and they get so much benefits and the 97 per cent gets nothing. Club players have the Club Players Association, but that group has not yet been recognised by Croke Park.

"Why are 97 per cent of the players treated like this? Surely I am not controversial in saying this and any right-thinking person would agree with me in this view. There are so many little perks they could give to club players like deals with mobile phone companies or car insurance companies."

"I think the CPA would be in a great bargaining position because you have so many club players and Croke Park needs to recognise the CPA as soon as possible.

"Make the club player important. I trained as hard for my club as I did for my county. I see the modern club players and the effort that they are putting in is huge."

And he is not a fan of having club fixtures back first on July 17 and believes the club players are "guinea pigs" in all of this.

"It would make more sense to have three per cent of players back playing first in the inter-county series. It would be far easier to monitor and county squads have very professional set-ups.

"Clubs have senior and reserve teams and you could have anything up to 80 players playing on small rural pitches all over the country which could be very risky as compared to the more controlled county fixtures".

"In a sense we are all guinea pigs and we are told there will be a surge in the virus in the autumn, so it makes more sense to start the inter-county competitions first. We are asking club players to play now Sunday after Sunday to get these competitions out of the way.

"Sadly, the big thing in the world today is money. We could have had a knockout championship in June and when 16 counties go out all of those players could go back and play with their clubs in the summer months which would be a great boost to the club scene.

"You would have reasonable crowds at club games with social distancing but today a county player does not play with his club and it is wrong."

In another life Eugene is a very well-known referee, having first taken up the whistle in the 1990s. The biggest game he got was an under-21 county final several years ago. Sadly, that was the match when a fellow referee verbally abused Eugene and the Sligo GAA CCC proposed a six-month ban. However, the Hearings Committee reduced this ban to two months.

In another instance Eugene gave a well-known Sligo county player a red card and that card was subsequently rescinded by the Hearings Committee.

"There were incidents in Sligo that I felt were wrong and if a person gets suspended, they should stay suspended and that was not happening".

And this was the background to his historic inter-county transfer to Donegal, in a landmark move for a referee.

"I had a choice to either give up refereeing in Sligo, which I enjoyed, or go elsewhere and whether people think I am right or wrong I will always be true to myself and I left Sligo on principle. I have no regrets as Donegal has given me a new lease of life.

"When I saw a six-month ban reduced to two months in Sligo, I just could not remain in that set-up.

"There are loads of fine people involved with the GAA in the county, for whom I have the height of respect, but in matters of principle there can be no compromise."

Eugene is now the oldest referee in Donegal, still whistling in his 63rd year, a testament to his fitness and dedication.

"But Sligo GAA means a lot to me and next to Mayo it is my favourite county and I have many good friends at all levels of the GAA in Sligo. In 2002 a great Sligo team almost beat Armagh who went on to win the All-Ireland. But the best player I ever saw was Mickey Kearins from Beltra, a great Sligo man.

"I am living in Sligo since the 1980s, it is my home, I have children and grandchildren here and I would love to see Sligo progress.

"I love the GAA. Next to my family and faith, it is the most important thing in my life, and I don't knock it just for the sake of knocking it, but only to make it even better in my own way. I don't drink or smoke and the GAA is my addiction.

"The greatest thing is the club, playing with your parish, your friends that you grew up with, argued with and these are the people who will carry you before you go through the door beyond the grave.

"It is about pride in your own, your own people and your own place. I am proud to have been part of all that and will be part of the GAA until I am no more."

Keep on writing and walking, Eugene.

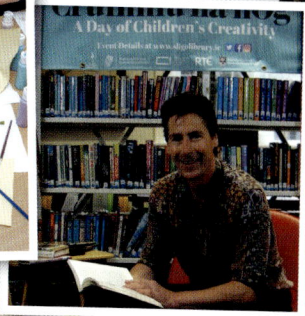

SLIGO COUNTY LIBRARIES

Sligo Libraries deliver library services
throughout its branch network:

Sligo Central Library
Ballymote Community Library
Tubbercurry Community Library
Enniscrone Branch Library
Reference and Local Studies
Mobile Library Services

ONLINE SERVICES

Sligo Libraries has a wonderful range of free online
services: eBooks, eAudiobooks, digital magazines
and newspapers, and eLanguage and eLearning
courses. Join online at www.sligolibrary.ie

FREE ONLINE RESOURCES:
E-books | E-audiobooks
Digital Magazines
Online Newspapers
E-Learning Courses
Online Language Learning

The Word: a collaboration
between Sligo Libraries
and the staff and students
of IT Sligo's BA (Hons)
Writing & Literature,
featuring author
readings, Q&A and
open mic

EVENTS

*Follow us to join our increasing schedule of home-grown
and free online events, including storytelling, health and
wellbeing seminars, art and craft activities, online yoga,
book clubs, music events, and The Word – pictured*

- **www.sligolibrary.ie**
- **facebook.com/SligoCountyLibrary**
- **@sligolibrary**   **@sligolib**

Sligo County Council
Comhairle Chontae Shligigh

MARY CULLEN

In December 2018, Mary Cullen was diagnosed with cancer – while she was expecting a baby. The inspiring athlete talked to Liam Maloney about what was her toughest year

PUBLISHED ON OCTOBER 17, 2019

THIS IS THE ONE RACE THAT SHE has to win. And, thankfully, for Mary Cullen, the finish line is in sight.

There will be no medal this time or a new personal best, but a chance at a happily ever after with her young son, five-month-old Ellis, and her partner Mark Smyth. Hoping that there is life after cancer.

Mary, from Coolbeg, Drumcliffe, has been coping with the toughest year in her life. The athlete, who has competed for Ireland and won a European medal 10 years ago, was diagnosed with cancer in December of 2018. But, at the time of the worst news possible, she and Mark were invigorated by the fact that Mary was eight

LEFT AND RIGHT: MARY CULLEN AT ATHLETIC MEETS

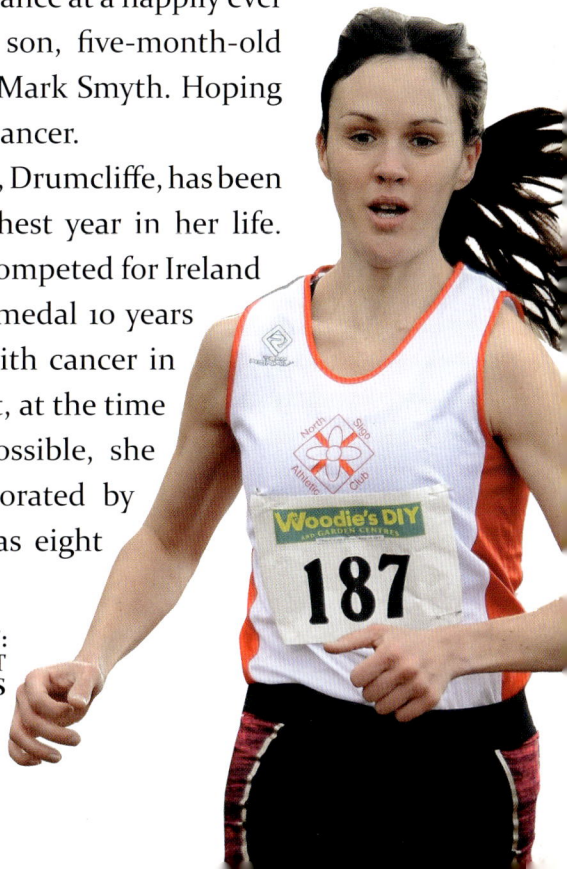

weeks pregnant. Anxious, terrifying months were in store: She juggled looking forward to having her first child with the difficulties of dealing with and overcoming a tricky cancer.

The 37-year-old reflected on the day she was told that what she thought was a hearing issue was actually a tumour.

Working in RunPod at the time, she jogged the short distance from Markievicz Road to JFK Parade, where the offices of Marcus Choo, a consultant ENT surgeon, were based.

"I remember leaving Mr Choo's office after being told that I had cancer and walking aimlessly around the town. I was walking over towards Dunnes Stores."

"Then I got upset because I rang mum [Geraldine] and I rang my sisters. Then I remember being in Dunnes and seeing people that I knew, I didn't want them to see me upset."

She recalled: "I was just walking around in a bit of a daze. It was a little bit like it was happening to someone else. I had the background of being a runner, of being fit and healthy. I wasn't feeling sick. I didn't feel like there was anything wrong."

Mary lost people close to her as a result of cancer. Her dad, Paddy, passed in July 2011 as a result of lung cancer (although Mary points out that he was a smoker) and her aunt, Mary Noone (a sister of her mum, Geraldine) died from cancer 18 years ago – just months before Mary headed off on an American sports scholarship at Providence College, Rhode Island.

For someone who, because of her running career, has had to adhere to a healthy lifestyle, getting cancer made no sense.

After getting used to the awful predicament came medical bulletins and test results. The tumour was located in the nasopharyngeal region (the upper part of the throat, behind the nose) with malignant cells also near the brainstem.

When it had spread to one of the lymph nodes behind her ear, a surgery procedure called neck dissection was required.

Ahead of that surgery on December 18, 2018, Mary realised that it wasn't just her life that was in jeopardy. Her unborn child was also at risk.

"I was told that the type of cancer I had was unusual and that unusual cancers do unusual things. The surgery I was going to have brought with it a risk of miscarriage – that is when my focus went on the baby more so than myself."

She got through that – with just a subtle neck scar as a reminder – and then it was a case of a nervous waiting game. Waiting until she was 35 weeks into her pregnancy so that the baby could be induced and delivered. Then the treatment for her cancer could begin.

There may have been no middle ground. If there were indications that the cancer was aggressive and fast-growing, Mary's baby would have had to be delivered after 28 weeks. If this had been the case there would have been potential or probable complications for the baby.

Being pregnant, however, meant that she couldn't undergo certain scans. The medical professionals didn't mince their words, giving her the worst-case scenarios.

"I was told along the way that there might not be a good outcome – for either myself or the baby. There was the risk that the cancer had spread further and there was a baby to be looked after – I wanted to be around for Ellis," said Mary, whose story reached a nationwide audience as a result of her featuring on an episode of RTÉ series The Rotunda.

Baby Ellis arrived five weeks premature, just under 2.5kg (around 5lbs) but healthy. This was a pivotal moment in Mary's life.

"Ellis is thriving. We've had him over in Germany when I was getting my treatment."

"Until he arrived safe and sound there was obviously anxiety involved. When I heard him crying for the first time it was a brilliant feeling."

"We always knew he was going to have be delivered early, we just didn't know how early. When he was delivered at 35 weeks – OK and healthy – it was a massive relief."

Mary then went from new mum to being treated for cancer in Essen, Germany. The treatment included radiation therapy and chemotherapy.

After undergoing almost two months of that treatment, there were side-effects.

"I went through a bit of a rough patch – the doctors, to be fair, had made me aware of this, that things would be bad before they would start to get good. I had trouble swallowing and I developed a lot of mouth sores – this made eating and drinking difficult."

She also had to be on a course of pain medication.

But Mary has turned the corner. It is over six weeks since the seven-week phase of cancer treatment ended. Further tests in December will determine if the dark days have passed or if there is more treatment required.

Mary has cried and got angry. She still does.

"There are still days that I will get upset, if my energy levels are that bit lower. I'm so used to being active – I've ran 90 miles a week – so not to have that means I could be bouncing off the walls."

"There were times, after Ellis arrived and I was going through the treatment, that Mark and I would ask ourselves why had we been given these circumstances – cancer and having a newborn baby."

"But, genuinely, I don't think cancer discriminates. It is one of those things that people can get and there may be no reason why."

People have asked her if she felt that having cancer while being pregnant changed her experience of motherhood.

"For me, being pregnant was a great distraction from the cancer. "I was a selfish runner, I would put all my energy into running and me – it was all about me. Then, when I got pregnant, I had still to be in a good place in order for the baby to be in a good place but I think it just gave me a different perspective."

She continued: "It is hard to say how I would have dealt with the cancer if I hadn't been pregnant but it would have been easier to have had a 'pity party' for myself.

"There would have been more questions of 'why me' and I think I would have been more down in the dumps about it. I knew that there was someone else to look after and care about."

Family and friends helped share her burden but she highlighted the impact of her partner Mark, himself a star athlete in his younger days and also a scholarship recipient.

"I was so lucky to have such support around me – from Mark, from the two families and all our friends. "We never dwelled too much on the tumour. We took things just one day at a time and tried to live in the here and now. Mark helped me to look at things that way – I would have had a tendency to look too far ahead and wonder how we would manage things down the line."

While the next stage of the waiting game is counting the days down until December's scan and test results, Mary, a member of North Sligo AC, maintained that her running background made a positive difference.

"Even getting out for a run during the pregnancy was great – it gave me some mental space. There were days when things were overwhelming and I just got out for a run while I was pregnant – so Ellis and I went for a run together!"

"Running gives you motivation and determination – qualities that you use for real life as well.

"I've had terrible races – I thought I was in the best shape of my life and races hadn't gone how I planned. You are down in the dumps but you have to come out the other side of it.

"From that perspective, days that were tough, even during treatment when I was feeling low, nauseous and had little energy, I had to keep going because I had experienced other things in life that hadn't gone to plan.

"I was able to lean on running in that way."

What she has gone through has also put her running career into perspective: The highs, the lows, setting records, winning medals and unfortunately not qualifying for three Olympics.

"I used to get so devastated when I had a bad race. I would feel that I had let so many people down."

"People put so much emphasis on sporting moments – they are amazing and they lift a nation – and sport also brings so many people together from different walks of life.

"Definitely, it reminded me what is important in life – what happens with family and friends – and how there is more to life than just running."

In saying that, the running community reached out to her during her illness, including those she had ran with and against during her time in America.

Will she run again as she once did? "I will always be known as a runner but now I'm a mum too."

"I sometimes think that I would like to get back to competitive running – but I don't know yet if that is possible. It will be a slow process back to that level – I am back running but going very slowly at the moment.

"I would love for Ellis to see me race, maybe in a couple of years. At the same time, my perspective has also changed. I know the amount of time and effort that has to go into running at the level that I ran at.

"I don't know, right now, if I'm in that head space to give that commitment back and give up certain things, with Ellis or my family, for that to happen."

In time, Mary hopes to glean a meaning from what she has gone through – and is still going through.

"Sometimes I wonder if I ever will get closure on it or, even better, clarity on it all. It is still so raw, I'm still in the recovery phase."

Mary, who has availed of the services at Sligo Cancer Support Centre in Sligo town, is already looking ahead to Christmas.

"It is going to be extra special with Ellis being here now. I hope by then, 12 months on from when I was first diagnosed, that I will have a greater insight into why I had to – and we had to – go through all these things."

"I think that sometimes we are given things that we can handle. Maybe these cards were dealt to me just because I could handle them.

"Maybe I will have a great perspective on things – not to sweat about the smaller things, like I would have done in the past.

"Even now I still wonder why I have to go through the side-effects of the treatment, because it is miserable. But it makes the good stuff in life really good – I appreciate life so much more now."

She won't admit it – she is too modest – but Mary is stronger now. More resilient. An inspiration, too. Sligo people cheered for her before, wishing her across the finish line. Now they are just cheering for her, wishing that she will make a full recovery.

"I was blessed, in a way. I initially had a blocked ear. I could have just sat on that and not done anything with it – maybe the cancer would have gone further. If anything, I was blessed in the sense that I got the chance

MARY CULLEN AT HOME IN DRUMCLIFFE WITH HER PARTNER MARK SMYTH AND SON ELLIS

to catch it earlier compared to other people, who mightn't have been as fortunate to get an early diagnosis for their cancer.

"I think of Ellis as a massive miracle. He arrived at 35 weeks and is healthy. Even during my treatments, coming back and seeing his little face was a great thing."

Mary is based in Drumcliffe, with things made easier in recent weeks because Mark's employers have allowed him to work from home and therefore spend precious time with Ellis and Mary.

She encourages anyone with a similar health problem to at least communicate with family and friends.

"I used running to help me, because that was my background, but I would encourage people to get out for a walk and to talk to people as well – as Irish people we are getting better about expressing ourselves, our feelings and talking about stuff."

Mary concluded: "Definitely for me, sharing my story and for people to reach out to me has helped. It is not good to keep things bottled up."

JOHN MULLANEY

Gentleman, poetry lover, salesman and historian – John Mullaney has been the face of his O'Connell Street shop for decades. Gerry McLaughlin chatted to him

PUBLISHED ON JANUARY 16, 2020

FOR THE THOUSANDS OF PEOPLE who have entered that great Sligo institution that is Mullaney's on O'Connell Street, there has been one constant since at least 1950.

And that is John Mullaney, a gentleman and gentle man, always impeccably turned out in a chalk striped suit, a steady gaze, a nuanced twinkle in the eye and an ability to make you feel that you are the most important person in the room.

And, while I know that John detests the cult of personality, I am speaking as a customer who has observed him in his natural habitat over many years.

It is very hard to believe that he is in his 88th year and that is not *plámás*, something

LEFT: JOHN MULLANEY IN HIS O'CONNELL STREET SHOP

he makes clear that he detests. It is a fact, just as it is a fact that his knowledge of Sligo going back over many generations is truly remarkable.

But for this relative philistine, the most striking part about John Mullaney is his clear love for all of the arts, for Beethoven and especially for William Butler Yeats.

John is now the only person who lives above their shop in Sligo's most famous street and his eyrie is full of books of all kinds, paintings, carvings and elegant furniture.

But he is at his finest when he is reading something from Yeats, something from long ago that has real resonance for today.

For John, the Sligo poet holds a special place in his heart and John performed in many of Yeats's plays as a younger man when he and his late brother Tom Mullaney were very involved in the Yeats Society.

But John is probably best known as a historian, a walking, talking encyclopaedia of the town he knows and cares for so well.

The ancient and highly poetic Irish language, for which he has a fine facility, and for which he has a high regard, would describe him as a fear cneasta, fear leannta, fear cineálta, ach go hairithe... fear uasal.

His memory is pretty forensic and observations remarkably balanced, a man who always sees the two sides and abhors brash glib analysis.

John can clearly recall the cattle fairs in Sligo in the 1930s and the Second World War and its impact on Sligo. And he has some interesting vignettes of some of the customers who have visited the shop, including former taoisigh like Charles J Haughey, Garret FitzGerald, Bertie Ahern, John Bruton and Brian Cowen who have all called canvassing.

Former New York mayor Michael Bloomberg, who bought an Aran sweater, was a customer, and "we promised him 30,000 Irish votes at least if he wore it on St Patrick's Day at the parade".

Lord and Lady Mountbatten were also occasional customers in the shop, as well as the current King of Norway, Harald V.

Mullaney's has also run a famous travel agency since John's father Michael bought John White and Son in 1909.

The Mullaneys had the agency for all the then shipping lines – Cunard, Anchor, Ellerman, White Star, Greek Line, North German Lloyd, American, Canadian Pacific, Orient and many others.

Part of the Mullaney building was owned by Wynnes of Hazelwood in the early 18th century and you can nearly smell the history from the unique rich aroma of timeless Donegal tweed and Barbour jackets in which they specialise.

But it is clearly a treasure trove of ancient documents of which John is largely the careful custodian.

Fast forward to a grey day in January 2020, and it is clear that while John has a deep respect for the past, he is a strong pragmatist and that is reflected in how Mullaney's has adapted to the modern challenges of the internet and the growth of online buying.

It is a testament to their tenacity and adaptability that the travel agency is still going strong, as is the shop with the famous mosaic at the front door.

John lists the traders and merchants who had businesses that existed until the last quarter of the 20th century – Blackwood, Bellew Brothers, McDaull the clockmakers, MacArthur, Nelson, Johnston, Lyon, Pettigrew, Pollexfen, Smith, Middleton, Harpur Campbell, Meldrum and Wood are among those he can recall.

With changing political parameters, in the late 19th century, a new Catholic merchant class came in to Sligo with names like Higgins, Keighron, O'Connor, Collery, Milmo, Foley, Flanagan, Down and Tighe.

Mullaney's took over from White and Son in 1909 and has been at the heart of retail life of Sligo ever since.

In a talk given to the Catacombs Centre in Calry Parish Church, John fondly recalled the number of shops that used to adorn his own O'Connell Street and adjoining streets.

He recalled the colourful Ms Gallagher's shop next door, where you could get heart-shaped conversation lozenges with phrases like "waste not want not", "give me a kiss" and "I think you are beautiful", which he described as "an unlikely mix of romance and wisdom".

John also recalled the "4.6" Mrs Beirne, which "had a raised gangway which allowed her to preside over a big selection of Fry's products".

In John Street you could buy a chocolate bar called "Half Time Jimmy" in Oliver Byrne's Shop.

"We were each equipped with one by my father on our way to Sligo Rovers football matches, but the discipline was that it must remain unopened until half-time."

John remembered Alfie Bree's shop next door to Byrne's as a treasure trove where you put in a penny in a mechanical crane and with "adroit manoeuvres" you could get a teddy bear or a stuffed monkey.

But this was also the place where a young John first encountered inflation. Jenny's was an upmarket spot with "mouth-watering marshmallows" and Michael Nevin's of High Street had lovely Macintosh Double Centres.

On this grey January day, we moved up the stairs into his inner sanctum, a book-lined oasis of culture.

John said: "I have been involved in this business for 70 years. I was born in this house and my father bought the leasehold in 1909 and I bought the freehold in 1960."

So where did the Mullaneys come from originally, I asked John.

"Our tribe were out in Beltra. My grandfather lived there and my great grandfather came down from the Sooey area to Beltra. But we have always considered ourselves Tireragh people. My grandfather Patrick was born there in 1826 and he was a farmer who had 40 acres.

"My father's name was Michael Mullaney. He served his time in the drapery trade in Howley's of Tubbercurry and he came from there to John White and Son, who were running this business from the 1870s.

"My mother's name was Mary Henry, from Coolaney.

"My father, who was born in 1879, worked for John White, who was a very interesting man who belonged to a Protestant sect. They were the Free Church and they built what is now the Library on Stephen Street.

"He was on the council of that church and his only son contracted tuberculosis in 1909 and John White sold the business to my father because he wanted to go to California, hoping that in the desert climate the tuberculosis of his only son would dry up.

"And the boy did survive, and his descendants still visit us here and I bring them around the house to show them where they lived.

"My father Michael and his brother Tom were partners in the business, but Tom stayed on as manager in Howley's, where both of them worked.

"My father initially went from White's to Moon's in Galway and his job in Moon's, among other tasks, was to go out and buy the woollens from the looms from the hand weavers.

"So that is why we have been into the hand-woven stuff for so long.

"They would send it to London for tentering and shrinking and washing before it was brought back here to the tailoring department.

"My father learned how to cut material as well and when he came back from Galway and bought this place along with his brother Tom he had up to 20 tailors at a time here. Both of them were men of extraordinary taste.

"I still stand in awe when I look at the old shop front. There are about five shop fronts in the town that are the work of Costello and Son.

"They are all beautiful fronts – Thomas Connolly's pub, Cavanagh's Bar across the road, Wehrly's – his work is just beautiful.

"We still have some of his descendants who come from England and ask to be brought out to the front door to show them where their great grandfather's name is written on the sign board.

"I have the original drawings for the shop front. The mosaic was done in London and the marble we have is Connemara marble and cannot be replaced, and we had to be very careful when they were laying the foundations for the new surface work in the street.

"The white marble at the front has cast iron spud stones for the gates, which we no longer use. But the spuds are there and they have oxidised into the marble and you could not replicate that. Costello finished the shop front in 1921."

John was born in 1932 and his earliest memories were of playing marbles in the gutter outside the shop and the horse traffic and the council sweeping up the horse dung.

He remembers "very organised" fairs that were held in the Fair Green.

John added that when a farmer would fail to sell in the Fair Green, very often he would bring the heifer back and tie it to the railings of the Stag's Head bar, which is where Carraig Donn is now.

One of the local "tanglers" would find out from the seller what was his price and from the buyer what was the best he was going to do. A bargain was struck with a spit on the hand and a handshake.

"That usually happened down in Tobergal Lane, which means the Bright Well in Irish. It was one of the sources of water until the plague of the early 19th century, when the spread was attributed to a number of wells.

"And when we were building on at the back of the shop, one of the things we found was a nine foot brick well. We put in an oversized pipe and drained it into the sewer which runs under the house and it never gave us trouble."

John went to primary school to the Marist Brothers on The Mall and from there to Summerhill, where he came out in 1950s.

"I always came out in vintage years as 1932 was the year of the great Eucharistic Congress in the Phoenix Park and it was the first major international recognition of Ireland as a state.

"The gift of the Irish people to the nuncio at the time was a carpet by the Yeats sisters in the Dun Emer Guild and they also supplied a carpet to Westminster and to the White House.

"In 1950 it was the Holy Year. The Mall school was particularly civilised, and we had Brother Bernadine and Brother Phelim, who later taught in St John's of Temple Street."

He liked school. But, he said: "In those days you did not ask so many questions – do you like this or that. it was there to be done and you got on with it. Summerhill was as good as a third-level basic degree today. You had Latin, Greek, Mathematics and all was taught as Gaeilge. There was a tremendous discipline in your thought, and you got a great classical training.

"We presented all the Shakespearean plays and they always cast the first years in the female parts as their voices hadn't broken. My first role was to play Hamlet's mother Queen Gertrude. I had to put socks in my bosom. Years later they brought in the Ursuline girls to, quite sensibly, play the female parts."

All the teachers were all very "very professional".

He said: "Some of them were doing it without ever having a vocation to teach but were disciplined enough to do it. Some of them were teaching because they loved it and some of them were teaching because they had eccentric ideas that we did not understand at the time."

He added: "One of them was way ahead of his time because he would talk to us about the 'Roaring 40s' – the famous trade winds in the southern hemisphere. He would ask us what we knew about the Roaring 40s and the wilder the story you could tell the better.

"You might say that when sailors came to that latitude, they had drink taken and were pretty well sozzled and that was the Roaring 40s. He would then ask for another story which would be a different story. But what we did

JOHN MULLANEY'S SHOP ON O'CONNELL STREET

not realise until much later, that nobody ever forgot what the Roaring 40s were and what the real meaning of it was.

"Now if he had simply tried to teach that to us nobody would remember it, but he was clueing you in with mnemonics."

"The principal at that time was Canon Casey from Roscommon."

John was in Summerhill from 1945 to 1950 and it was "an extremely hard time" to grow up in.

"The war was a very difficult time and we did not realise how much it impinged on our lives at the time. But all of the rationing system was dictated by the war, all of the farming system was dictated by the fact that you had legislation for the amount of land that was to be tilled and if you did not meet your quota you could be summonsed.

"And if you did not cut your ragwort, you were summonsed also.

"We lived in a much more disciplined society then and there were strict rules with rationing. If you came in here to buy a suit at 16 or 12 guineas you also had to have a page from your ration book with the right number of coupons."

In tandem with all of this, was the travel agency, which was there before the Mullaneys' time, and John has the books from 1906 with the list of those who left Sligo by sea and later by air, which is social history in itself.

There were old ledgers in an old store at the back of the premises and when they were pulled out a cat and her kittens had decamped there.

"She was there with a litter of kittens and I told the National Archive people that we should postpone the search and leave the cat and her litter of kittens in peace. The cat had got in behind the ledgers.

"Three years later a girl from the National Archive came in and said, joking, that she was here to enquire about the welfare of a cat and a litter of kittens.

"We had nobody on the Titanic as it was a maiden voyage and it was far too expensive for local emigrants. It was £6.10 shillings to go steerage to America at that time. We booked several people on the Lusitania but the Lusitania was coming from New York to Cobh when it was sunk so we did not have any local people on board.

"The travel agency is the only one within a drapery shop in the country and it is now also the only travel agency in the county. Ten years ago there were six. That is just change."

So has online booking affected Mullaney's travel agency?

"The whole thing with challenges in business is that you have to wait long enough for that to change back to what it was once again. And it has started to change once again.

"People are now booking very intricate cruise holidays and if you are parting with €3,000 to €4,000 you want to know things like is my state room under a dance floor or is my state room near a lift shaft.

"You have all the answers online but you don't have the questions.

"A sharp knife does not make you into a brain surgeon and that is how people are coming back to us.

"One man said, ah, I am back to ye, I did it myself the last time and I made a hames of it. He had booked an Italian coastal place where there were 75 steps down to the beach, and that is the kind of thing that you can run into. This is not immediately apparent online."

So what about the "personal touch"?

"Yes, there is traceability as we are government bonded and insurance bonded and we have 110 years of experience to show you, whereas there are a lot of people who are in the travel business today who are not really in the travel business, they are just jolly good advertisers."

John began his apprenticeship in 1950 and he was trained by Tom Nicholson, and John trained Tom Nicholson's nephew John Nicholson, who is in charge in the men's outfitting department."

"John Nicholson trained my nephew John and there is loads of tradition that we have."

Elsewhere, John has a great interest in all the arts, something that developed from his Summerhill time.

"Palgrave's Golden Treasury was common in Summerhill and we did not do very much of Yeats as he was not quite persona grata with the Catholic Church.

"My interests started in the Ursuline Convent attached to St Anne's School and they were way ahead of their time as we had a weekly elocution class and a weekly drill class, which was great training.

"We got our first poetry lessons and we started with simple poems like 'Christopher Robin Is Saying His Prayers'. I liked Shelley, Keats, Wordsworth and all of those poets."

John was later a member of the council of the Yeats Society for many years. His brother Tom was the honorary secretary of the first International Yeats Summer School and later became president of the Yeats Society.

This was around 1960. Yeats had been interred in Drumcliffe in 1948.

John acted in the Yeats plays and the ones he loved best were the masked plays, "The Dreaming Of The Bones" and "Purgatory".

He said: "The Japanese were very interested in the masked plays because they were conforming largely to the discipline of the Japanese Noh plays. Yeats was taken with the Japanese Noh theatre at the time. They still have Japanese students at the summer school."

The council of the Yeats Society was an entire cross-section of the community. There 160 students at the Summer School at the time.

When asked about any favourite Yeats poems, John said he has "several favourites." "One of my favourites is 'Sixteen Dead Men', and while I don't agree with all of the sentiments you don't have to to recognise genius."

And then he recites:

O but we talked at large before
The sixteen men were shot,
But who can talk of give and take,
What should be and what not
While those dead men are loitering there
To stir the boiling pot?
You say that we should still the land
Till Germany's overcome;
But who is there to argue that
Now Pearse is deaf and dumb?

And is there logic to outweigh
MacDonagh's bony thumb?
 How could you dream they'd listen
That have an ear alone
For those new comrades they have found,
Lord Edward and Wolfe Tone,
Or meddle with our give and take
That converse bone to bone.

And then he segues into another classic called "The Second Coming", one of the poet's great political poems:

Turning and turning in the widening gyre
The falcon cannot hear the falconer;
Things fall apart; the centre cannot hold;
Mere anarchy is loosed upon the world,
The blood-dimmed tide is loosed, and everywhere
The ceremony of innocence is drowned;
The best lack all conviction, while the worst
Are full of passionate intensity.

For John, that poem applies very much to Ireland today even though it was written back in 1926. John read Yeats's poems at An Tóstal many years ago and believes Yeats should be read by an Irish voice.

"Some of these actors do a great job of acting but they don't speak poetry. Bob Geldof did a tribute to Yeats and it was quite magnificent, and Bono and Edna O'Brien read Yeats from the heart. But the Irish language is very beautiful too and we have a phrase over the door, *Is giorra cabhair Dé ná an doras*, which means that "the help of God is nearer than the door".

"My grandfather, who was born in 1826 out in Beltra, spoke Irish as well as English. But my father had no Irish, it was lost just like that and he was born in 1879 and he was the last of 17 children."

And even though he is quite a historian, John is adamant that he does not want Mullaney's to be seen as a piece of history.

"The important message from my point of view is that this is a business and what is happening in the present because that is what we all live in.

"In looking at an old established business one has to realise that the older businesses which survive, survive because they are modern businesses using the tools of modern trade. We have an internet site and all communications are all state of the art, computer driven. We were the first business in Sligo to accept a credit card in 1950."

In his long career, John has met some interesting quirky characters.

"There was one Englishman who came into the shop, he was 6ft4ins and his Chinese wife was 4ft6ins. She was looking for a Barbour coat and I put on an extra, extra small Barbour jacket.

"You would have had to kill her to get it off her and I never saw a man going for his wallet as quickly and he was so delighted.

"He said they lived in Beijing and he had agency for the Morgan car in China. I asked if the Chinese bought the Morgan car as it is the rich man's toy, a hand-built aluminium car.

"Oh, he said, when you make your first million in China you buy a Rolls Royce, but when you make your first billion, you buy a Morgan."

So, what is the secret of a good salesman? John Mullaney has always been premier league in this department – I know of one person who came in to buy a Barbour jacket for her husband and the couple ended up buying two Barbour jackets!

"We always hope that our customers are impressed and we are always impressed when we hear the bell ringing on the till.

"People have been coming back to us for generation after generation and one customer flew over from London last year to have his son kitted out for his first Holy Communion because he himself had got his first Holy Communion outfit from us as well."

"The best salesman I have ever heard was the late Gay Byrne and if you watched him, his distinguishing factor above all others was his ability to listen. In my experience, it is the most valuable asset you have.

"If you listen to people, it does not mean you have to be dumb. If you listen to the nuances of what they are saying and observe them, you can understand the people. But if you are totally superficial in your judgment you haven't a hope in business. People have all sorts of depths in them. No man knows the whole of another man's story, a poet once said. It is not proper that he should.

When I was a callow youth back from a trip to America in 1960, I was serving a north Sligo farmer and he was a grand man. He said, you were away? I said I was on my holidays and when he asked me where I had been, I said that I was in America. And with all the brashness of youth, because I thought he might not have heard of it, I said I was in Arizona and I spelled it out for him – A R I Z O N A.

"He gave a little sigh and said Arizona, and I thought he was turning the word over in his mind. The farmer then said: 'When the copper ran out in the mine above in Butte in 1923, I came down with my pick and shovel to Arizona and with my five years' work there I made enough to come home and buy my farm.' I have always held that in my mind, that you never know the whole of another man's story and you never will."

John added: "It is totally about understanding what people want. You don't listen alone to what they tell you they want. You have to listen to what they are really telling you in the way that they talk about various things. You need to interpret what they are saying and if you don't genuinely like meeting people then you have no business in the retail trade.

"You could have a brilliant accountancy mind, be an expert in display and all kinds of administration expertise, but if you don't have an interest in people, you are wasting your time.

"Fergal Quinn of Quinnsworth had an amazing ability to understand people. But you need an actuarial balance as well between commercial and social intercourse. But people do respect you if you are giving them an honest opinion. It takes time, but a man who comes in to buy a pair of socks could go out having spent €1,000 given the right circumstances."

Indeed – I am thinking about those two Barbour jackets, John!

Long may you reign.

JOE COX & CON POWER

2020 was the 50th anniversary of the opening of IT Sligo. Alan Finn spoke to former engineering lecturer Joe Cox, who witnessed 40 years of change at the IT, and Con Power, its first president

PUBLISHED ON JANUARY 16, 2020, AND FEBRUARY 13, 2020

IN FIFTY YEARS, THE INSTITUTE OF Technology in Sligo has seen a lot of change. From one building to a sprawling, ever-growing campus and from 100 regional students to alumni from around the globe, it has proven itself to be one of the county's and indeed the North West's great success stories.

One man who has seen much of the transition is former lecturer Joe Cox, who worked in the Engineering department for 40 years. Joe walked through the doors of IT Sligo – then known as the Regional Technical College – for the first time on

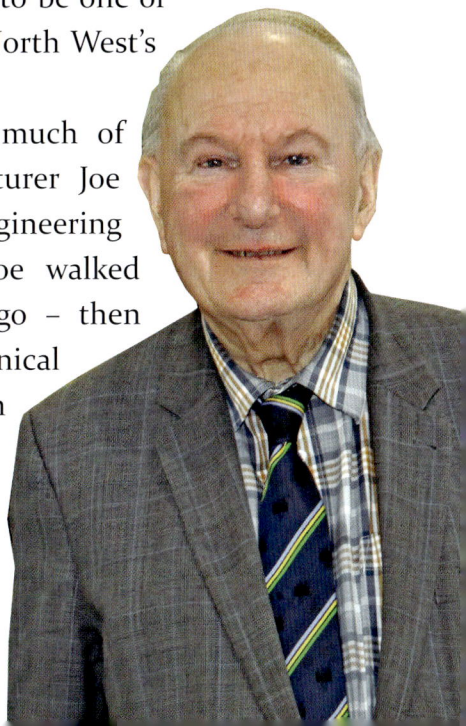

LEFT: JOE COX.
RIGHT: CON POWER

September 1, 1972. He recalls how it was in its infancy but already recognised as a potential gamechanger for education in this part of the country.

"The college opened in spring of 1970. It was one of a number of regional colleges which opened that year following a steering report which advocated an increased need for technical education in Ireland. Development of areas such as Finisklin was achieved in some way as a result of having technicial education in Sligo."

The courses available to students are varied and seem to be growing on an annual basis as they not only cater to more industries. Academic aspirations are very high in the region these days, but Joe recalled a time when there was a lot of barriers and little hope for the common person who wanted to enter higher education.

"When I arrived we had courses for apprentices in carpentry, joinery, tool making and motor engineering. We also had two-year certificate programmes in business studies, engineering and science, so they were technicians and could be employed as such. We were giving new education opportunities for people in the region, before 1970 your options were Galway or Dublin. This introduction of higher education in the region offered something for local people to aspire to because up until then it was very hard to enter higher education unless you had money or a scholarship."

One of IT Sligo's greatest strengths is its never-ending endeavour to enhance and improve itself and what it can offer students and the community. This isn't a new phenomonon however as the decade-by-decade achievements were steered forward by staff who had envisaged the institute we know today.

"In the 80s, we had our first three-year course with a diploma at the end of it, which is known as an ordinary degree. Traditional four-year courses were then developed in the 90s so students could leave IT Sligo with a degree. In the last two decades we have now been able to offer programmes such as post-graduate, masters and post-graduate doctors.

"Our greatest strength of all was our ability to provide a ladder of opportunity and the staff who drove that forward is something we are proud to be celebrating. The areas of strength were always built on the strength of individual lecturers."

The pursuit of a university status feels like it has been rumbling on forever.

"The relentless efforts that have been and continue to be made are necessary according to the Carrick-on-Shannon native who says that it would unlock a whole new world of possibility for the whole of Sligo.

"IT Sligo aspires to achieve university status and I believe that would recognise the work that our students, our people and our community put into it. That status is also criticial because when agencies such as the IDA and Enterprise Ireland as well as private individuals come to Sligo and ask if we have a university, we can say yes we have.

"A lot of decisions on bringing business to an area can hinge on whether or not there is a university in the locality, so it cannot be understated how important it is for the wider development of Sligo to be awarded this status."

What has been achieved in 50 years at IT Sligo is a great story of determination. It has emerged from being an educational outpost to being

STAFF MEMBERS AT THE IT IN THE 1990S. JOE COX
IS ON THE LEFT IN THE FRONT ROW

an innovator and leader in many fields and the graduates have been flying the flag for the region for a very long time as evidenced by a recent reunion.

"We overcame an underdog status and it was only very recently I was invited out for a meal with a class I taught in 1979.

"They told me they were lifted from a scenario in the North West where you had to go to England and work on the building sites.

"One of them told me an anecdote about when he had been qualified for six years and he had become a site supervisor. Somebody made a remark about him being a 'Paddy with a briefcase' as if he was an anomaly, but Paddy with a briefcase was a graduate of RTC Sligo who had done his technical qualifications and now was in a supervisory role rather than simply an operative role."

Joe retired from the IT in February 2012, but he remains very closely affiliated with his old workplace and rather appropriately is one of the head organisers of this year's 50th anniversary celebrations.

The programme for the year includes events such as a book launch, faculty reunions, the Connacht Fleadh, a concert by the RTE Concert Orchestra and a gala dinner.

For him however, the centrepiece of the itinerary is the UN Artificial Intelligence Conference taking place in March which he believes is the greatest symbol yet of how far IT Sligo has come.

"One of the highlights of the programme is that we are having a conference on artificial intelligence.

"It is a key development because it is an example of IT Sligo collaborating with and supporting a new leading edge technology business, LiveTiles, which selected Sligo as its European base.

"This conference will set the agenda for a United Nations world conference to be held in Geneva in June, so it will put IT Sligo on a world stage for artificial intelligence.

"A conference at IT Sligo has the potential to shape the development of artificial intelligence for the benefit of society around the world and that to me epitomises how far we have come."

CON POWER

In an institution full of innovators, there has to be a leader steering everything in the right direction.

At IT Sligo, that job often falls to the feet of the president whose very legacy is dictated by growth of the college as they edge ever closer to their Holy Grail of earning university status.

Some of the most significant strides forward occurred during their first decade of existence in the 1970s as what was then known as the Regional Technical College was determined to prove that it was more than an outpost west of the Shannon.

At the helm for much of the decade was Con Power, who was the first person to hold the presidency on a permanent basis.

Con explained that it is not a job he had anticipated he would take and was a spur of the moment decision based on the level of knowledge he had gathered of how the college operated.

"I had been a lecturer in the College of Technology, Bolton Street, and I was sent here to do research for the Department of the Environment on behalf of the college. I was due to return to Bolton Street as an assistant head of the department, but the Department of the Education had a rush of blood to the head and sent me back here instead."

Being the head of an individual RTC was a step into unfamiliar territory, but he revealed he did have a hand in helping roll out the programme which delivered such colleges around the country in 1970.

"I had already been in the education system for a number of years, I began lecturing in Bolton Street in the early 1960s. I had also been involved in the early discussions with the steering groups who would go on to open the many Regional Technical Colleges in the 1970s as Bolton Street was regularly consulted in those early stages of developing the plan to roll those colleges out."

He went on to describe the not so thorough vision of the steering group. This could have been a problem, but Con feels IT Sligo's ability to quickly establish its own strengths was a sign of a very promising future ahead.

"For me there was an element of going into the unknown. When the five original RTCs were established, the steering committee itself didn't really know in precise detail what was going to happen. These colleges found their own levels and kind of took their own shape. Sligo was designated as the national centre for toolmaking training and this was largely as a result of some of Ireland's foremost toolmaking businesses being located in the county.

"From this we moved into other areas thanks to the skills of our staff, accountancy for example was one of the earliest specialised courses we offered and Environmental Science was very big for Sligo for the time it was introduced as well."

Many courses founded in the 1970s still exist to this very day. Among them are in the area of Childhood Care, but the demand for this course emerged from an unexpected source.

"Things often happen in colleges in answer to a request and childcare is an interesting one. It came about here when a man who I had been in school with named Frank Dunne, an Assistant Secretary General in

the Department of Justice and Superintendent of Prisons at the time, approached me and said that there was a major problem with prison officers who would not staff Loughan House unless they are given a course in childcare. From that point on we recruited staff, put a programme together and our first childcare students were those prison officers from Loughan House."

Today, IT Sligo prides itself on both the number of counties and countries their students represent, something which was further propelled forward by their utilisation of online studying.

Con revealed that this was another impressive indicator of the success to come from IT Sligo as they have welcomed international students to their college long before it became the norm.

"In 1975 I started a campaign to have this place designated as a Polytechnic College. There was always a sense of vision here and if you look at a map of Ireland we were the only viable education institution north of Galway.

"I also think Sligo has had a very extended reach for much longer than people realise. In the early years we had students from all 32 counties in

the college in one year and we also had overseas students in the 1970s, they came from places like Iran, Iraq, Tanzania and Kenya. Back then it might have been seen as strange for these people to come to Sligo, but our attitude was simply 'why not?', we were delighted to have them attend the college and they were made to feel very welcome in Sligo."

Third-level education in Sligo was unknown before 1970 and getting through that decade may have been seen as survival, but for Con the 1970s was a time of great forward thinking that laid the foundations for not only the next few years, but the coming decades.

"In a strange way, the development I am most proud of is not only beginning of Environment Science but also the decision to employ Pat Timson who proved to be worth his weight in gold.

"I had a dream that I couldn't deliver, but Pat could. I knew what was needed, he knew how to do it. That became the first degree course of IT Sligo. The extension that was built in the 70s was also very important as it allowed us to grow our staff considerably. To look at it now as part of a large campus it doesn't seem like much, but at the time it was hugely important."

As Con Power stood in IT Sligo last month, he couldn't help but bask in the pride of what has been achieved in 50 years and was delighted to see the wide-ranging community who came along to celebrate the launch of the book celebrating their anniversary.

This was very important to him as he maintains IT Sligo becoming one of the region's biggest assets could not have been achieved without the goodwill and support of the wider public since the early days.

"I think in terms of influence within its own catchment area as well as national and international, this has been the showcase of all the Institutes of Technology in Ireland.

"The relativity stands up, this started in what could have been the most disadvantaged place in Ireland as the North West is often forgotten about, but IT Sligo never saw itself as an outpost.

"The people of Sligo never whinged that they were disadvantaged, there was always a constant 'let's do it' attitude and there was some enlightened leadership which viewed the RTC as a positive development, the other areas who got RTCs were not so fortunate as there was tension between them and the VEC. Gus O'Kennedy, who was the chief executive officer of the Sligo Borough VEC was one of the greatest promoters of the RTC here and that should be up in lights to everybody.

"The VEC was extraordinarily supportive towards us, they were very enthusiastic as were the Sligo Borough Council who always worked together for us, political differences were always put aside and that is something that always stands out in my mind, they treated us as a benefit to Sligo and I would safely say that same spirit here is as strong today as it was back then."

PREVIOUS PAGES: CON POWER, WHO CELEBRATED HIS 81st
BIRTHDAY ON THE DAY OF THE IT SLIGO BOOK LAUNCH IN EARLY 2020,
WITH PAST AND PRESENT IT SLIGO STAFF MEMBERS, CLLR ROSALEEN
O'GRADY AND COUNCIL CHIEF EXECUTIVE CIARAN HAYES

SEÁN MacMANUS

Seán MacManus told Gerry McLaughlin about how he helped to make Sinn Féin a party for the people in Sligo, Peace Process negotiations, and the death of his son Joseph in an IRA operation

PUBLISHED ON MAY 21, 2020

SEÁN MACMANUS OF SINN FÉIN IS the greatest TD that Sligo never had.

He came very close in 2002, and stood for election around half a dozen times since 1984 before retiring as a sitting member of Sligo County Council in 2017.

In between, Seán led a hectic life at the simmering face of Irish republican politics, beginning with his days of protest as an emigrant in London in the 1960s. He is a life-long republican for whom patriotism was never a game, but a consuming passion.

But the Gubaveeney, Co. Cavan, native, who retains the rich accent

LEFT: SEÁN MACMANUS AS A CHILD WITH HIS MOTHER ROSE. RIGHT: SEÁN MACMANUS

of his ancestors, has never been just about longing for the re-unification of his country.

He was largely responsible for building and making his party relevant to the community he served and especially the working-class community of the town he has taken to his heart. That took courage, determination and no little nous in a town not noted for a republican base.

But Seán MacManus has operated on a very simple but profound political philosophy. If someone asks you to do something for them, you make sure you try to do exactly just that. What you see is what you get, and he does not suffer fools or plámás at all.

He was first elected to Sligo Borough Council for the West Ward in 1994 and stayed there for 20 years until its abolition in 2014.

Seán was elected to Sligo County Council in 1999. That year he was also elected to Sligo Borough Council and stood unsuccessfully in the European elections. And he was elected to the County Council in 2004, 2009 and 2014 – remarkable achievements for a man who was on small finances and had no big PR campaigns. He was also Mayor of the town in 2000 and 2004.

Those are all proud achievements, but pride is not part of his armoury. He has always got more satisfaction from helping people to get what they are entitled to, from medical cards to homes. It does not matter who you are – he has treated everyone the same.

A love of history at national school in Barran, Blacklion, fostered a love of his native land and he read more as a boarder at the Marist College in Athlone in the early 1960s.

Like many others of that generation, he emigrated to England. At just 17 in 1967 he worked as a carpenter on the building sites, where "the money was good".

While there he became involved in republican circles and was on numerous protests in the summer of 1968.

He met Helen McGovern from Glenfarne in the Galtymore Ballroom and they married and had two sons – Joe, who was born in 1970, and Chris, who was born in 1973.

Joe, who was part of an IRA active service unit, was killed in a shootout with a UDR soldier outside Belleek, Co. Fermanagh, in 1992. Chris is a current MEP for Connacht-Ulster after serving for many years on Sligo Borough and County Council.

Seán said he was equally of proud of both his boys, but as a parent, "a part of me died when I got the news of what happened to Joe".

Seán and Helen came back to Sligo in 1976. Sligo in the mid 1970s had a small but active republican community and Seán became interested in the escalating situation in Long Kesh when republican prisoners lost their political status.

He was secretary of the County Sligo Anti-H-Block Committee, which campaigned in support of the republican prisoners and especially those who went on and died on the hunger strike of 1981. And he was involved in the election campaign for hunger striker Joe McDonnell and later for Leitrim republican John Joe McGirl.

Seán became a member of the Sinn Féin Ard Chomhairle in 1982, where he remained for over 20 years. He was national chairperson of Sinn Féin from 1984 to 1990 and was in the chair in the Mansion House at the Ard Fheis when the party voted to take their seats in Leinster House, which sparked a split that saw ex-Sinn Féin president Ruairí Ó Brádaigh and other republicans walk out and form Republican Sinn Féin.

After the IRA ceasefire in 1994, Seán was part of the first Sinn Féin delegation to meet publicly with the British Government in over 70 years.

These days he is retired, but still believes that his country "will be re-united".

He said: "Yes, Brexit has hastened it. It may not happen in my lifetime, but I deeply believe that it will come."

Seán was born in Gubbaveeney in west Cavan in June 1950 and went to school in Barran, where his classmate was one Brian McHugh – a life-long friend who went on to become the founder and long-time editor of the *Sligo Weekender*.

Seán said: "We started school on the same day and right through our schooldays we sat together, and we have been great friends ever since".

Seán's parents were John MacManus and Rose Fitzpatrick from the locality.

"I liked English and history and geography right through school and I was very interested in Gaelic football. Cavan was the team and the remnants of that great team were still around when I was in primary school – they won an All-Ireland in 1952. I like a lot of sports. Queen's Park Rangers are my favourite soccer team, and I went to see them when I was in England in the mid-1960s."

Seán went to the Marist College in Athlone as a boarder, which was "character forming" as it "toughens you up to a degree as you are away from your parents for the first time".

He said: "I also saw others being very upset by being away from home for the first time. But I don't think I would have liked to have either of my two sons to have gone to boarding school. I thought I had a vocation and at that time a lot of houses had some member of a religious community in the family. I was relatively religious, but I soon discovered that I did not have a vocation."

Seán came home and then headed to London in the summer of 1967. He had just turned 17.

"The fact that I had already been away from home for three years broke the culture shock, but at 17 you can take a lot of things in your stride. London was booming, and it was an exciting time as the whole pop culture had just exploded. I was not long in London before I met my wife Helen in the Galtymore.

Seán got work as a carpenter and he and Helen married in 1970 in Harlsden in London.

He said: "I always had a great interest in history and that was fostered by a teacher called Denis Harrington in Barran – he used to get mad when the people of our area would call this side of the border the Free State. 'This is a republic', he would say. He inculcated a great love of Irish history in me and that developed into an interest in politics.

"When I was in college in Athlone, I read a lot of Irish history and we always seemed to be winning an odd battle but losing the ultimate ones. That sense of injustice and unfairness started in me fairly early, the feeling that the British had no right to be in our country. Other things were influential on me, like Bloody Sunday and the Hunger Strikes."

At this time Seán was also involved in anti-Vietnam protests on a broader political front – a time when Bob Dylan wrote, and his girlfriend Joan Baez sang some of the greatest ever songs of resistance.

"The anti-war feeling was everywhere, and change was in the air. I was also very supportive of the Irish people's right to self-determination and then when the war broke out in Northern Ireland in 1970, I went to marches in London. I became active in republican circles, especially after Bloody Sunday in 1972."

Many things changed utterly on a January day in 1972 when 13 innocent civilians were shot down by the Parachute Regiment in Derry. For Seán MacManus, this hit like a thunderbolt.

He said: "It certainly brought it home to me that a person would need to be a bit more active in their opposition to Britain's rule in Ireland."

One of the Sinn Féin people that Seán knew in London was Brendan McGill, who later ran the Old Barracks pub in Ballyshannon. By then Seán and Helen had two young sons. One of the reasons they came back was to have their children taught in the Irish educational system.

The economy was picking up in Sligo and Seán got a job working as a carpenter – but there was a big drop in wages.

He said: "There were different stages of the houses being built in Cranmore, so work was plentiful. The money was much less, and I remember the first week's wages that I got was about £40 in 1976 – I had been getting at least twice that in London.

"Political status for IRA prisoners was cut off in the late 1970s and I became involved in a campaign to get it re-instated. That led to the hunger strikes, when the prisoners said they would not wear a 'convict's' uniform."

Sinn Féin had a structure in Sligo at the time, but it was mainly concerned with a united Ireland and had no involvement in community politics – something Seán MacManus later fostered and developed.

He said: "We were abstentionist and did not take seats in Leinster House, so we were outside the political process to a large degree."

Seán became secretary of the County Sligo Anti-H-Block Committee in late 1979.

"I was very active, and it gave me a profile that I was probably not aware of at the time. The H-Block organization at the time was not a Sinn Féin organisation, it was very broad-based. There were a lot of unaligned people and people from Fianna Fáil and the Labour Party, and Declan Bree was also involved. There were H-Block branches in north Sligo, Collooney, Tubbercurry, Ballymote and Riverstown – they were scattered all over the place. Some of them joined up with Sinn Féin in later years.

"The second hunger strike began in March 1981 and lasted until Bobby Sands and nine others passed away before it finished in October. I remember when Bobby Sands died. There were up on 10,000 people on the streets of Sligo. Nearly all the building sites, shops, factories and places of employment closed down for a period.

"The H-Block Committee had a good structure in some factories in Sligo, and as the deaths mounted, you could see people start to get emotionally tired – it was a very emotional time. Every evening when a republican prisoner was coming near death there would be a black flag vigil the length of O'Connell Street.

"There would be 300 to 400 people there of an evening between 5pm and 6pm in solidarity with the dying prisoners. That happened quite a lot

"After the hunger strike, I saw the need for Sinn Féin to become relevant and to be involved more in community issues. I became a member of the Sinn Féin Ard Chomhairle in 1982 and I became national chairperson. At this time, I was virtually working full-time for Sinn Féin.

"I was self-employed, but the work with Sinn Féin took me away from my regular work and it was lucky that Helen was working as well, and I am always very grateful for that. Helen and the two boys were also very understanding."

Seán was Sinn Féin chair up to 1990, which took him away from home quite a bit.

He said: "I chaired the session of the Ard Fheis when the split over abstentionism happened in 1986 and I was able to handle it and it was conducted in an orderly fashion.

"It was sad to see people like Ruairí Ó Brádaigh, and indeed any comrade who was involved, taking a different path. I was sorry about the split and when you left you were no longer at the forefront of the political struggle."

Meanwhile, Seán was also beginning his long career as an active local politician. He said: "I pushed from early on that we needed to be more visible to the people and to make ourselves more relevant. If people had problems about medical cards, housing or employment then we should be involved, and we made an electoral breakthrough in Sligo even before the Peace Process began.

"The first time I stood for Sinn Féin was a Sligo Corporation election in 1984 and I did not get in. I got a fairly decent increase on what the previous Sinn Féin candidate had got in 1979.

SEÁN AS MAYOR OF SLIGO WITH HIS WIFE HELEN AND SON CHRIS

"I had been involved in Joe McDonnell's election campaign in 1981 and John Joe McGirl's campaign in 1982, so I was getting used to elections. But is a very personal thing and you can feel that whatever vote you get is a personal reflection on yourself. I contested quite a few General Elections and I did not make Dáil Éireann. I came very close in 2002. The entry of Marian Harkin was crucial. But that's politics."

The split in Sinn Féin in 1986 "did not involve too many in Sligo".

Seán said: "The late 1980s were tough times for Sinn Féin activists. The Coalition Government were putting a lot of pressure on us and there were nationwide searches for arms and stuff. At one stage over 100,000 houses around the country were raided for arms.

"I was arrested on a number of occasions while going about my duties as chairperson of Sinn Féin both north and south of the border. That was a hard time on our family in Maugheraboy. When your house is invaded by a bunch of people who go through the most intimate of your personal belongings, tear the house apart and put children under pressure, it's very traumatic.

"It was very hard on my wife Helen as well of course. The guards would sit outside our house for maybe days on end watching the house. And I was always being stopped on the road".

1987 was also the year of the horrific Enniskillen Poppy Day bomb in neighbouring Co. Fermanagh, when 11 people died. It had a huge impact on the country and on the republican movement.

Seán said: "Going back to my time in England, republicans came under a lot of pressure after the Birmingham bombing. And the Enniskillen bombing was a most unfortunate incident for the loss of all those lives and the suffering of families, which I deeply acknowledge. It gave grist to the mill to those who opposed republicanism in the north. It was a bad time all around."

At the same time Seán was "up and down to Belfast every Monday" for a considerable time as secret negotiations had begun between Sinn Féin president Gerry Adams and SDLP leader John Hume.

Seán said: "I did not meet John Hume during those discussions but I was involved in drawing up strategy and exchanging papers between the parties. This was around 1988.

"This continued right into the 1990s. Certain columnists in the national media had awful spite against Sinn Féin, but despite all that negative rhetoric you could feel that there was a shift in the British position and that was transferred to the Dublin government.

"Things moved on and the 1990s was a very active time for me. It is a blur in many ways. It was hectic, and I contested six elections in the 1990s. I contested a local election in 1991, a General Election in 1992, I won my first local election in 1994 and I was there for 23 years until I retired in 2017.

"And in 1999 I contested three elections – Sligo Borough Council, Sligo County Council and Europe. I won the first two."

The IRA called a ceasefire in August 1994, and Seán was part of the first Sinn Féin delegation to hold public talks with the British Government since the days of Michael Collins in 1921. The others included the late Martin McGuinness, Gerry Kelly, the late Siobhán O'Hanlon and Lucilita Breathnach.

Seán said: "Obstacle after obstacle was put in the way of the Peace Process and the IRA ceasefire broke down in 1996, but while large sections of the Irish government were slow to embrace peace in the early 1990s, that changed when Albert Reynolds became taoiseach. I had respect for him.

"John Bruton was not as keen in developing the Peace Process in my view and I think he was a reluctant participant."

Seán was there in the thick of the action leading up to the historic signing of the Good Friday Agreement in 1998. How did he feel when the Agreement was signed?

"It was a big stepping-stone, but we then had to bring it back to our own people to gain their support, which was not easy. There were loads of meetings, but we kept briefing our people on every step of that process."

Seán won his first election to Sligo County Council a year later in 1999. He topped the poll in the Corporation election in the West Ward and got elected on first count in the county council election.

He said: "The local organisation in Sinn Féin bought into the need for us to be community activists as well as political activists. We had to make ourselves significant to the lives of people so that people could say that Sinn Féin will take on our problems and they will not back down.

Seán was elected first as Mayor in 2000 thanks to a pact with Fianna Fáil, but that only lasted a few years – the privatisation of bin collection "tore that alliance asunder".

Seán said: "I was the first Sinn Féin mayor anywhere in Ireland since 1968 – Norbert Ferguson was elected mayor of Sligo that year.

Seán was elected mayor again in 2004. It showed, Seán said, that "anybody could become mayor – a fellow coming from west Cavan could be mayor of Sligo".

He said: "I have always found the people of Sligo very decent and I know you could say this about a lot of places. I always found them very welcoming and they gave me great support, and this is a really beautiful county.

Seán contested every General Election from 1989 to 2007.

He said: "I could have taken a seat in 2002. Once Marian Harkin entered the race it took away a large segment of the floating vote. The last one I contested was in 2007. I got a heart attack a few days into the campaign and I was out of action for quite a while. My first heart attack was in 1993, the year after my son Joseph was killed. It was stress."

Seán has met many notables including Ted Kennedy, Patrick Moynihan, Tony Blair, Mo Mowlam, Bertie Ahern and David Trimble.

Seán called time in 2017 as he admires politicians who step down "at times of their own choosing".

He said: "I wanted to go at a time of my own choosing when I thought that I had done my best for the community and for Sinn Féin as much as I possibly could. I have watched too many people stay too long in politics and in the end, the public tells you that you're around too long – I didn't want that to happen to me.

"I wanted to spend more time with my family as I was heavily involved in politics since the late 1970s and only for Helen I would never have been able to do that."

But he has no regrets that he did not get a Dáil seat. He said: "By 2011 I did not want to be going up to the Dáil and sitting on the back benches".

These days Seán is very proud that his son Chris is now a Sinn Féin MEP and equally proud of his eldest son Joe, who died in an IRA action in February 1992.

Joe's untimely passing had a traumatic effect on Seán and his family.

Seán said: "Joe was a very extrovert and outgoing fellow and he was a normal, ordinary guy. He was big into football. He played both soccer and Gaelic and he was a medal winner with St Mary's. He played with Collegians for most of his soccer career. He was just 21 when he was killed

"I would not like to have come up against him, especially on the soccer field, as he was teak hard. He would take an odd pint and liked the girls and was into heavy metal music – a normal young lad.

"Joe was interested in politics but not to the same degree that Chris would be. Like Chris, from his teenage years he was subjected to harassment from the Special Branch.

"Joe would have seen prominent republicans like Gerry Adams, Martin McGuinness and Mairéad Farrell coming and going to our house and that would have had some influence on his political thinking.

"But the signal thing for him was Loughgall, when a number of IRA men were shot by the SAS in an ambush. I remember he asked me could he come to the funeral of Jim Lynagh, which was down in Monaghan. Shortly after that he became more active. Joe was also very active in Sinn Féin in Sligo as he used to sell the paper for us in the town.

Seán spoke poignantly to me about the last time he saw his eldest son alive. He said: "I gave him a lift to where he was staying a few days before his death. We were having the craic about football – he was an Arsenal supporter despite my best efforts to make him a QPR supporter. QPR were after beating Manchester United and we were laughing about that.

"The evening he was killed, two republicans called to the house to tell us he had been killed. I can still see it quite clearly. It is very fresh in my mind, and as a parent who loses a child, whether it be in a road accident or sickness, and particularly a young person in the prime of their health and the whole world before them, it just tears you apart.

"The hurt, the sorrow and the loss is just terrible and you are never the same again, and I am sure the same goes for Helen and Chris. I was never the same person again and something went out of life and something died inside of me.

"But I am very proud of him, as I am of Chris. He had the courage to follow through his convictions. He saw the situation in the north wasn't right and he tried to play some part in rectifying it. People of course have different views of that, but I am very proud of him."

Joe's younger brother Chris, Seán said, was "imbued in politics since he was eight or nine years of age".

Seán said: "Both of them, living in the house that they did, it was natural that they would be republican.

"We are very proud of Chris, who has worked very hard on the Corporation and is now an MEP. Chris knows that it is important that if you tell someone you will do something, you must try your very best to do it and your word is your bond. Chris is now an MEP and that is great news, but we never have any big celebrations – that is not how we are. We don't make a fuss about things."

Seán MacManus was never a man for show. He believed and largely proved that positive action speaks louder than words – and he is not bad at the latter either.

Finally, what is Seán's advice for budding politicians?

He said: "There are a lot of words and I have met some great people from all parties in politics, but the most important thing is being honest with people – honesty has to return to politics."

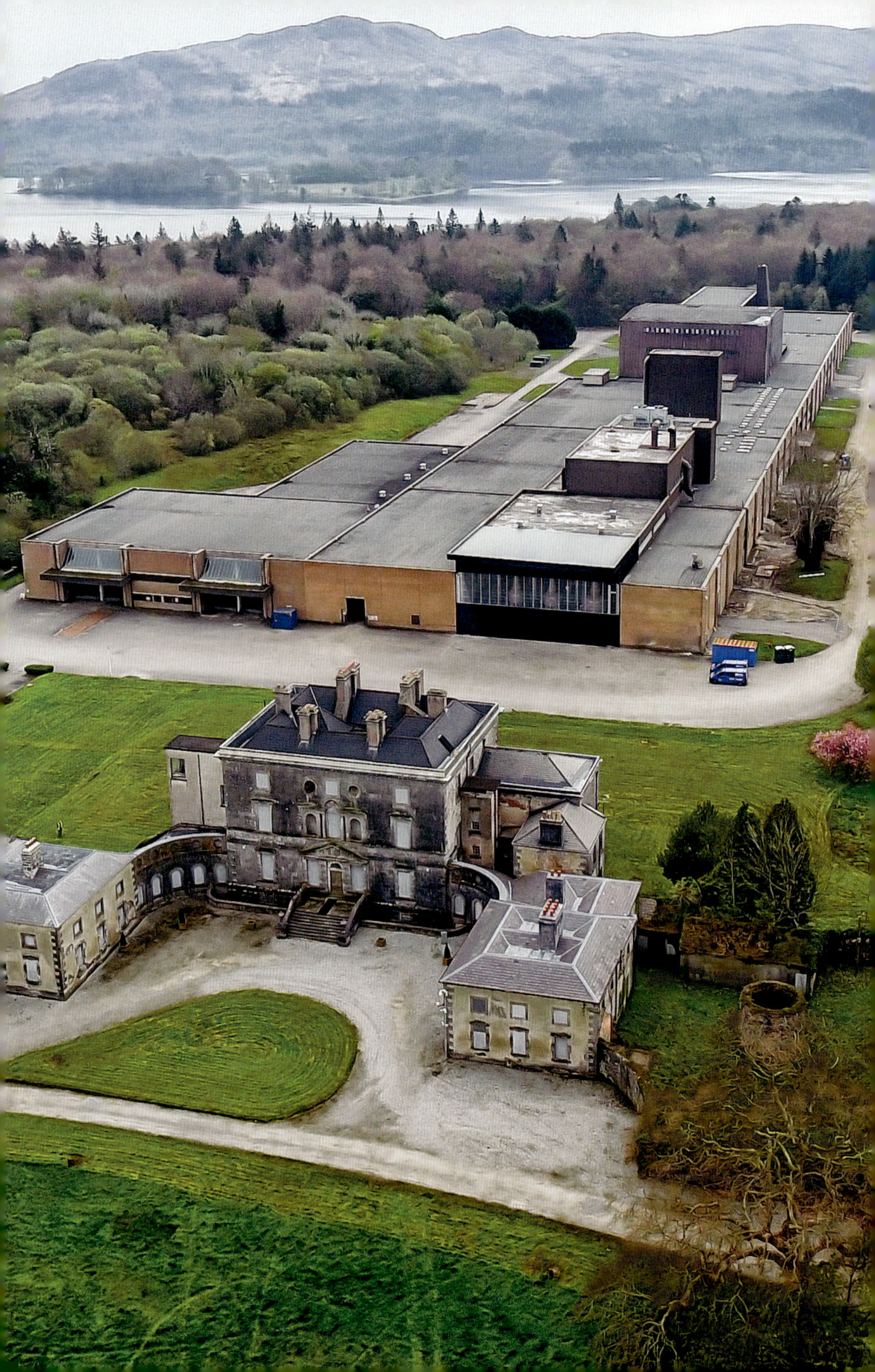

LIFE AT THE SNIA FACTORY

Brian McHugh remembers days, nights, colleagues, bosses, unions and sport at Sligo's biggest employer, Snia in Hazelwood, in the 1970s and early 1980s

PUBLISHED ON MAY 14, 2020

THESE ARE MEMORIES OF MY EARLY days in Sligo, and in particular my 10-year stint in the Snia factory.

In 1975, I married a young girl named Geraldine Cassidy, also a native of west Cavan, on July 5. Somehow, she is still with me, a patient woman.

The wedding reception was in the then relatively new Silver Swan Hotel, where the Glasshouse now stands. 'The Swan' was then an in-spot for weddings. We lived in a rented house at 11 Temple Street while our current home in Ransboro was being built.

Snia was the biggest employer in Sligo, with close to 600 full-

LEFT: THE SNIA FACTORY BEHIND HAZELWOOD HOUSE, WITH THANKS TO LOUGH GILL DISTILLERY. RIGHT: A HANDBOOK FROM 1975

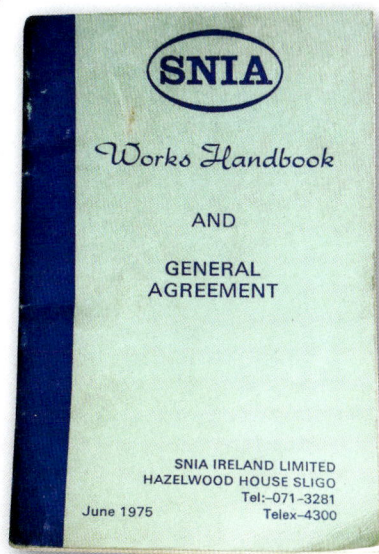

SNIA

Works Handbook

AND

GENERAL AGREEMENT

SNIA IRELAND LIMITED
HAZELWOOD HOUSE SLIGO
Tel:-071-3281
June 1975   Telex-4300

time staff at one stage, predominantly male. Over its 10 years in operation, taking staff turnover into account, at least 1,000 in total would have worked there at some stage.

Wages were good at the time especially for the majority of us who were on shift work. The factory ran 24 hours a day, 365 days year.

A majority of employees came from rural parts of Sligo and surrounding counties. A theory for this was that Sligo 'townies' were not prepared to give up their social life to do night shifts and weekends in Snia. I will make no comment on that one!

There was plenty of overtime available with some financially hard pressed staff working shifts on their rest days almost every week. And double shifts – 24 hours – were common. Many of the 1970s houses you see around today were built on Snia overtime.

However, life in Snia was not all about saving money. Back then regardless of which nights your time off fell on there was always a choice of places to socialise. It was the time of the big 'singing pubs' with music seven nights a week, and always a good gathering of Snia folk around.

Among the most popular of these establishments was The Blue Lagoon in Sligo town, Jordan's in Maugherow, Coolera House (in its heyday) The Happy Landing in Coolaney and the Coragh Dtonn in Skreen. The Irish House in O'Connell Street was good for smaller gatherings.

For some, socialising was not restricted to days off. It was not unusual for a few thirsty guys after finishing a night shift to head to Crystal's Bar in Sligo to quench their thirst and then go home for a few hours kip before going back in for another night shift. Crystal's had a docker's licence enabling it to open early.

Employees also had an active Sports and Social Club which as the name suggests ran all kinds of events for employees and their families.

A periodical newsletter brought staff news of various happenings around the factory. For a nylon producing company it was aptly named Snia Yarns. The editor was Seamus Storan.

The following are more who come to mind: Michael McGurrin, *Sligo Weekender* photographer, Seán Cassidy, living near Castlebaldwin, Gerry

Dolan RIP. John McLoughlin (died in drowning accident on Lough Gill) RIP, Martin Tivnan, Martin Boyce, Jackie Malee, Jim Hannon, Michael McWeeney, Sean Curneen, Jimmy Mooney RIP, Tommy Duffy, Martin Burke, Pauric Clancy, Pat O'Hanlon RIP, Pat Milmoe, Pat Kennedy, Stanley Latten, Chris Cunningham, Seamus Gillooly, Anthony Hegarty, Jack Downes, Eric Potter, Mick Downey.

Names of other people from adjacent departments that come to mind are listed below.

Those were the days, my friends.

A FEW OTHER NAMES

I mentioned above the names of some of those I worked alongside in the Spinning Department.

Here is a small selection of others from I recall from various departments of the factory.

Drawtwist: Eamonn O'Donnell, Ronnie Clancy, Mick McGuinn, Sean Kennedy, Paul McManus, John McManus, Tom Curran, Joe Gildea, Nicholas Clancy, Stanley Clarke, Peter Rooney, Peter Barry, Martin Loughlin, Lawrence Loughlin, John Brennan, Paddy McHugh(my brother) Phonsie Travers, Ronnie Hanney, Padraig Loughlin, Connie Gallagher, Thomas Cassidy, Paddy Dixon.

Polymer: Pauric McGowan, Pat Mulligan, Tony Fox, Frank Clancy, Michael Sweeney, Jim McDonald, Jimmy Giblin RIP., Jim Marshall, Peter Mulvaney, Austin McDonnell, Packie Conlon.

Laboratories; Anna Craig, Ann O'Donovan, Teresa O'Neill, Rosaleen Ownes RIP, Marian McNulty, Concepta Lynch, Caroline Cox.

Office: Mary Clancy RIP, Jane Whyte, Claire Whyte, Lovel Clarke.

Maintenance: Dick Molloy, Jim Foley, Kevin Gallagher, Martin O'Grady RIP., Tom Kennedy, Bob Ryan, Noel Mulligan, Jackie Kelly, Noel Kelly, Chris Benson, Johnny Gallagher, Chris Rutherford, Paddy Bannon, Pauric Coyne, Denis Mahon,

Various: Tom Haran, Michael Mulvaney, Gerry McManus, Michael Vickers, Paddy Joe Conlon, Marcia Coyne, Breege Gordon, Mary Wynne, Josephine McDermott, Frankie Rainey.

General Manager: Jim Somers. Personnel Manager: Noel Davis. Italian managers: Dr Berti, Dr Cavalli, Dr Richichi, Dr Meda.

SOME BOSSES I REMEMBER

Among my 'bosses' or supervisors in the Spinning Department were: Jim Purdy, a native of Belfast.

Brian Parke, Strandhill. Brian later went on to become president/chairman of the large Unifi textiles firm in North Carolina in the US.

Other Supervisors: Brian Devaney, famous as the Dame in Coolera Dramatic Society Panto; Tony McLoughlin, now-retired TD; Willie Carter, Strandhill; Seán McGuire, Cranmore; Mel Farrell RIP; Seán Traynor; Joe White RIP.

Mick McGuinn, Calry: Mick McGuinn has the distinction of being the only person whose work spanned all the years of the Hazelwood industry. He worked in Snia, was security at the factory when Snia closed, and continued on security during the years Saehan Media operated in the factory.

THE UNIONS AND NEGOTIATIONS

As in all big employment places, Snia had labour relations issues.

There were several trade unions representing the various categories of workers. The ITGWU, later to become SIPTU, was by far the biggest union there, catering for all the general production workers.

Each shift in each department had their own shop steward. At some stage – I cannot remember when – Frank Clancy from Cairns Hill and myself were elected secretary and chairman of the ITGWU for the factory.

We could get some of the smaller issues sorted out easily, perhaps by a casual chat between the worker(s) and supervisor involved.

When things got more serious, we sought the support of a full-time ITGWU official based in the Union Hall at Lynn's Place in Sligo. The Union

Hall is long gone; it was demolished ahead of the building of the Inner Relief Road. It was located near to where the closed-down TD's pub is now, close to the town end of Finisklin Road.

All of the Sligo branch union officials we dealt there have since passed away. They were former Mayor of Sligo, Tommy Higgins, Tommy Callaghan, Noel Kilfeather and Tony Ayton. They have gone to where they will not have to fight for their rights.

When serious difficulties arose we had many long negotiation sessions around the large conference table in Hazelwood House, which was the factory head office.

The General Manager Jim Somers, a Kilkenny native who lived at Larkhill Road in Sligo, would lead the company side. He would normally be backed

**A FOOTBALL TEAM MADE UP OF MEMBERS OF
THE MAINTENANCE DEPARTMENT STAFF**

up by a number of his fellow managers and sometimes by Italian officials, bearing in mind that the parent company was in Milan.

On the other side of the table would be the full-time Sligo branch union official at the time, joined by Frank Clancy and myself, together with shop stewards from the department concerned in the dispute.

Most times negotiations would be successful. If not we would take it to a hearing with a Rights Commissioner in Dublin or the odd time it would go to the Labour Court.

Jim Somers died in Dublin in 2011. RIP.

The most difficult rows were the ones that blew up overnight – perhaps when tempers would flare on a night shift. A few times this led to an

ONE OF THE ITALIAN MANAGERS WHO WORKED IN THE SLIGO FACTORY, ANTONIO RICHICHI, LIKED SLIGO SO WELL THAT HE MADE A RETURN VISIT TO THE TOWN IN 1980. HE IS PICTURED ON THE LEFT WITH HIS FORMER WORK COLLEAGUES BRIAN DEVANEY AND TONY MCLOUGHLIN, THEN MAYOR OF SLIGO, IN HIS MAYORAL ROBES, AND ANTONIO'S WIFE. BRIAN DEVANEY AND HIS LATE WIFE CATHERINE ALSO MADE A SURPRISE VISIT TO ANTONIO IN ITALY, WHERE THEY WERE WARMLY GREETED

unofficial picket on the gate in the morning, with the cars of incoming workers not passing the picket lined up for a mile out the Hazelwood Road.

These disputes had to be resolved quickly while the continuous process factory would be kept running by staff who had worked all night. But they always got sorted, mostly by an agreement to lift the pickets pending talks later.

Down the years there were disputes, big and small. But considering the number of employees involved and the fact that we were spread out on various shifts and factory departments, Snia would not have been known as having a problematic labour relations history.

STAFF ROMANCES AND WEDDINGS

Snia was not all about work. Romance blossomed among employees there too. Among the marriages that flowed from Snia were Chris Benson and Breege Gordon, Ronnie Hanney and Mary Wynne, Paddy Dixon and Rose Cunningham, and Ronnie Clancy and Mary Clancy (RIP).

SOCCER, GAELIC AND BASKETBALL

Snia workers showed their prowess in sporting activities in a number of codes. In soccer, Snia had the distinction of winning the last MacArthur Cup Final played back in 1976. This was a highly regarded and very competitive Sligo inter-firms competition. To get to the final, Snia outclassed a side from the Post Office in the semi-final. In the final Snia were up against a strong team from CIE-Henderson's. The final, played at Summerhill College, ended in a draw. To great excitement, the Hazelwood team emerged winners in the replay after a competitive game.

Snia's home ground was to the front of Hazelwood House with high-standard dressing rooms located in the basement of the historic house.

The factory also had a strong gaelic team. In 1979 they reached the semi-final of an inter-firms competition against the gardai, who went on to win the competition.

Another old undated sports report tells of Snia Gaelic coming out tops against a North Western Health Board side, winning by 3-10 to 1-7. The report credits Brian Devaney and Peter Barry with powerful displays in the centre.

Not to be outdone, a group of Snia girls formed a ladies' basketball club in 1980. Concepta Clynch and Caroline Cox were the driving force behind it. The team was coached by members of Sligo All-Stars.

THE 1976 FIRE

It is Tuesday November 23, 1976. I am on a 'rest day' having come off night shifts a day earlier. I volunteer to go in for a shift of overtime to help pay for the building of our house at Ransboro. The foundations for it are in and block-laying has started. But there is much to be done and we are on a very tight budget.

The overtime shift turns out to be one of the most dramatic days of my life and a traumatic one for all the 500 staff there. It is the day of the big fire in the factory, one of the largest ever seen in Sligo.

On arrival at 8am I am assigned to work upstairs in the Spinning Department, in an area known as the Quench Floor. It is an extremely warm place to work, the manufacturing process demands that the temperature be kept very high.

Halfway through the shift, my colleague on the floor is on his lunch break and I am on my own. It is time to go further upstairs in the tower to record some routine readings on machines. I am on the third floor, there is nobody else around, just the heat and noise from machines running.

Suddenly I hear what I remember as a loud thud and a vibration that brings white dust down around me. I run down the stairs, by-passing the lower floors, to check what's happening. On reaching the landing at the ground floor, someone is standing in a nearby door opening on to the outside. He shouts, "come on get out quick". I ask what's wrong, he shouts the "the spinning tower is on fire".

I turn to run back up one flight of stairs to the Quench Floor to retrieve my jacket, but I'm again told to get out, "the fire is raging up there". I do as I'm told. When I get out everyone else is gathered in bunches standing on the grass area in front of the factory. I join them and look up at the tower from where I had come from minutes earlier.

Flames and smoke are coming from various openings on the floors just below where I was working. I realise I'm the only production worker who was above where the blaze started. I'm probably the last person evacuating the factory and all I lost is my jacket!

Quickly we hear the sound of sirens approaching. Fire engines, ambulances, gardai. The emergency services have activated their major incident plan.

More and more fire-fighting appliances arrive, first from Sligo, then from Ballymote followed by ones from surrounding counties. None of us ever saw as many blue lights together before.

The blaze goes higher and higher. We are moved further back to escape the heat. Fire crews are spraying water on the inferno from all directions.

When they seem to be getting it under control, we hear mini-explosions as barrels of oil and other chemicals catch fire, re-igniting the blaze again and spreading it further up the tower.

Eventually the blaze is extinguished, just thick black smoke remains, and the heart of the factory is burned to a shell.

Meanwhile, word about the big fire has spread throughout the town. Everyone has seen and heard the dozens of emergency services vehicles racing through the streets with sirens blazing.

Family members of employees working on the day are worried sick about their fate. There are no

THE FIRE OF
NOVEMBER 23, 1976

mobile phones, there is nobody answering the 071/3281 sole landline to the factory. In the absence of any knowledge of what's happening, people naturally fear the worst.

My wife Geraldine, then pregnant with our first child Ciaran, is among those trying desperately to get in contact. She is working on The Mall, which was then the main route for the siren vehicles rushing out to the blaze.

After some time we are allowed to make our way past the fire engines and walk across the large car park to the Snia security hut where we join a long queue to use the only working telephone on that side of Hazelwood estate. We get to deliver the news that we are safe.

It later emerges that two maintenance men were treated in Sligo General Hospital, thankfully their injuries were not serious.

Investigations afterwards show that the fire started after a chemical leaked on to a hot motor and ignited.

After weeks of speculation as to whether the factory would re-open, its owners in Milan give the go-ahead and construction work starts to rebuild the fire damaged building. Some of the burned rubble is removed to form part of the foundation for Henderson's Garage on the Bundoran Road.

After about a year on lay-off, staff are taken back on a phased basis. During part of the time I was off I got temporary employment working as a petrol pump attendant for John Peyton at Duck Park filling station, which was where the Feehily Funeral Home now is.

The cost of demolishing and rebuilding the damaged building was in the region of £6 million.

CLOSURE IN 1982

Snia in Sligo died without those working there knowing for sure if it had passed away. In August of 1982 production was "temporarily suspended" for what we were told would be a six-week period, and all staff were laid off.

We were told that the lay-off was necessary due to an international decline in the market for nylon. It was obvious to all of us that there was a problem – the large stores for the completed product were full to the roof. While we were assured that the lay-off would be for only six weeks, many doubted if the factory would open again.

I remember making my way out from my last shift and looking back over my shoulder at the factory and asking myself: after 10 years, is this the end?

Many in Sligo and the surrounding area shared our fears. As we made our way to the car park on that final day, we were met by national and local media representatives seeking comments.

I was approached by the then RTÉ western correspondent Jim Fahy and a cameraman. To be honest, I cannot remember what I told him – personally I had my doubts, but I was also speaking as a trade union representative.

Our worst fears were realised, the six-week period came and went, the weeks turned into months, Christmas came and went with no news of reopening. We were in an ongoing state of limbo.

The issue was repeatedly raised in the Dáil and at local authority meetings. It made the front page of the Sligo Champion almost every week with comments from Sligo ITGWU branch secretary Tommy Higgins, and senior shop stewards Frank Clancy and myself.

Finally, on October 11, 1983, after 14 months of temporary lay-off, confirmation came of what we all suspected.

A letter arrived from Snia, signed by general manager Jim Somers. The opening paragraph read: "Dear Brian, I regret to inform you that I have been instructed by the Board to advise you of its decision not to re-open the Hazelwood plant." It came on my birthday – not the present I wanted.

The letter went on to explain that since the lay-off the company had made every effort to find ways of resuming works at the factory but this was not possible due to a continuing decline in the market for nylon.

The closure was a massive blow for employees and for the Sligo economy. Ireland was in a recession. Many Snia employees were left with big mortgages taken out on the expectation of ongoing well-paid work in the factory. There was a frantic search to find alternative jobs that by and large did not exist. Some set about creating their own jobs. There was doom and gloom. As for myself, I had by then considered starting a local newspaper. The letter on my birthday expedited that plan.

REACTIONS TO THE FEATURE ABOUT LIFE AT SNIA

My trips down memory lane via the road out to Hazelwood in the three-page feature last week met with sizeable reaction from former Snia workers and from their family members, *writes Brian McHugh in his McHugh's Views column of May 21, 2020.*

I had enquiries about the origins of the picture of the 1976 Snia fire smoke in last week's feature, pictured below – apparently there are few such photos still around. It was taken by the late Willie Ward from a vantage point at his home across the river at Holywell Road. Thanks to Willie's son Gerry, who now lives in Australia, for sending it to me.

Gerry was only three years old at the time and remembers seeing the blaze and all the drama from their garden as onlookers gathered there. The trees were lower then so the blazing factory was visible from the Ward cottage on the other side of the river.

Obviously this was many years before the days of mobile phones, but Gerry said that somebody must have shouted to him, "get the camera".

Willie was an employee of Hanley's and died in 2003 aged 81. He was a big supporter of the local Aughamore rowing club.

Speaking of his family home from where the picture was taken, Gerry said the family have lived there for as long as anyone remembers going back to the late 1800s.

Locals know the hill as "Ward's Hill", a steep incline coming out of town directly opposite Hazelwood.

Meanwhile, another former employee of the factory recalled the fire: Maugheraboy native Pat Kennedy said he was working that day in the Spinning Department.

He was on a break in the smoke room at the time and Noel Trotter of the maintenance department came in and shouted: "Get out, the factory is on fire." When Pat raced outside he found there was more smoke there than was in the smoke room.

One of the names mentioned in last week's feature was Doug Luck. Sadly, he passed away on the day before the paper was published.

Doug was the production manager in Snia for a number of years before it closed in 1982. He was then a resident of Calry. He moved to Clondalkin in Dublin some time after the factory closed. He died at the Hermitage Medical Clinic and his funeral was in Clondalkin on Friday last. RIP.

Sympathy to his family, including his daughter Gillian, who lives in Sligo and works at Sligo University Hospital.

Finally, I received the following email from Tony Flynn regarding the Snia team having won the MacArthur Cup: "I have just read your feature in today's *Sligo Weekender* and thoroughly enjoyed it. However, your piece on the final of the MacArthur Cup is incorrect. Yes the final ended in a thrilling draw but there never was a replay of that game. CIE-Henderson's were unable to field a team due to injuries and work commitments. The cup was then awarded to Snia without playing the game, so to say they won it is untrue. This ended the MacArthur Cup competition and God only knows where the cup is now. I played in that final for CIE-Henderson's."

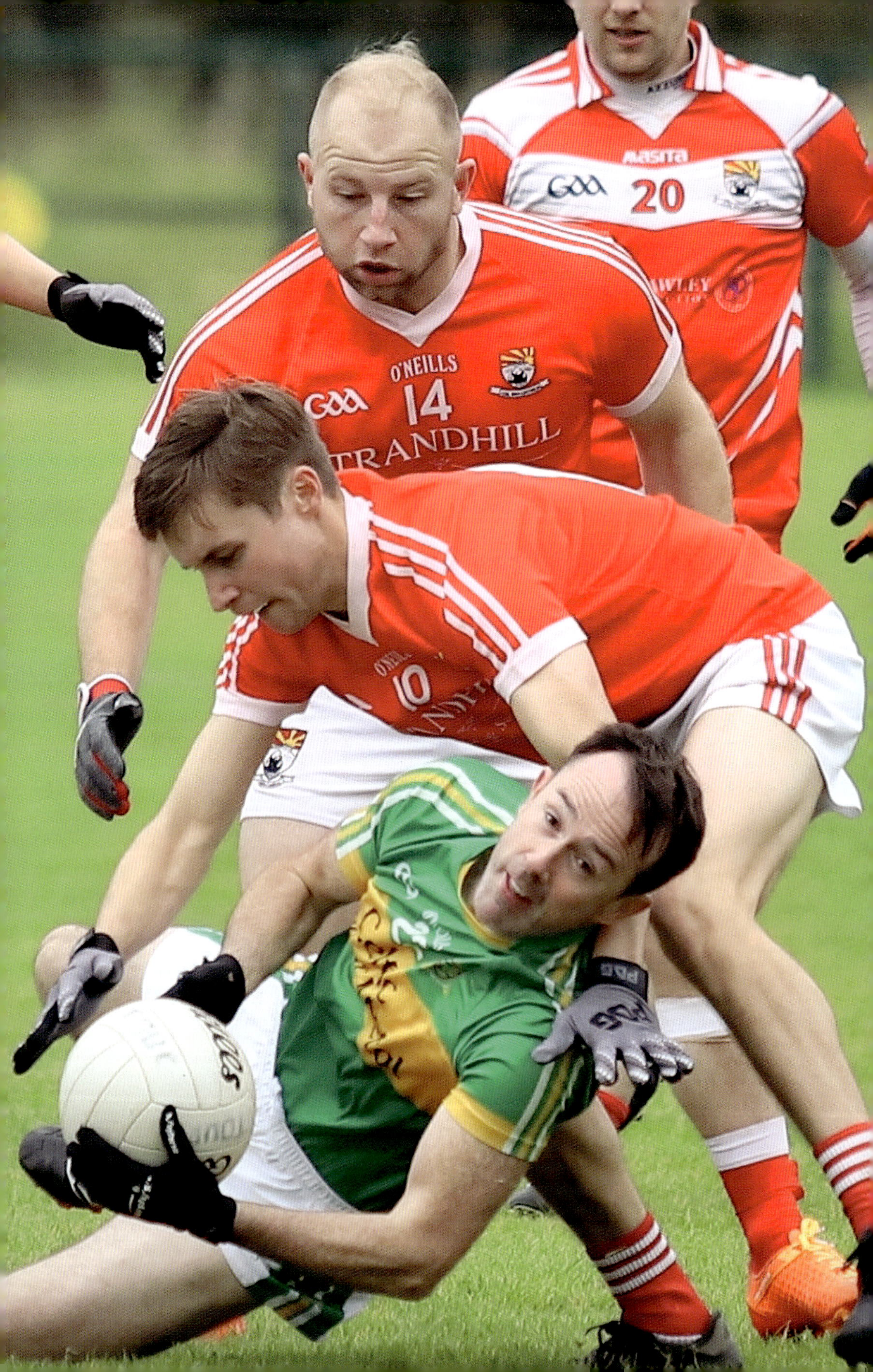
MASITA
GAA
20
O'NEILLS
GAA
14
TRANDHILL
O'NEILLS
10

JOHN MARREN

Long-serving forward John Marren has been a key player for Tourlestrane, winning 10 Senior Football Championships. Liam Maloney spoke to the unsung hero of the south Sligo club

PUBLISHED ON APRIL 9, 2020

FOR JOHN MARREN, IT HAS ALWAYS been about doing his best as a Gaelic footballer: for himself, his family, community and, of course, *the* club – Tourlestrane.

The Banada native is just one of hundreds of players who've been immersed in Tourlestrane's GAA religion over decades.

But what makes the 37-year-old unique is that he's been there for 10 of the club's 15 Sligo Senior Football Championships.

Promoted to the club's Senior squad in 1999 – when aged just 16 – by then manager Neil Egan, this was Marren's first taste of success. When Tourlestrane won a fourth title in succcession in 2019 this was Marren's

LEFT: JOHN MARREN – WITH THE BALL – IN ACTION AGAINST COOLERA-STRANDHILL IN A COUNTY SEMI-FINAL TWO YEARS AGO

10th medal. His record is bettered only by teammate Shane Dunne, who, two years older, was part of the Tourlestrane side that won the county final in 1997.

Marren, for years a diligent, hard-working forward always capable of sniping a vital score or two along with winning crucial frees, is only realising now what a brilliant difference he has made in the green and gold.

"It is a huge privilege [to have that many medals] for myself but, to be honest, it would be all about the team. Personally, though, it is a great achievement to be playing for that length of time."

"1999 was when I won my first medal and to be able to be there, so many years later, not just still performing but to see the club develop – is a source of immense pride."

A member of the title-winning squad in 1999 – Tourlestrane defeated Easkey in the decider – he didn't make his championship debut until later that year when he featured in a Connacht Club Senior Football Championship game against Leitrim's Glencar-Manorhamilton.

Marren, who would end up being part of a Tourlestrane dynasty, had to wait five years for his next Senior Football Championship medal, though.

"At the time I thought titles would come frequently. But it turned out that we didn't win another county title until 2004. In my playing career, that was the biggest gap in between titles. It was strange because the club had started to become a force, they had won it in 1994 and again in 1997."

He continued: "We had good teams then but the Sligo Senior Football Championship was very tough, very competitive in those years."

Indeed, in between Tourlestrane's sixth and seventh titles there were four different winners of the big prize.

"Myself and Colin Neary never headed off on a J1 visa to America in those years. We stayed at home, thinking we'd be picking up more medals!

"But it wasn't until 2004 that we made the breakthrough again under Anthony Brennan. He took over the team, started to drive us on again and got us back on track."

While Marren can recall all 10 of the county finals that Tourlestrane won when he was involved, two campaigns, in particular, stand out: 2009 and 2017.

Tourlestrane were seemingly heading for the exit door in 2009 when they found themselves a woeful 10 points adrift in a county semi-final against St John's, then the new kids on the block.

But Tourlestrane scrambled a draw – Marren kicked the equalising point from a late free having taken over the free-taking duties due to Gerry McGowan going off injured – and won an equally tense replay that went to extra-time. They beat Eastern Harps in the final.

"That drawn game stood out for me because it showed what Tourlestrane are all about. Players led from all over the pitch – to get a draw and know that we drove on from that is a special memory."

St John's, who had never contested a county final, were emboldened at that time to do justice to the memory of the late Johnny Stenson.

Marren reckons that had St John's overcome Tourlestrane in that semi-final it could have sparked a silverware sequence for the Carraroe outfit.

The 2017 campaign saw Tourlestrane retain the Owen B Hunt Cup for the first time in their history. Eastern Harps were the runners-up.

This was also the first time that a club had won back-to-back titles in the Senior Football Championship since St Patrick's achieved this feat in 1988-89.

However, Marren's recollection of 2017 centres on the passing of his sister, Mairead, in September of that year. She died in a tragic accident when on holiday in Spain with her husband, Sean Davey.

The long-serving player says that Gaelic football was a source of solace during an horrific period that changed things forever for the Marren and Davey families.

"That county final win was tinged with emotion for myself and my family because we lost my sister, Mairead. It was a very difficult time for my family, particularly my parents, Michael and Kathleen, who had been such a driving force in my football career. Winning that final, and it being a two in a row, was special. A huge achievement for the club, the community and the families. That success touched us all."

Marren, who has two other sisters, Kathleen and Geraldine, could have easily stepped back from playing. But he chose not to.

"I think being involved in football did help me at the time. I had to wait a few weeks in Spain before we could bring Mairead home – that was tough. But keeping in touch with the lads and the team getting back into the swing of things gave me an outlet.

"I might not have talked a lot about what was going on but I knew I had teammates to rely on and that the community was there for myself and my family. Football definitely did help. I think I needed the football, it is such a big thing in my life.

"There was no pressure on me to go back playing. When I got back into the routine, be it at games or at training, players just sat down beside me as normal in the dressing-room. You might have got a tap in the shoulder but nothing needed to be said."

He went on: "It is unfortunate that other families in the club would have had their own tragedies so there was a kind of understanding there.

"It has been tough. Time does help, although it doesn't heal. You can never forget what happened, but you can only think of the positives and the great impact Mairead had during her life. Even in terms of sport, she was part of one of the first Tourlestrane Ladies Gaelic Football teams to win a Junior title."

"You have to stay positive and live your life as best you can."

There was further sadness surrounding the team due to the death of Jackie O'Hara in October of 2017 – Jackie's son, Eamonn O'Hara, was (and still is) Tourlestrane's joint-manager along with Gerry McGowan.

Marren, a past pupil of Banada Abbey, was only ever on the losing side once in a Senior Football Championship final. That was 10 years ago.

"In 2010 we were going for two in a row. We were playing Eastern Harps in the final. We got two injuries in the 10 minutes before half-time – David Durkin and Eamon Haran. We were three points up at the time. Harps pushed on in the second-half, fair play to them. Michael Doddy had a great game. He was someone that we would always have been aware of when we were playing them."

Marren's 10 SFC medals have come at the expense of five clubs: Easkey (1999), St Mary's (2004, 2016), Tubbercurry (2013, 2018), Coolera-Strandhill (2011, 2019) and Eastern Harps (2007, 2009, 2017).

But it is a club not on that list, Tourlestrane's neighbour Curry, that Marren says is its biggest rival.

"When I started out at Senior level that rivalry was probably a bit more over the top than it needed to be. There is a huge respect between the clubs. Curry weren't that successful in the 1990s but when it came to the next decade, the 2000s, they brought it up to a new level [Curry featured in four county finals in six years, winning two].

"That is the club that we would have had some very competitive matches with. We always wanted to beat each other. It is good to have a rivalry like that. But a lot of friendships have developed between the two clubs. We also would have gone to secondary school with a lot of the Curry lads. We also had some great battles with Harps."

Marren, a Project Manager with CBE and a part-time farmer, played both soccer and Gaelic football for University of Limerick during his Third Level studies there.

He also played soccer locally for Aclare Celtic, a club driven on by Tommy Gaughan and with Barry Price as its star striker. Marren's niece, Farrah McDonagh, was goalkeeper with the Sligo Rovers women's U-17 team last season.

Gaelic football is the number one sport for Tourlestrane folk. Marren says there is no secret formula to explain the club's capture of 12 county titles in 26 years.

Lots of hard work, a dash of good luck here and there and, most importantly, a competitive edge throughout the squad. Everyone who plays for Tourlestrane wants to be in the team. Period.

Marren also hails the club's underage structures and those selfless coaches who nuture the next generation of Senior players.

"There is no reason why other clubs can't do what we're doing. We've had a bit of luck along the way but a huge amount of work goes in. The underage structure is very important. When I started off my dad [Michael] and David McVeigh were over teams that weren't successful but they kept the players involved.

"Players are also given their chance at Tourlestrane – it doesn't matter who that player is or what their family is, if they are good enough then they know they'll get a shot at making the team. That helps to drive on people and create that winning mentality.

"Success breeds success and that is the one thing we have been fortunate with. We've kept winning and the kids have turned up at the pitch – all looking forward to playing for the club in the future."

He highlights Tourlestrane's policy of almost always appointing a manager from within the club has helped, too.

"A local management, with knowledge of the players, is huge. They can talk to the players, one-on-one, because they know them. A local manager will know your character as much as your football. That is a huge thing."

Neil Egan, Anthony Brennan, Michael Henry, Eamon Haran... then Gerry McGowan and Eamonn O'Hara – they know us all. They always had the players' respect because they had done it for the club as well.

"You might disagree with a management decision, but they always wanted to do the best for the club because it was their club. Compare that outlook to other club players who've had a merry-go-round of outside managers. Some clubs go with that idea that you have to go outside the club to get a good manager."

He mentions that he has only had two 'outside' managers during his time playing for Tourlestrane's Senior team, both Mayo men: Frank Noone and Raymond Dempsey.

Marren has always tried to sustain his sporting appetite despite the passing of the years and the emergence of other forwards just as hungry and talented. He still wants to play for Tourlestrane in 2020 but at the moment sporting hopes – along with everything else – have been put on hold by the dreaded Covid-19.

One regret is that he never pushed on at Senior inter-county level, having represented Sligo on various underage teams. He was briefly in the Sligo Senior panel at the start of 2005 – when Dom Corrigan was at the helm – and played in an FBD Connacht GAA Senior Football League game against Leitrim.

"I would never sit on a Tourlestrane bench just to win a medal. I've always trained to be at my best. I would always have felt that I could be in the starting 15, even to this day."

"I think you have to have that mentality and belief if you want to succeed and you want to do something, both for yourself and the

TOURLESTRANE'S JOHN MARREN WITH HIS WIFE VERITY AND HIS PARENTS MICHAEL AND KATHLEEN

team. As my career has gone on and I've gotten older maybe I don't get the chance to start games but I can still come on and try to make an impact."

"Over the last few years it has been incredibly difficult for our management to pick the team – there could be up to 10 lads on the bench with four or five county medals each, and they aren't starting. They all feel that they should be on the team."

"From 2000 to close to 2016 I would have started nearly every championship game, maybe missing only two or three games through injury. When you get to a stage where you are not starting it is difficult to get used to, at first, but you have to embrace it."

"You have to realise that there is more to it – it is about developing more players along with yourself. In the modern game, which is about the panel just as much as it about the team, the older players can be the ones pushing on everyone else to be their best."

"I think players and management will see the squad members who are doing that and it is appreciated."

Tourlestrane certainly appreciate what John Marren has given to them.

Despite Covid-19, Sligo GAA had a club season in 2020, and Marren played his part in it. He was Player of the Match in the Junior 'A' Football Championship final as Tourlestrane overcame Owenmore Gaels and he was a late second-half substitute in the Senior Football Championship decider – Tourlestrane defeated Drumcliffe-Rosses Point to complete a record-breaking five-in-a-row

THE SPANISH FLU IN SLIGO

In 1918 and 1919, soon after the end of World War I, the world was hit by the Spanish flu – also known as the black flu. John Bromley looks at its terrible impact on Sligo

PUBLISHED ON MARCH 26, 2020

THE LAST PANDEMIC TO DIRECTLY affect Sligo in the way that Covid-19 coronavirus has the potential to was what became known as Spanish flu over 100 years ago.

The 1918-19 flu pandemic affected most parts of the world and, according to one historian, it "killed more humans than any other disease in a period of similar duration in the history of the world".

In County Sligo around 350 people died from the flu in the space of about 18 months.

They were among millions worldwide, estimated to be around 50 million, who succumbed to what is still considered the worst epidemic ever.

The political upheaval of the time and the First World War has tended to overshadow the flu epidemic in terms of Irish history. The

Westminster election of that year saw the election of 73 Sinn Féin candidates, including Sligo's Countess Markievicz, who was the first woman ever elected to the British parliament. They refused to take their seats at Westminister and instead formed the first Dáil.

Despite its name the epidemic didn't start in Spain but became known as the Spanish flu because Spain was the first country to report openly on the spread of the disease, due to its neutrality in World War I. In other countries, news reports were censored because of the war and stories of large numbers of people dying from the flu was considered bad for the national morale.

Many Spaniards were not happy with it being called the Spanish flu and called it the Soldier of Naples (after a popular song which was said to have spread like the flu), while the Japanese called it American influenza.

Within the British army on the Western Front it was known as Flanders Grippe, while the German army called it Blitzkatarrh.

There were varying opinions at the time as to where it actually originated. Many related its origin to a military camp in Kansas in the US or to a major British army base in northern France. Others suggested it originated on the battlefields of northern France because of the use of mustard gas or a German biological weapon.

However, in recent times it has been suggested that, like Covid-19, it originated in China and was brought to the Western Front by Chinese labourers hired by Britain and France for manual work to free up troops.

Ironically, the ending of the First World War, in which millions lost their lives, is thought have been a major factor in the spread of the infection worldwide.

It was thought that soldiers coming home from the war brought the flu into Ireland. It first showed up in Dublin and Cork, where troop ships docked. The first recorded outbreak was among soldiers and sailors on a US vessel, USS Dixie, off Cobh in May.

The flu spread across the country in three waves, the first in spring 1918, the second in October-November 1918 and the third in spring 1919.

Throughout Ireland, many public buildings were closed to limit infection. Schools and libraries were closed, court sittings were adjourned and many businesses closed for periods due to staff illness.

In Dublin many people stopped using the trams for fear of catching the flu and streets were washed with disinfectant in an attempt to try and remove the infection.

In many places markets and fairs were called off and some dance halls and theatres were also closed.

Ireland doesn't seem to have gone as far in infection controls as in Arizona and Virginia in the United States where handshaking and kissing were outlawed, while in Chicago, the police were under orders to arrest anybody who sneezed in public.

Unlike Covid-19, which so far seems to have a more severe effect on older people and those with underlying health conditions, the Spanish flu primarily killed healthy young adults, most in the 25 to 35 age group, sometimes within 24 hours of being infected.

THE FEVER HOSPITAL

The fact of those considered the most healthy being at most risk added to people's fears, as did reports of cases of discolouration of victims, which led to it being dubbed the "black flu".

Apart from a darkening of the skin, other symptoms were sore throat, headache and fever.

Hundreds of thousands of people throughout the country were infected, with estimates as high as 800,000. Often whole families were affected.

Official figures put the total number of deaths from influenza in Ireland between 1918 and 1919 at over 20,000, with just under 10,000 dying from pneumonia.

In Sligo the number of deaths from flu in that period was just under 332, according to the reports of the Registrar General of the time.

More people in Sligo died in the third wave of the flu in spring 1919 than in the first two waves in 1918, with 232 deaths recorded in 1919 as against 100 in the previous year.

However, even the number of deaths in in the autumn and winter of 1918 was very worrying locally.

A news report from November 1918 spoke of how "the prevalence of influenza is casting the shadow of gloom and depression all over the town".

"We had hoped that the disease in the mild form we had known it at first would pass away without fatal consequences. The opposite has been the result and this week it is our sad duty to record a number of deaths as a result of this deadly malady."

"In some cases whole families were stricken down, a feeling of nervousness and depression has spread all over. No one seems immune from attack. Even those who were formerly seized with its grip cannot feel secure in the thought that their first illness is innoculation against a second attack."

The report stated that there had been more than 20 funerals the previous Sunday, and "many who are on the sick list cannot be regarded as out of danger".

It was reported that doctors, nurses and chemists were having a busy time and "every effort is being made to cope with the plague, as it has been justly described".

"One shudders to think of young men who a week ago were the embodiment of youthful vitality now lying cold in death."

Sligo didn't fare as badly as Dublin and other larger urban centres where there were larger groups congregating together.

Although Sligo's population was larger than now, at around 79,000, it was largely rural based and spread throughout the county, which helped greatly to ensure better social distancing at a time when the phrase was unknown. Although there is one historical report from Donegal of a woman speaking about being told as a child to walk on the other side of the road from a house where it was known there were people with the flu.

Large numbers of deaths from the flu in any year was not uncommon at the time but in his report for 1918 the Registrar General, Sir William Thompson, commented on "the excessive mortality from influenza and pneumonia, deaths from influenza amounted to 10,651, as compared to an average of 1,234 for the preceding 10 years".

At that time another disease of the respiratory system was a big killer every year. In 1918, tuberculosis was responsible for 9,576 deaths nationally, with 149 of those in Sligo.

It has to be remembered, too, that compared to now the health services were not as well equipped, facilities were not as good, hygiene and infection control was not what it is now and many of the medications we have now were not available.

At that time people also died regularly from conditions which now are rarely fatal and indeed rarely encountered in this country.

Nationally in 1918 over 1,000 people died from whooping cough, 640 from measles, 219 from diptheria, 91 from scarlet fever, 40 from typhus, 13 from dysentery, while enteric fever (typhoid) killed 267 nationally, with nine deaths in Sligo.

At the time of the Spanish flu the only medical hospital in Sligo was the fever hospital in Sligo town, which stood where the orthopaedic wing of Sligo University Hospital is now.

The hospital was almost 100 years old at the time, having been opened in 1822. It was built to accommodate only 50 patients but often held more than that.

It was completely overwhelmed during the cholera outbreak in 1832 and during the Famine it often accommodated three to four times the number of people it was built for.

Again during the Spanish flu epidemic the hospital was unable to cope with all the cases locally.

It closed as a hospital in 1958 but was used as a medical residence and a nurses' home until 1978 when much of the building was severely damaged in a fire. It was demolished the following year for the building of the new orthopaedic wing for Sligo General Hospital, which opened in 1982.

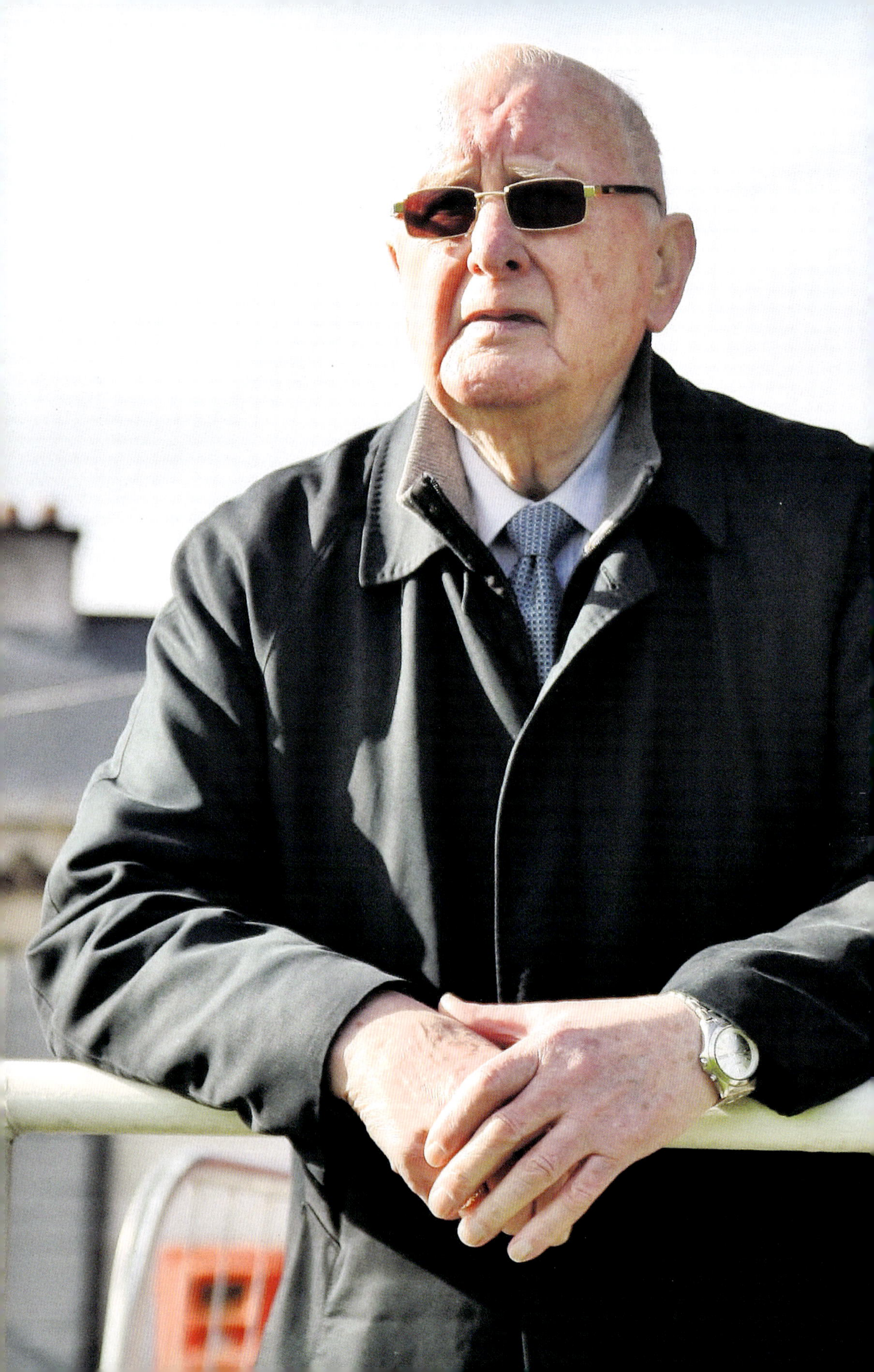

PADDY GILMARTIN

Alan Finn chats to Sligo Rovers stalwart Paddy Gilmartin, who recalls being one of the club's first bus drivers, and how his time as secretary led to an unbreakable friendship with a Bit O'Red legend

PUBLISHED ON MARCH 9, 2017

BUS DRIVER. COMMITTEE MEMBER. Secretary. Vice-president. These are just a few of the jobs performed with pride by one of Sligo Rovers greatest stalwarts – Paddy Gilmartin. The Bit O'Red have played a big part in the life of this Temple Street native for the best part of almost 77 years, and he wouldn't want it any other way. Despite his undying passion for his beloved club, Paddy did not come from a footballing background, instead being introduced to Rovers by a close family friend.

"A man called Filan who worked with the Corporation brought me to the my first

LEFT: PADDY GILMARTIN AT THE SHOWGROUNDS

game. He used to call around to our house for dinner and he was a mad Sligo Rovers fan, so he brought me out to my first game and we kept going to them, he was on Harmony Hill and I was on Temple Street, so it was handy for us." Paddy is perhaps one of the first ever fans to experience Sligo Rovers away trips, and to this day he still makes many treks up and down the country in tow with another familiar Showgrounds face.

"I have been going to games since I was 10 years of age and I have been going to away games for at least 40 years now, the only one I haven't travelled to recently is Cork City away, but I get to all the other ones. I do travel to them with Noel McCloat and I think they are the only games he actually gets to see because he is so busy for matches in The Showgrounds with the shop."

While his love affair with the club had just begun, a combination of World War II and league restructuring meant that Sligo faced a number of years without their football club, a scenario which puts those lengthy off-season periods into perspective.

"I remember when we were booted out of football in the 40s. I was on Temple Street and a man came over to me and shouted 'we are back in football!', the off-season does be long enough, waiting for the new season to start, so you can imagine what it was like for us to have to wait year after year for another game."

Bus drivers in this part of the country were a rare commodity in the 1950s, so Paddy's licence and access to a minibus were enough to earn the responsibility of driving Rovers to their away games. After over a decade behind the wheel, Paddy remembers the dire conditions of the roads, going out of their way to pick up commuting players and the laughs along the way.

"We used to have a player called Jackie Quinn, he was living in Athlone and I used to dread having to go down to collect him, it was an awful stretch of road and normally we wouldn't have to go through there anyway. No matter where we were playing, the drive was always longer then than it is now because you had to take all of these back roads. Another time I remember was when Gerry Mitchell and Dessie Gallagher were acting the mick on the bus. They must've got fed up with it because all of a sudden Tony [Bartley, the manager] asked me to stop, and next thing all I saw was Dessie getting taken off the bus and chucked into the river."

Like many supporters of his generation, Paddy fondly remembers the famous FAI Cup tie with Shamrock Rovers in 1955 and the Austrian sensation who etched his name in Rovers folklore that day.

"I remember that game well. I was stood near the goal when Albert Straka took the penalty and I'll never forget that when he scored it, he took off down to the dressing room because everyone ran towards him, but he must've thought he was going to get beaten up or something. He came with a pedigree, he was a very good player and scored a few goals. His style was probably ahead of the league for that time."

When the name Paddy Gilmartin is mentioned to supporters of a certain vintage, the name Johnny Brookes usually follows.

Paddy's pursuit of a goalscorer lead him to British shores where he was put in contact with the soon to be Rovers legend.

The then secretary was dogged in his determination to secure Brookes' signing, a move the forward would not regret as he praised Paddy for saving his career, sowing the seeds of a strong friendship which remains today.

"I was secretary at the time when I got Johnny Brookes. I used to ring the English papers and I got in touch with a fella called Tony Harrison, he was a sports writer, I asked him if he knew of any centre forwards looking for a club and he said he'd call me back.

"He rang me back the following day and he said 'I have a man here, he is thinking of retiring, he is fed up because he isn't getting a right go at his club.' He gave me Johnny's number, so I rang him and asked him if he would like to come over and the first thing he said was 'Where's Sligo?'.

"I told him we were looking for a centre-forward and he said he would think about it. I rang him a few times, I kept at it and eventually he said he would come over.

"He ended up signing and in his first game he got a hat-trick. While he was here, he recommended Mick Walker to me so I rang him and he ended up signing. Another player I got was Paddy Byrne from Dublin.

"Johnny loves Sligo – it gave him a new lease of life. Myself and Johnny are still in contact. He lives in South Africa now but he does come over here the odd time, he does ring me every month and I do ring him, he does call me his older brother!"

Although Johnny did not settle down in Sligo, he was far from the first player to fall in love with the west of Ireland. "Players like Chris Rutherford, Gary Hulmes and Tony Stenson have never left Sligo and even now you look at Joseph Ndo and Anthony Elding, they are still around. I don't know what it is that keeps them here, but they obviously seem to like it here."

As a volunteer of many years, Paddy is full of praise for the efforts put in today – a far cry from some of the more curious tasks undertaken in times gone by just to ensure a game could go ahead.

"I remember one time we had a match on a Sunday and the weather was terrible, very frosty. Paddy Munn got us to put tyres on the pitch and that stopped it from freezing. There is a great crowd there now, much better than years ago when we were practically begging, that has all changed now for the better."

Fans young and old retain the height of respect for Paul Cook, who laid the foundations of the club's golden years.

Cook is highly thought of by Paddy who was mesmerised by his team's style of play.

"Cookie really brought a bit of spice to it, especially the cup games. The quality was fantastic but what he had was a good balance of both young players and older players, you want a general on the pitch and that is something that we miss now if the game in Limerick is anything to go by."

Despite being utterly disappointed by what happened in Limerick, Paddy still places his faith in Dave Robertson but believes there is an unwanted level of negativity among certain quarters of The Showgrounds, present even during the club's most successful period.

"It took eight matches last year before they won and you saw what happened then. You hear people saying 'get rid of him, get rid of him', and that is why I never go up to the stand during games, I don't like the hassle and negativity you constantly hear there. You always get someone who finds a flaw no matter how they are playing." In 76 years, Paddy has seen The Showgrounds undergo major face lifts which have greatly enhanced the stadium, a shining beacon the club can be proud just over a decade after being compared to a "farmer's field".

"I had old videos of games here and I was looking back on one of them and you wouldn't believe the cut of the pitch back then when you look at it now, players were up to their knees in muck but there is a different speed to football now, it is much faster and you wouldn't play like that on those pitches, but the facilities now are just fantastic."

In his final anecdote of a fascinating chat, Paddy returned once again to his close friend, who asked an innocent question which perhaps best highlighted the divide between English and Irish football in the 1960s.

Paddy collected Johnny Brookes at the train station upon his arrival in Sligo and immediately brought him for a look around the Showgrounds. He took him down around the pitch, to which Johnny remarked, "is this the training pitch?"

MELODY URQUHART

When Melody Urquhart visited Sligo in 1993, she discovered a magical place with a rich history. Soon she returned for good. Gerry McLaughlin learned about the park she set up – and how she shared her talent for dance

PUBLISHED ON JULY 23, 2020

THIS IS THE STORY OF A LANCASHIRE lass who had an *aisling gheal*, a bright vision – and the talent, tenacity, courage and character to make it come true.

Melody Urqhuart is certainly a woman you don't meet every day and while she is 72, she has the mien and energy of a much younger woman.

Melody has the feet of a dancer, the soul of a poet and the heart of a lioness as she sits in her lovely home in Kilmacowen under mighty Knocknarea and the Ox Mountains.

LEFT: SIXTEEN-YEAR-OLD MELODY AFTER BEING AWARDED THE ANNA PAVLOVA TROPHY FOR CLASSICAL BALLET

Melody has been living in Sligo since the mid-1990s, when she swapped a high-powered career as a hugely successful dancer, choreographer and manager of a number of famous dance troupes in London for the mystical balm of Knocknashee, the Hill of the Fairies.

There, in the heart of the home of the famous Tuatha De Danann, Melody created a magical monument to the dawn of time, to the warriors and wizards of this truly wonderful world.

Melody's vision lasted for almost 25 years and was called Gillighan's World, a very special place in Sligo that celebrated a storied past where giant figures like Lugh Lamh Fhada, The Daghda, Balor of the Evil Eye, the Morrigan and Breas the Beautiful once again rode the wind in Melody's very own Celtic Twilight.

It was a huge challenge for someone who had shone in both the artistic and corporate worlds. But there is loads of grit as well as natural grace in this true force of nature.

Melody, whose ancestors were a mighty fighting Scottish clan, whose castle was on the banks of Lough Ness, has danced for all the captains and the kings and for the British Royal family, and has performed in La Scala of Milan as well as the London Palladium, fuelled by graceful ability, ambition and searing determination.

She is both a dreamer and a doer and not only loves history with a deep and genuine passion but has actually lived it in the way she re-created the past in Gillighan's World.

Melody has a burning passion for Irish mythology and history. She is a constant philosopher and it is clear that Ireland, especially Sligo, has a special place in her soul.

She is a very spiritual person and has a deep connection with her adopted home and believes that the landscape can determine many different moods.

But in tandem with this Celtic odyssey, Melody has run a very successful Dance Academy in Sligo that caters for around 100 pupils, from age four to 18, in a lovely, warm wooden building at the back of a home brimming with a cornucopia of books, a fish pond and her own bonhomie.

Thousands of Sligo children have been under her tutelage over 20 years and she has choreographed a number of musicals.

In her native England she progressed from being a very driven, successful ballet dancer to choreography, to managing dance companies, to becoming an examiner of dance – and gained a PhD along the way.

But there isn't a snobbish bone in her body as she retains the distinctive Lancashire burr of her native Blackpool.

In Sligo she has found her true Land of Heart's Desire and the landscape and its people have a very special place in her big heart.

Melody Urquhart was born an only child in Blackpool in 1948.

She started ballet dancing at eight and "that has been my life really".

Melody came from a "working class family" and her mother and father were "in confectionery". They named a company after their precocious daughter. She ran a shop for her father at the age of 15.

Melody began with ballet and she had "wonderful teacher" called Hope Sherwood, who gave Melody the passion to be a great dancer

Melody said: "She knew how to challenge me and get it out of me. To her I owe my love of dance along with my mother. It was not just a case of being a great dancer, there is the feeling, the passion, the emotions that went with it and these have helped me through my life.I was dancing every day and my first big gig was dancing at the Royal Court Theatre in Liverpool at a pantomime, which was less than perfect in the early 1960s.

"They were great days. But when you were 16 to 18 in those days you were much younger than similar age groups today. It was a time when people were rebelling against past restrictions and they wanted freedom and they wanted new things so there was this culture thing going on.

"But it was a marvellous time for people who were creative and people who wanted to live an alternative style of life and there were so many opportunities and no safety net. That was the thing and that was the adventure and now when you get that type of person, there is a lot of red tape around it, planning it and overanalysing it.

"In those days if you wanted something, go out and get it, take the risk – and if it went wrong you just paid for your mistake."

Melody then went to London. Her mother died of a brain haemorrage on June 1, 1964, which was a big blow. Melody was only 16 and it was "like facing the world alone".

She said: "But my mother's teaching in my early life has been the pathway for my ethics and morals all my life and I was lucky to have had her. She taught me how to love nature, to respect people, how to love flowers and she was a huge part of my life."

While Melanie also has an amazing work ethic which has stood to her, artists also suffer from insecurity.

"People see you on stage and they see confidence, your art and you look so self- assured because you are passing it on to others, but there is great deal of insecurity there, too.

"Your work is like your costume – you are playing a part and that is you, playing different characters within your life span. But when you hear that applause it shows that people liked what you did.

"It is the most wonderful feeling of approval and you are wanting people to like you, understand you and accept you and that is the motivation.

"A lot of people might think you are arrogant because you have a strong work ethic, but it is not about that, you just want to be the best you can be and pass it on for future generations".

Meanwhile, Melanie has worked at La Scala in Milan, the London Palladium, the Victoria Hall and on television in ballet, all the performing arts, jazz, tap, Greek, lyrical and all forms.

So when did she get into management? She said: "It was in the 1970s when I became a licenced agent for 17 to 18 years for major companies, worldwide."

She recruited dancers, artists and it was like "head hunting, finding the right people for the right job".

"It took me into the corporate world, and it was tough as I was inexperienced and each new role was like starting at the bottom, having some success and some failures.

"You know you have to fail at some things, otherwise you will not really succeed, but it is how you deal with those mistakes that help build your character. It is how you get yourself out of the situation you have got yourself into. People always want to hear about what you succeeded in, but the success story is in surviving".

Melody had Melody Urquhart Management in the 1970s and she had some of the best dancers in England.

"These were people with real bite. They did not come from any pampered background in London – they came from the fighting hard working-class of people from the north of England. Working-class people have the hunger to succeed."

Meanwhile, Melody's growing business took her to Iran, Malta, Italy and Spain.

"I was learning to get in with agents and see how the business worked so that I could create and sell what I had, and it put me in with big companies like London Management and the London agents.

"I created groups of well-known dancers like Touch Of Class and Good Vibrations. I knew Pan's People and Hot Gossip, but they came after us. We had theatres and I also opened a complete performing arts school in the end. That was a government scheme. The best way to train someone was to get that young spirit and guide it in the right way. The school was for everybody, not just the rich or the privileged. It gave a chance to any young person we felt had that talent and, most of all, the hunger to succeed.

"This was bringing dance to those who would not normally be able to do it. It was a tough school, but it taught them the skills of life. It taught them how to survive and live in the world, how to deal with agents and how to handle currencies, laws, rules and commissions. There were dancers, singers, actors and comedians and a complete variety school."

By the 1980s she had three companies, Melody Urquhart Management, Melody Entertainment Leisure Services and The Melody Urquhart Master School.

She said: "We were called investors in people as hundreds and hundreds went through the doors of the companies and all of them were successful".

And then, at the height of her fame, the voice of Ireland and more specifically Sligo came calling. Melody became the 'baroness of Leyny' – Leyny covers large tracts of County Sligo.

She said: "In 1993 I had heard about a history of the barony of Leyny. I wanted to be a historian and was interested in the source of religions and beliefs and how we have gone from there to here.

"I am a very spiritual person and mythology to me is very motivating and emotional. The barony runs to Beltra and right to Charlestown and I bought the title, something that has been done for centuries.

"A very wise lord once said to me: 'Titles of themselves mean nothing, it is what you do with them and what you contribute is what matters. It is a responsibility and it is a work'."

Melody came to Ireland in 1993 and "from the moment I arrived here I fell in love with it". She came to Sligo and stayed in a little B&B on the N17 and she had her little girl with her, Chantelle, who was then 11.

"It had got very exhausting, running three companies, and I was also an internal and external verifier for colleges and the government. I remember sitting in the Venue in Strandhill, and there were so many friendly people there and they were showing Chantelle the Irish punt at the time.

"It reminded me of my childhood, where the doors were open, and you could go into each other's houses. You felt part of a community and I ended up in Killoran's in Tubbercurry, which is an absolutely wonderful place. It was magical and there was music and there was a grandad dancing with the little girl and a son playing on the bodhrán. It was so different to London.

"I started to read about Sligo in Wood-Martin and O'Rourke and was up at night reading and I found out about Knocknashee – and Gillighan's World was later established.

"The stories, legends and folklore got into my soul, like a ballet. Here were amazing stories and after five days I went back to England, but I found I could not work as my mind was constantly on Sligo. The richness of the history here fascinated me, and it was as if I had been given a chance later in life to do what I wanted to do and I took it on as the biggest hobby going. And then by 1995 I decided I was going to come here and build the park. I was going to live this story and I was going to live my life totally and I was never going back."

Little by little it came together with a park of many unique features, a man-made pool with water flowing down from the hill above and a cottage restored to its former glory. The ring fort on top of Knocknashee, which was partially ruined, was rebuilt.

A discovery trail was built, including special flora and fauna, and in keeping with its imagination, miniature villages and fairy abodes were placed in a wonderful botanical garden and Melody did much of the hard graft herself.

"The Gillighans originally owned the property going back to the 1930s and Dominic Gillighan moved back into Sligo and they had a pub here, I believe. The first day the park opened was amazing and it was really like 'The Field Of Dreams' – and I wondered, would the people come?

"It was around four and a half acres and we turned a field into fairy gardens. We used every single stone in the place to build the walls, create the features, the art, the archway, the tunnel going in. We restored the fairy ring and we breathed some life into it and made it into a painting really and a ballet in motion.

"And the people started to come, and 20 odd years later they were still coming. It was a spiritual place and it became different to what I first planned, and I realised this was not a money-making venture.

"I met some wonderful people like Séamus Conway and Peter Kivlehan and they told me the stories of the area. It was fascinating. I loved the whole Celtic mythology, and those men told me to pass the stories on when they were gone. It was Séamus who allowed me to buy the land and he trusted me and he was just like my grandad and I absolutely loved that old gentleman. He was so bright and so intelligent, and his son is still my friend and a very sincere person."

Melody was very much hands-on and did not want to destroy the place's original character. She said: "Magic was already there in the moss and twisted trees, and I didn't want this place to be phoney. So I worked with the land and let the land tell me.

"We were open seven days a week from May Day to September. It would always take four or five weeks re-doing the ground after the winter. It could get cold and windy and wet up there. I had to re-build the garden. It was never meant to be just a children's park. Children love fairies – it is an escape and a fantasy, and their imagination can run riot. And while it was hugely popular with the children, it was also geared towards adults.

"I was shocked that so many people did not know the history or did not know about their monuments. In the past Ireland was one of the most learned places in the world, the island of saints and scholars. Everybody knows about the Egyptians, the Greeks and the Romans and their great empires. Very few people knew that at one time, Ireland matched these places in terms of culture and learning. The Greeks and Egyptians came here to learn, and I created a little amphitheatre with stones in a semi-circle and I would tell the visitors stories and I would also have speakers on history in various groups.

"It was a means of passing on a rich heritage and telling people to cherish their history and heritage for future generations. Nobody knows about tomorrow, but these stories should be passed on – they are in your blood and they are of your people."

Melody is very conscious that she had come to a special place when she arrived in Sligo in the mid-1990s.

She said: "It does not matter where you came from, but when you arrive in a place you can feel it, respect it, love it and take an interest in it. It is what you see in your heart and that is what you want to spend your time doing in that place.

"This was totally a labour of love. I had to close it last year as I am getting older and the clearing of the land became physically impossible. At its peak we had thousands of visitors and we did three Christmases there and they came from all over the world to see it. It was emotional – we had music in the mountains as well as Santa, and it was all about embracing each other. It was purely magical and very moving.

"Three years ago, they had an archaeological dig and I was telling the story of the people of that hill and my proudest moment was when Knocknashee made the front page of Archaeology Ireland.

"There is now a walkway to the top of Knocknashee and I am a bit sad that for 20 years I waited for that day but I could not do that. My hope is that I can get someone to take the park and continue what we started.

"I would sell or lease but only to someone who would keep its essence and not spoil it but carry it on. I do feel like its guardian and I have a responsibility to the land and to the people who supported me and trusted me. My son Dane was often in the park and he has loads of stories from when he was a very young, but he went back to England in 2018."

Gillighan's World is currently closed but Melody hopes someone will carry on the flame she lit so brightly.

Meanwhile, Melody bought her current lovely home in Kilamcowen in the mid-1990s.

She said: "I did not think I would be living here permanently, but I made a choice and I chose here.Both of my children, Chantelle, 11, and Dane, seven, came over with me and that was a big part of my decision."

In tandem with Gillighan's World, Melody has been running a very successful dancing school since coming to Sligo.

She said: "When I came here dancing was my whole life, but I said to myself, I am never going to dance again as I am just going to build my park. I was going to be the new Melody and I was living in a place where my children would grow up in a place that was so much about community.

"We were all in each other's houses, in other's gardens, there was music and singing and it reminded me of my childhood. This is a wonderful area and it was buzzing. My neighbour Rita down the road had a little girl and her little girl wanted to dance and so did a couple of the others and they got to know that I taught dance. They said why don't you teach ours to dance? She said, Melody, if you are going to live here among us, then you have got to play your part. And if you have got a skill and you can dance and teach the children in the community and that is what you should be doing.

"I thought, she is right, so I started off with six or seven little girls from the village. I said I would give them six weeks during the summer to see if they liked it.

"What they learned through the dance is to fight, independence, pride in themselves, and coping with exams – it helps them in school and in life. It gives them confidence, and someone has believed in them.

"It will not be easy, but that encouragement, correction and guidance makes them into really successful people when they grow up.

"We used to hire The Sally Gardens in Ballisodare, Coolera House, anywhere that would take us, and 20 odd years later I still have around 100 children per week."

She tells the story of a spirited little girl called Nicola Gallagher who got to achieve her dream with the help of Melody and the *Sligo Weekender*.

"She was with me from a very young age and she had the hunger, but of course nobody had planned that she would take up dancing as a profession. So, we organised it with the *Sligo Weekender* and Noel Kennedy the photographer. I said, this girl can go to college, the same one my daughter went to in Leicester, but we have no money.

"So, we set up a 'Chance To Dance Scheme' and we raised money everywhere. The *Sligo Weekender* held the bank account and we went out and sold tickets and we got enough money to get Nicola to a performing arts school in England for three years. She graduated and now she has a life in Mexico, has a beautiful baby boy, speaks fluent Spanish, has set up a huge dance agency in all the Mexican hotels and she is a great girl.

"I had the most fantastic children and fantastic mothers, they were pioneers, they were spirited, and we went up to the North and they walked away with nine trophies for a variety of dances.

"The Irish people like to expose their children to a variety of things like football, hurling, swimming, horse riding and music. They only like to go from September to May – not during the summer.

"I had to change my ways to make it fit and we do as much in eight or nine months as any other school that is open 52 weeks a year. I do it all on my own and my friend Maisie does the music for me. All these children are being trained to a worldwide standard. Those exams are stepping stones for a child and when they go out and do this, they know they are great.

"We closed the dancing from the end of May to September, which allowed me to work on the park in the summer months. I have put hundreds of dancers through my hands here and I have been operating from here for the past 14 years."

Melody is an adjudicator for many types of dancing but has great respect for Irish dancing and she knows 32 different international dances.

Sligo continues to be very special to Melody. She said: "Sligo is one of the most spiritual places in the world. I pick up vibes when I go to different places all over the world. I can sit here and I can feel it and some people don't stop long enough in life to take it all in.

"Lough Talt is very atmospheric and that is what I love about here as around every corner there are different places. Lough Gill, Glencar, Benbulben, Knocknashee, Muckelty, Knocknarea and the Ox Mountains are all completely different and Dooney Rock and Hungry Rock all have their own character, but there is a thread that you can feel running through them all. It is an energy and it inspires me totally.

"I feel a peace and a calm here and I feel this spirit, this fighting spirit, and I found myself here. There is a beautiful peace about Sligo as if I have come to where I needed to be to find who I was, and I am genuinely happy. I had to give up a lot of things that meant a lot to me, but at 72, I can say that I am so grateful that I made the choices I made at that time. And I am grateful to Ireland for giving me a home and a place to do what I do, and I have been a very lucky guest here for 25 years."

Ireland and Sligo are certainly richer for meeting the mesmerising Melody.

MELODY URQUHART

CON LEE

Gerry McLaughlin spoke to Con Lee about his extraordinary life in the Garda Síochána – and how he gets on his bike to help cancer sufferers

PUBLISHED ON APRIL 2, 2020

THE SCOURGE OF DRUGS HIT IRISH towns like a tsunami from the 1990s on.

It killed, maimed and scarred so many of our young people, tore many families asunder, and made fortunes for strutting gang lords who revelled in the power of life and death they had in communities.

So many promising lives have been lost, and even a relatively small town like Sligo has not escaped.

But we had one police officer who took the fight to the drug godfathers in the North West on the streets of Sligo, a man who showed vision, courage and character and put his own safety on the line so that the rest of society could be protected.

This was dangerous work, but from around 1997 to 2007, Sergeant Connell

LEFT: CON LEE

Lee was at the coalface in the fight against the dealers in death in the North West, and that continued when he was assigned to murder investigations as a detective sergeant until his retirement from the force in 2015.

In between, he had been at the heart of drug busts, robberies and over half a dozen high-profile murder cases.

There is hardly any other officer with the same level of experience of serious crime in the town the Donegal native has grown to love so well.

Con and his team have hidden in a graveyard, raided sacred places and carried out hundreds of searches in their battle against the ruthless drug gangs. And Con knows personally of so many families that the drugs scourge has affected through his long years of service, and many still speak of his kindness, understanding and humanity. Even those he pursued had a respect for an officer who was also a gentleman.

Con and his teams had some major successes. They seized as much as €4m of drugs – including a €1.6m heroin haul in Carrick-On-Shannon in 2008 and a £500,000 haul of cannabis and amphetamines in Tubbercurry in 1999. The latter was the largest find in the North West to that date.

In that period Con and his colleagues dealt with armed and dangerous gangs, and on one occasion he was lured to a potential death trap at a quiet location outside of Sligo.

He got a call to go to a location from a caller who said he had some valuable information – luckily, Con had the foresight to have a back-up car in the vicinity. He said: "Shortly after I got there, four men pulled up in a car and were about the get out when they saw the back-up and took off at speed." It later emerged that at least one of the occupants of the four-man car was armed.

On another occasion the windows in Con's car were smashed, and he recalls picking glass out of a child seat in the back of the car.

These were testing times for Con and his much-loved late wife Fiona – and one of his children once asked him why some people were writing things on the walls about their dad.

On the plus side, this was a sign that the forces of law and order and Con's drugs squads were making an impression. He was issued with a personal firearm at that time, which he carried 24/7.

Con was deeply involved in the investigations into the infamous four murders in Sligo from 2005 to 2008: Hughie McGinley, Sam Smith, Tom Ward Jr and David Lynch.

He was also involved in the investigations into the murders of tragic teenager Melissa Mahon and Sligo pensioner Eddie Gillespie.

It is a source of great regret to Con and his hard-working colleagues that nobody has yet been brought to justice for the murders of Hughie McGinley, Sam Smith, Tom Ward Jr and David Lynch.

Con knew all of their families and his heart went out to them all.

But close to home, he has had to deal with the personal tragedy of losing his lovely wife Fiona to cancer in 2016. They had grown up just a few doors apart in Cluan Barron in Ballyshannon.

Fiona's death was a terrible blow to a father with a young family, but he has coped courageously and has made a huge contribution to Sligo Cancer Support Centre through his many cycles with the Innisfree Wheelers, which has been a big part of his very active life for many years.

That life began in Glenties in Co. Donegal, where he was born in 1961, one of 11 children to the John and Roisin Lee, who is still hale and hearty. The family moved to Ballyshannon in 1963.

Con's late father John was a garda and Con joined the force in 1982, the year after his Galway native father John retired. John had joined in 1946.

Two other brothers Patrick (who was in boarding school with this writer) and John also joined, and John is still a serving member.

Con's first posting was to Blacklion in the early 1980s, an exciting and dangerous time. It was also a sad time – an RUC officer with whom Con had been in contact just a week previously, Alan Corbett, was shot dead by the IRA.

Con went back to Blacklion as a sergeant in 1992.

But there were happy times too and Con was accompanied on his first stint in Blacklion by the now Inspector Denis Joyce and the current

Ballyshannon Superintendent Colm Nevin. Both were later colleagues of Con's in Sligo.

These days, Con is living in Ransboro with his sons Dara and Fergus. He also has another son, Oisín, and a daughter, Blathnaid.

Recalling his youth, Con remembers walking home from dances at Horslips and The Memories in Bundoran in the early hours of the morning and meeting his father John at a checkpoint on the roundabout in Ballyshannon in the late 1970s.

Con passed out in Templemore in December 1982 and he was posted to Blacklion on the Cavan-Fermanagh border.

He said: "I remember there were train strikes and bus strikes and I remember us getting taxis. We arrived in Blacklion at 1am in the morning and the first man I met on the checkpoint was fellow Ballyshannon man Walter Doyle. We had a great oul chat."

He was there for three years until 1985 and it was a hectic time.

He said: "Back then in Blacklion there were 29 officers and we had the army with us as well, as there was a permanent checkpoint. They were exciting times and there were six pubs in the village and you also had the Customs and the prison officers. It all meant there was a lot of activity in the village."

Con and Tom Doherty were transferred to Sligo on the beat in 1985 in Unit A. He said: "The first Neighbourhood Watch scheme was set up in 1988 and I was appointed community garda in Cranmore. Those were very happy days and I still have friends from there from that period.

"Chris McDonagh, whose wife was sadly killed in an accident, asked me to be best man when he remarried. He was involved in community work. There were 500 houses in Cranmore then, it was just a young estate and it had a population of 2,000. They were wonderful people and it was and is a small minority that tarnishes places all over the country. The vast majority of people that I dealt with were honest and decent people and you would not get better."

Con was delighted to be promoted sergeant to Blacklion from 1992 to the mid-1990s, and he enjoyed his time there. Belcoo and Blacklion were like one village and he was due to work there at 6pm when the IRA Ceasefire was announced in 1994 and the checkpoint was taken down. I remember going out that night in Blacklion and the whole community was celebrating their freedom. That was a great night."

Con was back in Sligo around 1995 as unit sergeant. This was the 1990s and drugs were becoming rampant at parties and raves, with ecstasy being particularly prominent.

"I always had an interest in the drugs situation. I was asked to set up a dedicated unit, which I did in 1997-98. Back then, it was Pauline McDonagh, Séamus Kearins, Willie O'Neill and Charlie Jordan. We worked very hard and I would like to think that we did some good work too."

This was the first dedicated drugs unit in Sligo.

Con said: "We did have some successes and we made the national headlines on a number of occasions. And we were recognised as one of

FERGUS, CON, OISÍN AND DARRAGH LEE AT THE CAROL SINGING AT SLIGO COURTHOUSE IN DECEMBER 2016

the best units in the country and I would like to thank, Pauline, Seamus, Willie and Charlie – who is still serving – for all their hard work".

"We had a huge seizure in Carrick-on-Shannon in 2008 when we seized €1.5m of heroin – and there was an element of luck involved. We got information that the drugs were being moved from Sligo to Dublin and we set up an operation in Carrock-on-Shannon and we waited all day, and nothing was happening. Sometimes you get the hop of the ball and I remember getting the call from Detective Inspector John O'Reilly that this was just not happening and to stand down.

"And two of the lads that were working on the operation with me went into Supermacs in Carrick-on-Shannon for something to eat. And while they were there, didn't the car that we were looking for come up to the drive-through and a person of interest came in looking for food too and we hit the jackpot. If he had kept driving on that night, we would have missed him. The lads had a photograph of him and they checked the Black Mercedes and found the drugs".

Back in 1999 Con's unit seized £500,000 of ecstasy tablets and amphetamines in Tubbercurry.

He said: "That was our first major seizure and we had good intelligence on this one and then six months later another £500,000 of drugs was got at Holyhead and a local criminal apprehended. That was to replace the one seized in Tubbercurry and it was a major success.

"Ecstasy was the whole scene then and we used quite a few 'clean street' operations where we brought teams down from Dublin to go around pubs and clubs in Sligo doing test purchasing, undercover work."

"Looking back, it was 24/7 and we were getting calls at all hours of the day and night. You could get a call at 1am or 2am and you were off. I remember we found a drugs cache in a remote area outside of Riverstown. We staked it out for 11 nights and there were ecstasy tablets to the value of £40,000 found. Another time we found a hideout at the holy well just outside of Carraroe and we watched it for four nights.

"We also found a hideout in Kilmacowen Graveyard in March 2006. We had information that it was being used and myself and Michael McGrath, who was with me on the unit at the time, and we had no more concrete information. We went out on spec and within half an hour I found the hideout. So that night we set up an operation and six to eight officers staked out the place. Within an hour, two men got out and went straight to the hide and I called 'Go, go, go!' There was €20,000 of cannabis resin found in that hide and the two men were convicted."

One drugs gang in the North West were the main players and 70 to 80 per cent of Con's team's efforts were taken up with curbing their extensive activities. The gang had considerable ties with drugs gangs elsewhere.

The Criminal Assets Bureau seized quite an amount of items related to the gang and one key figure was caught with drugs and sent to prison.

In the early 2000s, there were four major gangs operating in Sligo. Con reckons that the drugs squad seized up to €4m from the gangs.

But those seizures represent only a percentage of the drugs that get through, "something which is the same all over the world".

He said: "But it is all about supply and demand and if the demand is there you will get dealer and that is a sad fact of human nature. I have seen both sides and I remember some families coming under terrible pressure from the gangs and some young lads carried out robberies to pay off drug debts. Families were terrorised into paying off the drug debts of their children. It is not just the addict. Sections of entire communities have been held to ransom."

And Con was even targeted himself, which was a testament to the inroads he and his team were making on the drugs gangs.

"I remember on one occasion there were eight or nine of us on a drugs raid and I parked my own car away from where we were searching. When I came back, the front and back windscreens of my car had been put in. I remember coming home that night and my wife Fiona was very upset. There was a baby seat in the back covered in glass.

"They were also writing about me on the walls in Sligo, about what I was doing, and I remember my daughter Blathnaid, who was only nine or ten at the time, coming home and asking why they were writing about me.

"I remember another occasion shortly after I started in the drug unit. I was working plainclothes and there was a shooting in Sligo, and I got a call from someone who said they had information about the shooting. The caller asked me to meet them at the holy well at 10pm at night and the caller asked me to come in my own private car. I went out, but I had some members of the drugs squad in another car as back up. When I arrived four men in a car pulled in beside me, but when they saw the drugs car behind them, they sped off. They were later stopped in the town and one of them was carrying a nine- inch knife.

After that Con was sent on a firearms course and he was issued with a gun for personal protection.

Con is retired from the gardaí since 2015. But in a recent letter to the Sunday Independent he voiced his experienced thoughts on the escalation of the drug problem.

In the letter he said: "I have seen the scourge drugs have in families and societies, but what is happening now has brought it to a new level. Communities across the country are living in fear of drug gangs. The government should bring in legislation where on the evidence of a chief superintendent, drug gang members can be convicted. This legislation was used before to convict persons regarding IRA membership.

"Also, every Garda division should have a mini CAB unit targeting middle-range dealers in gangs and seizing their assets. Divisional drug units are operating with three or four members, which is not nearly enough.

"One garda told me recently that they could be working 24/7 as the drug scourge has got so out of hand. Gardaí need to be given proper manpower and resources. As we have seen recently, when they are, they get results.

"Yes, it will cost millions, but better that than spending it later on drug-related crime and on the mental health of young people as a result of their addiction. It also takes a terrible toll on other family members who have nothing to do with drugs."

It is a source of deep regret to Con and his colleagues that there have been no convictions for the brutal murders of Hughie McGinley, Sam

Smith, Tom Ward Jr and David Lynch in that frantic period from May 2005 to January 2008.

Con said: "The murder of Hughie McGinley stood out as it was in the middle of the afternoon in the town centre with loads of people around, and nobody deserves that.

"I was off that day and I got a call to come in and James Kearins was the Inspector at the time and he put in a huge amount of work into those cases. But it is one thing to know who is involved and who pulled the trigger – you must find evidence that will stand up in court.

"Sam Smith, Tom Ward Jr and David Lynch were all horrific murders. It was a scary time. You would be stopping cars late at night and stopping individuals that you knew had access to firearms. It was always in the back of your head – would they use those weapons?

"There was a lot of work put into all of those investigations. There were people who knew what had happened but were afraid to come forward and make statements, and that is understandable.

"Sligo is only just a big town, and everybody knows everybody else and there is fear.

"There was a certain amount of forensic evidence in those murders and we did send files to the DPP recommending prosecutions, but they decide based on the chances of a successful prosecution in court. Of course, we have to face the families, and it does affect you as a policeman that these families are not getting the justice they are entitled to.

"And they did not get that justice and I remember in particular the sadness of Tilda McGinley and Mary Smith at the death of their sons and it was the same for the Ward family and the Lynch family."

Con and his colleagues were deeply traumatised by the horrific murder of Melissa Mahon and happy that they managed to get a conviction after a shocking murder that resulted in a high-profile trial in the Central Criminal Court in 2009.

He said: "That was truly horrific and affected a lot of people and I was deeply involved in that investigation. And but for some vital information that we got early on that would still be a missing person case."

And then Con arrested the killer of 67-year-old Eugene Gillespie in 2012, a killing of a highly respected gentle man that shocked Sligo to its roots. The popular pensioner had been beaten and tied up in his house for a day before he was found.

Con said: "The killer was in the station on another matter around that time, and he was very agitated. He asked for a particular garda to talk to and when that happened, he made a full admission. The killer had drugs issues and all he got in the house was €40."

But it was not all doom and gloom for Con as he still has happy memories of his time as a young garda in Cranmore with the youth of that area.

"I really enjoyed being on the beat and helping to make changes in people's lives for the better and that is why gardaí have to get in among the community to know what is going on, to prevent situations developing and making people feel safe.

"You are doing a job but at the end of the day you are a human being with all that entails and I believe that we have one of the finest police forces in the world, and we still police by consent rather than by coercion."

The force has endured the Morris Tribunal and the Maurice McCabe affair but the vast majority of gardaí are of the highest integrity, Con said.

"Those four unsolved murders put us under pressure too, but it was not for lack of effort that we did not get convictions and they happened in a relatively short period of time."

Con took early retirement at the age of 54 in 2015 and is now 59.

"Sometimes you just get burned out and I was detective sergeant and I was stuck in the office and I would have preferred to be out and about meeting people on the street. I was in court a lot too and there were loads of cases to be dealt with over the years."

But the super fit Con has never been idle since he joined the Innisfree Wheelers Cycling Club in 2006.

"I always liked cycling and back in the 1980s I did seven or eight of those Mara Cycles from Dublin to Belfast. It is a big part of my life now and we have done a lot of fundraising and, in our existence, we have raised over €250,000 for various charities."

Con is also very involved with the Sligo Cancer Support Centre, which was a big help to his family during his wife Fiona's illness.

He said: "Some of our cyclists did a Dublin to Bantry cycle, a 400km cycle over two days, and we did a Wild Atlantic Challenge cycle which was a 540km cycle over three days, and we raised €25,000 from those two events.

"When I retired in 2015, I was asked to come on the board of directors of the Sligo Cancer Support Centre and I have been on it since. Fiona was 39 in 2002 when she was first diagnosed with cancer. She was teaching in Ransboro NS and retired on health grounds. The cancer came back a second time and she passed away on August 5, 2016."

Her passing has left a huge void in her family.

"When Fiona passed away the four of our children were living at home and some of the children were doing important State exams. It was a difficult time. But I was delighted that I had that 15 or 16 months with her after I retired. "She was always very encouraging to me in my work. We grew up just six doors apart in Cluan Barron, Ballyshannon.

"There were 11 of us, eight boys and three girls, but I did not meet up with Fiona again until I was in Blacklion and I was staying at home, and we got married in 1988. Her mother and my mother were very friendly, as were our families. We lived in Cairns Road in Sligo first and then moved out to Ransboro.

"My mother Roisin is still alive and is in the Sheil Hospital in Ballyshannon – where they have stopped all contact. But, do you know what I did – and I have not done it for over 30 years. I sat down last weekend and I wrote her a letter just to tell her exactly how much I loved her and I sent her some old photographs.

"My mother is a very creative spirit with her songs and recitations, and she won the Allingham Cup about five or six years ago, as did my sister Roisin last year."

Cancer has had a huge impact on Con and his family. Is he concerned that the coronavirus will have a devastating effect on the many cancer sufferers?

He said: "I know that our centre now is closed at the moment, but we are still providing online support and video calls. I know from talking to our manager Brigid Kerrigan that we have more than 1,700 people on our books between the centre in Sligo and in Tubbercurry. At times like this people are very afraid and they are in the middle of treatment and are very vulnerable.

"It is the whole uncertainty and there is a lot of fear and everyone thinks of their own mortality. I suppose and I believe we are getting great advice from the HSE and the top medical people and the government, and I think they have done a great job this past few weeks."

But he said he does not believe that cancer patients will lose out on vital treatment.

All of Con's active work is a fitting memory of his own Fiona.

Sligo has been a very big part of Con's life since he moved to live here in 1985.

He said: "It is a wonderful town, great people and stunning scenery and I have enjoyed my life here. I am still enjoying the cycling and the racquetball in St Mary's – well, up until recently anyway.

"Faith does play a big part in my life too and I go to Fiona's grave every week and I light a candle there for different people. The family are a great comfort to me. We had a few difficult years as they were all very close to Fiona and we all still miss her.

"I lead a very healthy life and last Sunday I did 100km and on Thursday I did 90km. But I will be stuck in the house now with this lockdown."

What does Con think of the lockdown?

"I think it is the right call and hopefully we will get the benefit of this lockdown in a few weeks' time and deep down I believe we will come out of it. We are brave nation and a great people, and we have always stuck together in times of crisis and we are world leaders and we will continue to be world leaders in so many different aspects of our lives."

Stirring words from one who knows – and there are few braver or better than our own Con Lee.

Sligo County Council
Comhairle Chontae Shligigh

Sligo.

Supporting Communities
Promoting Enterprise
Delivering for Sligo

071 9111111   info@sligococo.ie

071 9141119   www.sligococo.ie

Fire Services: 999 or 112
Housing: 071 9111324
Roads: 086 8569416
Irish Water: 1850 278278

f sligocountycouncil   🐦 sligococo   ⭕ sligocountycouncil

RAY MacSHARRY

For Sligo, he's the greatest taoiseach Ireland never had. The extraordinary businessman and politican told Gerry McLaughlin about his remarkable life – and his views on the Covid-19 crisis

PUBLISHED ON APRIL 9, 2020

THIS IS THE STORY OF SLIGO'S OWN "real taoiseach". And many of his supporters say that Ray MacSharry, proud native of St Patrick's Terrace, Sligo, was the greatest taoiseach this country never had.

There is no doubt that this tall, dark, dealing man with the charisma of his mother's people, the Clarkes from the green fields around Dromard, had all the attributes to be the country's first citizen.

His father sold insurance and the Clarkes were noted cattle dealers – so MacSharry DNA for a career in politics, the profession the Greek philosopher Aristotle described as "the art of the possible", is impeccable.

Ray MacSharry always had ability, acumen, ambition, razor sharp, succinct

LEFT: RAY MacSHARRY

intellect and natural eloquence – a man who was and is an alpha male, a leader of leaders and a man well used to being in charge.

But he is also a man with the emotional intelligence to know when "to hold 'em and know when to fold 'em", a very grounded man who had the ability to survive and ultimately thrive in the jungle of Irish and European politics.

And that was because he never forgot where he was from, never forgot his own or those who elected him, and delivered in spades in many projects in his native Sligo and for the country.

But he will always be a hero to the small farmers of Sligo and the rest of the country for his achievements for them when he went to Europe, first as Minister for Agriculture, then as an MEP and then as European Commissioner.

MacSharry always loved a good scrap and successfully took on the British Government, who wanted a cheap food policy. He made sure the Irish farmers got a good deal for their produce in the bearpit of Europe.

Agriculture was an ideal fit for MacSharry. Unlike some of his more academic colleagues he knew the difference between a bull and a cow, he knew how farms and farmers worked. It was in his blood and he had and has a passion for the land and for getting the best possible deal for those he represented.

He was also a very capable manager of marts and ran his own haulage company. And he has a genuine gratitude for the people of Sligo who kept electing him from the mid-1960s to the late 1980s.

But it is one thing to know the price of a bullock or a heifer. It is quite another to know how to get things done, to deal with different types of people, different egos and various bureaucracies.

But there are few greater psychologists than the breed of the dealer, for Ray MacSharry drove a hard bargain for his county and his country and always knew when to reach a consensus. The supreme pragmatist had been practicing this most valuable of arts since he was a teenager.

Add in a ferocious work ethic and can-do approach and you see how this Sligo champion went so far.

And that is why he also made a very effective Minister for Finance when he earned the famous title "Mac The Knife" when he took over in 1987 and the national debt was £24bn.

But it was not all about cuts, as he explained in a long and entertaining interview with this reporter.

Probably his greatest achievement was stabilising the finances of the country at a time of high emigration and mass unemployment. That stability helped to create the conditions for the Celtic Tiger when, as he calmly says "people went mad". But he did help lay the foundations.

His profession is littered with the corpses of hopefuls who died on the swords of their own or their opponents' ambition. But this never happened MacSharry. He was too brave, too bright, too single-minded when necessary, and he did not know the meaning of defeat.

He is one of the very few politicians to leave on his own terms in the early 1990s to pursue his true metier in world of business, where he has also been pretty successful.

Ray, who came from a non-political family, was first elected to Sligo Borough and County Council in 1967 and was elected a TD in 1969. He was re-elected in 1973, but Fianna Fáil were put out of office by Fine Gael and Labour and he was appointed opposition spokesman on the Office of Public Works.

In 1978 he was appointed Junior Minister of State at the Department of the Public Service after spending a lengthy period on the back benches.

His star rose dramatically in 1979 when Jack Lynch resigned and MacSharry proposed Charles Haughey as Taoiseach. He became Minister for Agriculture and started delivering for Irish farmers in Europe.

In 1982 he was made Minister for Finance and Tánaiste in a year of three General Elections, a year when he had to make some unpopular decisions. Fianna Fáil lost out and another period on the back benches ensued.

But MacSharry showed his resilience by bouncing back and getting elected an MEP in Bundoran in 1984, the night Neil Blaney lost his European seat.

Ray said: "I tried to get him to come back into the Fianna Fáil party, but it did not happen."

Ray was back again as Minister of Finance in 1987 and it was then he made all those famous but necessary cuts.

He resigned as an MEP, but was back in Europe again in late 1988, this time as a very successful European Commissioner. He re-negotiated the Common Agricultural Policy to a major degree in 1992.

Ray left politics, unusually well ahead on points, and got involved in various ventures. He has been on the boards of Bank of Ireland and Ryanair and was chairman of Eircom for a period, as well as a non-executive director of Irish Life and Permanent.

And although he is 82 this year, he remains an eloquent, fit and feisty character.

Ray was born in the front room of 30 St Patrick's Terrace in Sligo in 1938. He went to Scoil Ursula and then to St John's. His mother Annie Clarke was a teacher in a school in west Sligo near Dromard, where the Clarke family came from.

Ray said: "She always brought two out of the ten of us with her, five boys and five girls, so myself and Pauric were brought out with her in her Baby Ford car. I was there for two years, came back to St John's school, finished there and then went on to Summerhill College."

Ray remembers the Second World War and the ration books which were necessary for shopping.

"We used to go down to Bellew's at the time and we had ration books for everyone in the house and we were carrying the messages back and then going through the Market Yard we wondered where all the ration books had gone to. We remembered that we had put all the ration books inside Pauric's shirts so they would not get lost, so the panic was over.

"Ration books were like gold dust at the time. My mother had a Baby Ford car as she was teaching 15 miles west of Sligo and she had coupons because she was a teacher for three or four years of the war.

"But for the last year she did not go, so the car was pushed up to the back garden and lay there until the end of the war. I remember the number plate was EI 3322. We pushed it down St Patrick's Terrace, down Adelaide Street, over Wine Street, and there we changed it for another Baby Ford, IZ 3534".

Ray's father, Patrick MacSharry, was born in Killavogie in Co. Leitrim and came to Sligo town when he was 12. He worked in insurance. Patrick's father was a shoemaker and there was not enough business to keep going out in Leitrim, so he started as a cobbler in Sligo.

Ray said: "The Mercy College was there, the laundry and the orphanage were all there in Sligo at that time, and one of the first orders my grandfather got was to make shoes for all who were in those places. My grandfather also made shoes for the family. When my father Patrick was 16 or 17 he started selling insurance and he used to cycle out to Killavogie and Dromahair collecting insurance from all his friends and relations out there."

RAY MacSHARRY, EDEL MacSHARRY, MARIAN MOORE AND TD MARC MacSHARRY AT THE 'THIS IS YOUR LIFE' EVENT FOR RAY IN SEPTEMBER 2019 IN THE SLIGO SOUTHERN HOTEL

Ray's early connection with his mother's farming people out in west Sligo went back to a great early interest in animals.

He said: "I used to keep hens at the back of the yard and sell the eggs to my mother for the house. I used to sell the roosters for slaughter to Flynn's in O'Connell Street. I used to raise 50 chickens every year and I spent most of my holiday time out in Lismacbryan with my grandfather and my uncles. I took an interest in farming and agricultural activity and while I was still in Summerhill College I had something like 50 sheep out on land in Calry. I was also renting land."

Ray left Summerhill after his Inter Cert because he "wanted to go out and work".

These were the crazy days of De Valera's compulsory Irish, when you could fail the entire exam if you did not pass Irish.

He said: "The first job I had was weeding trees in the forestry out in Hazelwood, myself and Dominic Smith, when I was only 13 or 14 years. Before I left Summerhill, I worked briefly for the ESB in the rural electrification in the Drumshanbo area. My job was putting the meters into the houses. When I finished school, I went working for my uncle Matt Clarke and Benny Cosgrove, who were partners in the buying of cattle and sheep. They were exporting to Scotland and northern England and I stayed with them right up to the time I was elected to the Dáil in 1969".

These were exciting times for a young man as the mid to late 1950s were the peak times of the famous fairs, and Ray and his uncle travelled all over the country.

He said: "I was never in bed after 6am and we used to leave earlier for early fairs in Balla, Mayo and Roscommon town. We used to leave Sligo at 2.30am in the morning and they were all held on main streets and they were nearly over when people got up for their breakfast."

And then in the 1960s, before he was first elected to Sligo Borough and County Council, Ray got involved in the newly formed marts and managed marts in Ballina, Claremorris and Tulsk.

"There were cattle markets every fortnight and we helped out in Ballymote as well when it was starting up. These marts were initially boycotted by many of the dealers and it took some time to get them established, and thankfully most of them are still there."

There was no tradition of politics in Ray's family, which makes his achievements as the classic self-made man all the more remarkable.

Ray was in the Junior Chamber of Commerce in Sligo and they did quite an amount of charitable work for orphans,

He said: "We visited old people in nursing homes and gave them presents at different times of the year. And we found that there was a lot of red tape, so the Junior Chambers of Ireland decided to put forward candidates for the local elections. We had three candidates from the Sligo Junior Chamber – Terry Beirne and Johnny Ryan. Lord rest both of them, and me. They pulled out and I got elected to the Corporation and the County Council in 1967. We were delighted, the Junior Chamber was delighted, and Fianna Fáil was delighted as I had their nomination.

"Housing was a huge issue in Sligo at that time as there had been no houses built since 1956. Jobs and telephones were also huge priorities, so all those things had to be looked after. Infrastructure too – roads were always a problem. There is not much change from then except that broadband is a big issue as the world changes. The roads are still being complained about and there are definitely not enough houses.

"Two years later in 1969 the sitting Fianna Fáil TD Eugene Gilbride retired and I did not even know where the Dáil was, only that it was somewhere in Dublin. Many people were urging me to put my name forward and there were six candidates: Seán 'Red' McManus, Albert Higgins, Mickey Kearins [Sligo GAA star and Ray's first cousin], Bernie Brennan and Willie Farrell.

"Mickey flew back from the US and had great publicity and would have been a great candidate and later got elected as a county councillor. But he did not particularly like politics, and I won the nomination at the convention."

This was a big day for Ray, and all of his large extended family worked hard to get him elected, as did the Fianna Fáil party and his friends.

He said: "I will never forget the contribution made by all three."

He remembers his first day in the Dáil in Kildare Street and was "very proud to be representing the people of Sligo and Leitrim".

So what was the magnet that attracted Ray to politics?

He said: "I was always interested in helping people from my days in the Junior Chamber of Commerce, where I had been working with all the charitable efforts that the Chamber was making.

"I went in to streamline that support, mainly for poor people, the unemployed, the disabled and all of those people who were helping through the Junior Chamber. So that is what motivated me to get involved, and then when you get in you have to take on board every other interest of every other individual and community. You work very hard to resolve the problems of the day."

Ray was re-elected in 1973 and was appointed opposition spokesman on the Office Of Public Works.

"That entailed making sure that all of its activities were kept up to speed and you talked with the Junior Minister in Finance, who deals with these matters. You are progressing many activities in your own constituency and nationally in areas that were the responsibility of the Office Of Public Works. There was a lot of activity in the area of parks and wildlife area, the islands and maintenance of a whole load of areas that were in State control. And they were also concerned with government building in the area."

Ray was then appointed Junior Minister at the Department of Finance and was in charge of public works.

Did he find that his great dealing DNA and experience of farming and finance were a help in politics?

He said: "Of course. But the main skill is recognising what people's needs are, seeking to support them in solving those problems. Problems are the same worldwide no matter what level you are working at, whether it is for Sligo County Council, Dáil Éireann or the European Commission or the European Parliament. I found that the problems are the same all over the world. Unemployment, incomes, housing, infrastructure and jobs of course.

"In the mid-1950s, there was just no work and that is why I later set up my own haulage business. Jobs are always a problem as the population increases and most people would like to stay at home.

"Many of them had to emigrate, but thankfully many of them have come back to live here in all walks of life despite the difficulties of recessions and austerity budgets that I was involved in personally.

"The people held on, the people are very resilient and give them half a chance and they will make it and that is what has happened Ireland. It is a great country, there is no doubt about it, and we will overcome this coronavirus too.

"We got over the last recession ten years ago and now just as we are getting out of it, we are hit with this terrible virus, but we will overcome that no matter what the final cost.

"Whatever money is needed to fight the virus should be set aside and not to be used for re-booting the economy again. We won't forget about that sum, but we should use whatever money we have to boost the economy to get employment back up to the level that it was at."

What does he think of the Covid payment of €350 for those who are out unemployed and the €410 for those who are placed on furlough by firms who pay the difference?

"That is a very positive step but of course many people will still be short by the constraints that are on them in feeding their families. But they should be able to do that, and they won't be able to pay bills or mortgages or rates. The banks and local authorities will have to be lenient and constructive and sympathetic towards all concerned and hopefully this pandemic will only be of temporary duration."

1979 was a big year in Ray's career as taoiseach Jack Lynch stood down and Ray nominated Charlie Haughey as the new taoiseach.

He said: "I was a Junior Minister in the other candidate George Colley's department, working with him very closely, and he was a good friend and remained a good friend, but I felt that, at the time, the best person to lead Fianna Fáil and hold the support we had under Jack Lynch was Charles Haughey. That is why I proposed him and it turned out to be true. We always had 44 to 50 per cent of the vote in this constituency during his time and we are at 27 per cent now."

He was then given the ideal job as Minister for Agriculture.

He said: "I loved that, as agriculture was going through a very difficult time. But we were in a position to negotiate in Brussels reasonably good deals for our farmers at the time and keep the show on the road and I was glad to make that contribution."

What were the main highlights of his tenure?

Ray said: "The Common Agricultural Policy had been there for years, but there were aspects of it that people were seeking to change, which could mean the elimination of small farmers. That was anathema to me and there was no way I was going to tolerate that.

"What we did was to gear those supports more towards the small farmers, as I also did many years later when I was European Commissioner."

Ray added: "I hope that contribution that we made was helpful. And we are lucky that for the last number of years we do have the cheque in the post, which I succeeded in implementing many years ago to supplement farmer's incomes.

"And that was nearly being the only income they have had in recent years. But were it not for the fact that the CAP was reformed by me in the 1990s then we would have all this money going towards cold storages and the big tycoons that were running agriculture in the beef and dairy sectors.

"Now, at least the prices are controlled going to the community for their food and that the farmers have an income supplement coming through via the cheque in the post.

"I started that as EU Commissioner in the 1990s. We also had the Disadvantaged Areas Scheme in my time which I was involved in.

"We brought in a number of supports like the common organisation of the sheep market at the time when I was Minister for Agriculture and protected the payments that were coming and sought to improve them each time there were negotiations every year."

Three years later, in the infamous year of 1982, Ray was promoted to Minister of Finance and was also made Tánaiste.

He said: "They were very difficult times and there was a lot of uncertainty and instability within the country as there were three elections in the space of 18 months.

"We won one and lost two and I had to take very difficult decisions to try to manage the public finances so that the country could stay on the road.

"We did our best in that, but we were beaten because I brought in a supplementary Budget in October and there was a General Election and Fine Gael and Labour came in. When I left the Department in December 1982 the National Debt was £12bn, and when I came back in 1987 it had more than doubled to £25bn. It is relatively small in today's terms but there were 100,000 fewer people working in 1987 than were working in 1982, so 1987 was even more severe."

In the interim, Ray's career took a new turn in 1984 when he became an MEP for the Connacht-Ulster constituency – and at that time you could be a TD and an MEP.

He said: "I spent a few days in Brussels and a few days in the Dáil every week. Then I had my weekend meetings in the constituency from Clare to Donegal and I was very honoured to be there."

And Ray holds a unique record as he was the only Irish figure to be a member of all three European institutions, the European Parliament, the European Council of Ministers and in the European Commission as Commissioner for Agriculture and Rural Development.

Ray was elected in Bundoran, when he said that "even the great Neil Blaney was defeated in that election and he did not like it a bit".

Ray said: "I tried my best before I was a candidate to get him back into the party and I sought the approval of the organisation.

"But he was not going to be coming back and thankfully his nephew Niall Blaney has now been elected to the Senate for Fianna Fáil."

What was it like representing Ireland in Europe?

Ray said: "It was huge, with 600 to 700 people from 15 countries at the time and it was a very difficult type of area to have your presence felt. There were 18 of us from Ireland including Ian Paisley and John Hume from

Northern Ireland. But we all worked together in the interests of Ireland as a whole and all other differences were set aside."

Ray got on "extremely well" with the late Ian Paisley, who had strong farming interests as well.

"We worked in the interests of our people and he was a public representative as well as the man we knew as 'Ulster Says No'. But beneath that he was one of the best public representatives you could know."

When Ray was Agriculture Commissioner, he and Ian Paisley were in contact every week about some issues about agriculture.

Ray said: "At that time, we in Ireland were getting support from Brussels as every £100 that was spent, we were getting 75 per cent of it. In the UK every £100 they spent they were only getting 25 per cent from Brussels, so the Exchequer in London were not as much in favour of supporting agriculture as we would have been. They had an opposite cheap food policy, where we would be looking for the Irish farmers to have a better income.

"Ian Paisley was always anxious to ensure that what the small farmers in Republic of Ireland were getting, the small farmers in the North would be getting the same, and there were quite a few of them as well. We worked very closely with him and John Hume to ensure that every time I made a proposal as Commissioner to the dislike of the British Government it was always for the 32 counties of Ireland."

Practical patriotism in action!

"And we got it through and the first man to oppose me on that was always the British Minister for Agriculture, telling me I was interfering with national politics of the UK. I said no, I was making a proposal for the island of Ireland and it had nothing to do with politics. It was for all farmers to benefit."

Ray was also involved in reform of the Common Agricultural Policy in 1992.

He said: "That was to do with the GATT, since 1985 the General Agreement on Tariffs and Trade was seeking to put the agricultural programmes under the rules and disciplines of the GATT. The supports that were being given caused many countries in the world to complain about them and that they were distorting trade.

"Those negotiations went on from 1985 to 1992, and I was involved on behalf of Europe. After reforming the Common Agricultural Policy in the way we wanted, changing the supports to business to the individual farmer through the cheque in the post, it enabled us to show to the people of the world, the 144 countries, that we were not supporting increased production. We were supporting the income of the poorer and smaller farmers and we got it accepted and that breakthrough led to the agreement of the World Trade Organisation."

Ray was in Europe for seven years as a Minister, three as an MEP and four years as a Commissioner, thus spending 14 productive years on the continent.

Meanwhile, at home, Ray was given the post of Finance in recession-hit Ireland in 1987. With a national debt of £24bn, many saw the post as a poisoned chalice.

But Ray MacSharry, as always, was ready for the fight, and he left Europe to try to put out some fairly big fires at home with Mark Killilea of Fianna Fáil replacing him in Europe. Fianna Fáil were on a high and they won three of the four seats in Sligo-Leitrim. Ray's corrective actions earned him the title "Mac The Knife".

He said: "There was a serious situation in the country at the time and then I went back to Brussels as EU Agricultural Commissioner in 1988 after preparing the Budget for 1989. It wasn't the cuts that I was making that got me the name Mac The Knife. I think it was the overall strategy, which was to control finance. We hadn't the money to spend. We were borrowing too much and the debt-GDP ratio was over 100 per cent. Even in the last recession it hardly reached that figure.

"We brought it down to 60 in three years, so it is somewhere between that in recent years. We had to take those actions. Some of them were severe but the good thing about it was that in March 1987 when we brought it the Budget, it was tough but caring.

"We still looked after the poorer sections of the economy at that time and it began to work very quickly because it was seen in the world order that there was control of the finances and interest rates dropped by five per cent in five months.

"So everybody had some amount of money to spend because interest rates were as high as 17 to 18 per cent at one point during that decade.

"Anyone that had a loan or a mortgage had more money to spend and interest rates dropped further because the public finances were being brought under control. There was more money to spend, so there was more employment, more VAT and more income tax coming into the Exchequer and borrowing was down.

"That did eventually lead to the Celtic Tiger, but unfortunately in the Celtic Tiger when things went wrong, we continued to spend money rather than saving it, and we paid a heavy price for that in 2008."

Ray finished in Europe in 1993, left politics and went into the private sector working for himself.

"I was a board member of Bank of Ireland, Smurfit, Ryanair. I saw Ryanair grow in my time on the board there from 700,000 passengers to 44 million passengers and I was chairman of Ryanair for three years before it went on the Stock Exchange."

Ray was chairman of Eircom when it went on the Stock Exchange.

He said: "The launch was very successful. Sadly a year later the whole technological world collapsed and the people who had invested in Eircom lost some money.

"Some people lost a lot of money. Some people made money, those who sold early on – the price of the shares had gone up initially. But then shares of all technological companies came back and in Germany Deutsche Telekom lost more than 50 per cent of its value and people lost 50 per cent of their money. Here, we sold Eircell to help reduce the loss.

"In Ireland the average investment of everyone in the country was £900 and they lost £300 of that, which was a third which was one of the least losses of any investment in telecoms at the time. Very few people bothered to analyse that at the time, but I am telling you the factual situation."

He said: "We are just after coming out of a world recession and this virus is now putting us back into another one.

"I worked for 60 years and I finished in 2006-2007, and have done a bit of farming and gardening since then, and I also look after my grandchildren. I had 50 acres of land in Dromard and I had 15 acres down at Rosses Point and I rented two farms of 30 and 50 acres as well. I used to feed over 100 cattle in recent years. I started buying cattle while I was still in Europe and I did it on weekends when I would be home February or March. I had very good neighbours who looked after them when I was not around. But when I was at home I loved going out and walking the land and looking at the bullocks.

"I see all these people that are running on the roads and on concrete, it destroys your knees and hips, but if you walk and run on the land it will not affect you too much."

What are the highlights for Ray for his native Sligo?

He said: "I was delighted that we were able to progress a number of services here. We built a huge number of houses. When I started first in politics there were no houses in Cranmore, there were very few houses in Tonaphubble, there was nothing in Markievicz Road, there was nothing out the Sea Roads, Maugheraboy or Cartron. All of those houses were started in my time and were supported by me all through my political career.

"We also started with three or four industrial estates thanks to the IDA, Enterprise Ireland and successive governments, and we got many jobs. Of course, we had losses like Snia and GWI, but many of that expertise are still working Take GWI. There were 600 people working there, and now you have as many people working from home with various skills and doing very well. It was the same with Tool and Gauge and Basta in Tubbercurry".

"There are many difficulties still around and there will always be difficulties. No matter who we are or what we are, we would like to improve ourselves and improve our families. Maybe have a better house or a better farm, a better job or more income, and that is what life is about. And sometimes that can be easier than others.

"We have had a very severe 10 years of austerity, but the Irish are a great people and we have a record of over two million employed before this virus hit us. Let's hope that most of them will get their jobs back when this virus has passed so that we can get back into growth and prosperity again."

I asked Ray what Sligo means to him.

He said: "Sligo is my home. I have a great family. I was lucky to have been married to a great lady, Elaine Neilan, who sadly passed away 12 years ago. And I am lucky to have had six children and all are doing very well.

"My son Marc is doing very well in politics and he is a very able public representative who is interested in progressing Sligo-Leitrim and the welfare of the people here. And my nephew Tom MacSharry is also a very capable public representative in Sligo.

"In latter years I went on to marry another lady, who is a nurse in practice with the HSE. I have no complaints, I did not do everything right and people can criticise about what is happening now.

"But when you look back at the day that those decisions were made, they were different times to now, so I was glad to take the decisions that were necessary on the day, to try to help the country and the economy and its people. And I am satisfied that everything I did was relevant to that philosophy at that time.

"I saw the country grow substantially since then and I saw the farming community improve its numbers, not in the numbers of farmers but in the numbers of livestock. Of course, there have been ups and downs in the dairy and the beef sector as well, but I believe that the beef sector should have more support coming from the EU.

"It is up to us to ensure that we get the benefits we are entitled to, enough food for the people in the European community, and not have our food, as England wants, coming from Brazil, Argentina, Australia or New Zealand. We are here on their doorstep, but we must get our European prices as we sell our product to England.

"Unfortunately, that has changed recently, but with the support of our government and the EU this will help our farmers to have a good livelihood."

What is Ray's advice during this coronavirus crisis?

He said: "It is exactly as what the health authorities are telling us. I am isolated myself for the last three weeks, nobody in or out, and I get messages from Christie's and the supermarkets. I am happy to spend my days in my lovely house on Pearse Road, of which I am proud.

"I was greatly honoured by the achievements that I had and was greatly honoured to represent the people of Sligo and Leitrim and I thank them sincerely, as without their support I would never have been in the Corporation or Council, the Dáil or the EU."

Thank you, Ray. You are definitely Sligo's "real Taoiseach", and you made your own road in life.

TED MALONEY

Affable west Sligo man Ted Maloney told Gerry McLaughlin about his long-time commitment to Castleconnor and county GAA and the ups and downs of 18 years as a traffic warden in Sligo town

PUBLISHED ON AUGUST 6, 2020

BEING A TRAFFIC WARDEN REQUIRES the hide of a rhino and the nuanced, diplomatic skills of a Jesuit. As thankless jobs go, it is right up there with tax men, customs men, gardaí and referees.

But the affable Ted Maloney has been both traffic warden and referee, and he's certainly no masochist.

For over 18 years, from the mid-1990s, this tall, powerfully built figure strode the streets of Sligo and became one of the most instantly recognisable faces around the

TED MALONEY AS A MEMBER OF THE SLIGO MANAGEMENT TEAM AT THE LGFA ALL-IRELAND INTERMEDIATE CHAMPIONSHIP SEMI-FINAL MATCH BETWEEN SLIGO AND TIPPERARY AT NOWLAN PARK IN KILKENNY

town. Significantly, his second name was seldom used – he was just our Ted and there was no need for surnames.

Ted comes from a clan of people who were in business in various spheres and has all the attendant empathy, social skills and common sense of his people. And, while he upheld the law, he always believed in giving people the benefit of the doubt and was very kind to the vulnerable.

It is very easy to issue summonses, but not every case is the same and common sense and common decency are also valuable skills which he has in abundance.

Ted was and is witty and wise with a ready quip, a smile and ability to defuse a tense situation in a heartbeat, a skill honed in his previous career in various forms of sales.

He met a number of famous people and none greater than Alex Ferguson, the then Manchester United manager, who was over for an event honouring Sligo Rovers soccer great Seán Fallon.

And when he and friends like the great thespian Frankie Brannigan shot the breeze in the Courtyard just across from Sligo District Court it was an education in rapier-like wit and repartee.

But he is also a great GAA figure, becoming chairman of his native Castleconnor club while he was just over 21, was involved in major fund-raising in getting a new field and also became a GAA and soccer referee for a few decades.

He was chairman of Sligo-Leitrim soccer referees for four years and was a very well-known GAA referee for many years also.

At a very fit 72, he is still refereeing Ladies Football matches – something very dear to his heart as Ted was a major figure in the growth of the women's game in the Yeats County.

Ted is a former chairman of the Ladies County Board, a former vice-president of the Connacht Council and a former selector for the Sligo Ladies Junior side.

Ted was also a county board delegate, Connacht Council delegate and Central Council delegate and is currently an All Star selector.

He was also a prime mover in a hugely successful Coolera underage ladies' club that made a clean sweep of underage titles in the Yeats County.

Ted was also involved with the St Mary's Ladies Football team, who became a very successful side in later years. His daughter Karen was an outstanding player and athlete and is still playing the game her father did so much to promote for almost 25 years.

He has three other daughters, Tara, Laura and Sharon, who are twins, and the twins have played underage football with Sligo.

Getting Ladies Football off the ground in Sligo was not easy as there were still some old attitudes, that ladies were best at making tea. But Ted had the nous and diplomacy to get around such crass behaviour and really helped to put Ladies Football on the map over several years.

And, in 2006, when Sligo won a memorable All-Ireland Junior Football title, captained by Angela Doohan after just losing out the two previous years, Ted was development officer.

He has worn all the T-shirts, from managing, coaching, collecting at gates, organising transport, PR and was involved with Gaelic 4 Mothers in St Farnan's in recent years.

Ted was born in the wonderfully named townland of Attycree in picturesque west Sligo, not far from the Mayo border. From the Irish it is *áit uí chroí* – the place of my heart.

Ted was born in 1948, in a family of nine. Vincent, the eldest, was big into journalism and photography and was a local correspondent for newspapers. Another brother called Michael has combined a career as a barrister and a songwriter.

Michael's first song was in commemoration of 1966 and it featured on Junior Magazine. He also wrote 'Back Home To Donegal', 'My Old Sligo Home', 'An Irish Harvest Day', 'Spring Time In Ireland' and 'My Enniscrone', and they were recorded by various artists.

His father was Martin and his mother's name was Brigid and the family used to call her "the small little proud Mayo woman" who never forgot her roots.

The house was full of music and the family had a gramophone which was often taken down.

Ted went to primary school at Carrowgarry and second level at Corballa Vocational School and then when he worked in Ballina, it was for the great John Feeney who recorded several ballads later in the US.

Football-wise, three young men from Ted's home place won an All-Ireland Vocational GAA title with Mayo. Gerry Barnes captained the team, and Jimmy Cullen and Seán Foody and Theo Hanley were great footballers.

The club in Castleconnor was disbanded in the 1950s but a young Ted was central to its revival in 1969. They had no field and they got the use of the field from a local lady, who had given it to them in the 1950s. She agreed and her only condition was that they put on a gate.

"We ran sports that lasted five or six weeks and my brother Vincent said it was time that we register a club. I was chairman of the club in 1969 and I was chair in 1972 again. We started doing fundraisers of all sorts, in Carra Hall and we got Margo (sister of Daniel O'Donnell) and the Keynotes to play and they were popular.

"We bought some land, which was 14 acres, and I collected most of the money for Castleconnor in Mayo where I was working. The parochial house and a new school was built in Castleconnor also in 1983. They raffled a pony and took in over £30,000 and it was great going. We also built a community centre."

Ted's association with Castleconnor went on for many years and the famous Barnes and Christy Murphy were among a number of Murphys to play for the club, according to Ted.

"I played at wing-forward, but I loved the game and I would die for it."

He emigrated to Luton and worked in sales in the 1970s – the first of a number of sales jobs in his eclectic career.

"I was on about £300 a week and I stayed there for a year".

Ted came home to a family cleaning business for a period in the 1980s and he went working for Cahill's Bakery in Ballina for around 13 years.

Ted got married in 1984 and moved to Cartron and then to Kilmacowen. He played for Coolera for a few years before injury cut short his career.

Meanwhile, Ted began his refereeing career in the early 1980s, which began with an under-14 game in Ballina.

He said: "I have been refereeing for almost 40 years. I got into Cumann na mBunscoil games first. And then I refereed all over the county for many years but left because I felt I was not getting support for a decision of mine that was overturned at a higher level of the association. Referees should get backing."

Ted then took up refereeing soccer seriously in the 1990s.

"Gaelic has loads of rules and a lot of them are not implemented while soccer does not have as many. I always tried to use common sense and I refereed at all levels of soccer in Sligo and refereed All-Irelands and also at the IT. I liked refereeing soccer. It is a slower game, but the offside rule was a bit tricky and I only retired from refereeing soccer matches a few years

TED DURING HIS TIME AS A TRAFFIC WARDEN

ago. The disciplinary system in soccer was much better because if a player was banned, he stayed banned.

"In Gaelic we have hearings committees and too often they overturn 'valid' proposed suspensions by the CCC. The only way around this 'parochialism' is to have the Hearings Committee from outside the county, to ensure neutrality."

Ted began his long association with Ladies Football when his daughters began to play the game in Ransboro National School in the late 1990s.

"Karen was a very gifted player and we trained underage teams in Coolera. Rose Cawley, Teresa Henry, Eileen Sheridan and me trained the underage teams. We won title after title, including Community Games, and my daughters were also into athletics".

Meanwhile, Ted got involved with the Sligo county sides from around 1990.

"Marty Duffy, the referee, was the first Ladies chairperson, and then you had Kathleen Kane, Tom Kane, Martin Seery and I was chairperson from 2008 to 2010".

He added: "It was hard to get the game off the ground as people in men's football would say that women should not be playing the game at all. But I would say, why don't you go and look at the game. There were some very heated debates in the early days."

Ted's group of girls in Coolera-Strandhill were a gifted bunch and apart from underage, they also won a Junior county title.

"And then they transferred to St Mary's, where they won two senior county titles and a junior title."

Ted was involved in the management of these teams with Pauric Mannion and Richard Mannion.

"There were great facilities there and we beat the mighty St Nathy's a few times and we got to two Connacht finals as well as those girls were a very talented bunch. Róisín Devaney, Joanne O'Connell and Fiona Maye were among a group of very gifted players."

The county team was not doing well at this stage.

"Frank Gallagher, Tom Kane and Kathleen Kane were involved with the county Junior team and I was asked if Karen and a few of the other girls from Coolera would come to join the county who were playing Roscommon in the qualifiers. Karen was only 14 and this was around 2002 and Celestine Cawley also joined us along with Natasha Muldoon and I brought them to the county team to Frenchpark and we won it by a point. We ran a good Donegal team very close also."

Ted was part of Paddy Henry's backroom team when Sligo won an historic All-Ireland Junior title in 2006 by beating neighbours Leitrim.

This victory was most sweet as the Yeats County had lost in the previous two year's finals.

Two years later Ted became county chairperson, a post he held for three years until 2010. And he had to use all of his diplomacy and imagination to get a pitch for the county team to train in.

"We had no pitch and we were under pressure. We got the field off a man called Wally Burke but we had no place to change. We asked Bob Roemer if we could have a container and told him he could have an advertising hoarding on the side of it, so he agreed and that was a major problem solved for us in the field. The county team trained there for a few years."

Sligo won two NFL titles in this period also, a memorable time for Ted and his co-volunteers. Through all of this, Ted also helped with match reports for the local media as well. Ted then got involved in the Connacht Council where he was a delegate and also a Central Council delegate. He was also vice-president of the Connacht Council and he chaired the meeting on the big bust up in Mayo between Carnacon and the county board in recent years.

He said: "That was a tough one to deal with and I took no nonsense. We suspended some players."

Ted is currently on the All-Star Selection Committee and attends matches all over the country as well as Central Council Meetings in Croke Park. Sligo has had only one All Star, when goalkeeper Katrina Connolly was honoured in 2006. And, Sligo had Stephanie O'Reilly, Bernice Byrne among others on the Team of the League.

He is still involved with Ladies Football as a referee.

Meanwhile, Ted began his long career as a traffic warden in the hot summer of 1995. He had just finished a stint with the Ormeau Bakery in Belfast.

"I decided to give up the sales and my wife asked me if I would apply for the job as traffic warden. I did an interview and did not get it on the first attempt, but I later got a call to start work and it was Tony Fox who was my first mentor. I remember my first day with Tony. My attitude was to give the benefit of the doubt where you can, but then you are new, and a new broom sweeps clean. My experience in sales and dealing with the public helped me in this job".

"Sometimes people would say we will get you, but I used to say: You better join the queue because there are hundreds ahead of you. I generally got on well with people, and I always tried to be reasonable. You could have a mother with children, who was under pressure and had forgotten to put up a disc and I felt sorry for them. And she would only be in the shop for a few minutes, so you had to use your discretion.

"It was a great way to get to know Sligo and there were all sorts of excuses like rushing home as there was a cow calving. Some of the stuff was hilarious. A lot of people would give out about us, but we often searched and found lost keys, and this was all part of the service."

But there is one sad story that will never leave him.

"There was a young girl in Wine Street car park and she was not able to start her car. I borrowed a set of jump leads and got a man to jump start the car, but that young girl was killed in a road traffic accident in Mayo some time later.

"Not long afterwards a man came looking for me and said: 'You don't know me, but didn't you help someone get their car started with jump leads some time ago. I said I did, and he said, 'that was my daughter'.

"Another time a woman wanted to get back up to the hospital and had no car with her and I drove her to the hospital. So we were not always handing out tickets.

"I believed in treating everyone the same and I always tried to talk to everyone, and they are all some mother's child. I also spoke to the people who were on the streets. But I loved the work and the banter with people."

When asked about the current state of the traffic in Sligo, he said it was "a disaster".

He said: "Last week, I was going to referee a game in Drumcliffe, an under-12 match. I left at 5.45pm and at 6.30pm I was still stuck in traffic."

During his time, Ted has met some famous people, including former Manchester United manager Alex Ferguson, who he said was the "best conversationalist" he ever encountered.

Ted is "sceptical" about politicians but is mainly a positive person. For him, life is to be lived and not endured.

And he has certainly made his mark on the streets of Sligo and on various spheres of sport in the town and county he has such great time for.

Keep her lit, Ted – and keep on smiling. Just the ticket!

MICKEY KEARINS

Mickey Kearins, who played football for Sligo in the 1960s and '70s, left an incredible record, scoring 1,158 points for the county. Gerry McLaughlin sat down with the GAA legend who had magic in his boots

PUBLISHED ON JANUARY 30, 2020

MICKEY KEARINS HAD MAGIC IN HIS boots, and he was the Georgie Best of Sligo GAA from 1961 to 1978.

There is no other way to describe Sligo's greatest ever Gaelic footballer, who had a lion heart and had a bit of the maverick in his soul.

But the really great thing about this witty, wry Beltra legend is that he has never taken himself, or his terrific talent, too seriously.

As he speaks to the *Sligo Weekender* in his lovely home, it is clear that this a most grounded man, a modest man, an exceptionally shrewd man with all the

LEFT: MICKEY KEARINS

emotional intelligence of a great dealing man and a charismatic man, who was and is a born leader.

The feisty 76-year-old was never afraid to fire from the hip, take on the establishment and say what he meant throughout his long career.

But then genius often makes its own rules.

And it was another Sligo GAA legend, the late Joe Masterson, who perhaps best captured the essence of the mighty but extremely modest man from St Pat's Dromard.

Joe wrote: "Everything he did had the hallmark of genius – he fielded beautifully, faded from the tackle superbly, zig-zagged his way past bewildered opponents on scintillating solo runs. He seemed to have an in-built radar for the posts. In my opinion, Mickey Kearins was the greatest wing forward I have ever seen play in 40 years of attending Gaelic games."

Mickey's stats are also truly amazing. He scored 36 goals and 1,158 points for the Yeats County in a period from 1961 to 1978 in his 215 games for Sligo.

He was named on the 'Non-All Ireland winner' Team of the Century in 1984 at right half forward. He won an All Star with Sligo in 1971 and it was a crass injustice that he did not get another similar gong the following year.

And he played for his province of Connacht from 1963 to 1975 with all those great All-Ireland winning Galway teams of 1964 to 1966 – but Mickey was an automatic selection and this achievement is a record in Gaelic football.

Mickey won two Railway Cup medals in 1967 and 1969 and was inducted into the Hall of Fame in Croke Park six years ago.

In 1981, Gaelic footballers from all over Ireland, including Kerry's peerless Mick O'Connell, came together in Sligo for a "This Is Your Life" special.

And what a life it has been, as he was also a very early player and manager of Sligo in the late 1970s and early 1980s, to be succeeded by a great Castleconnor man called Barnes Murphy, who cajoled him to give it another go in the black and white jersey.

But Mickey was also the linchpin and player-manager of a great St Pat's Dromard team, who won seven senior county championships, two junior titles, numerous league titles and a plethora of tournament titles against some of the best clubs in the country.

However, it is his immense scoring feats, like 0-14 against Galway in a Connacht Championship match in 1971, when a great Sligo team just lost out.

Mickey could hit points with the right and left foot, could win his own ball, and was often on the receiving end of some very rough treatment.

And this makes all those great scoring records even more remarkable as he was often double-teamed, but to little avail.

Mickey got that elusive Connacht medal that he so richly deserved when Sligo defied all odds and beat the mighty Mayo in Castlebar, after a replay when all the experts thought they had blown their chance in the drawn game in 1975.

By then Mickey was 32, and confesses that he and his colleagues did some fairly significant socialising and were not really prepared for a terrific young Kerry team in the All-Ireland semi-final.

When asked to name his happiest day, he is unequivocal when he says: "The day I first pulled on a Sligo jersey as an 18-year-old in 1961 and we beat Cavan in an NFL match."

But he continued to serve the GAA as a referee right through the 1980s and refereed the All-Ireland SFC semi-final in 1989 between Dublin and Cork and is still not too happy about not getting the final.

"It was said a Connacht man could not get this game, because Mayo were involved, but the previous year Tommy Sugrue of Kerry refereed an All-Ireland final that involved Cork."

A man of principle, Mickey resigned at what he still regards as an injustice.

Mickey was born in April 1943 in Portavad, a few miles from his current home in Larkhill, Beltra. He was one of ten children, and he names them: "Dympna, Myself, Helen, Nuala (RIP), Peadar, Mabel, James, Noel, Sheila and Deirdre."

Mickey's father Jimmy Kearins was a cattle dealer and Mickey remembers being at a county final in Ballymote in 1951 when he was just seven years of age.

"There was a Fr Moore playing for Skreen-Dromard at that time and it was level pegging and we had a 50-yards free and it hit the crossbar, and that is what I remember most from that match, and they played against Keash. There was a family of Jameses up the road and the six of them were playing and two of them are still alive – one of them is 90 and the other is 95."

Mickey's father was on the Skreen-Dromard team that won county championships in 1934 and 1945, so the GAA was strong in the Kearins household.

"I remember going to a match between the great Tuam Stars and St Vincent's in Tuam stadium, a challenge match, and you could hardly get into it. That was in 1958."

Mickey went to primary school in Ballinlig and Mickey played under-12 with Dromore West in 1955 and won his first county medal, and won again at under-14 level.

Mickey went as a boarder to St Muredach's in Ballina but "hated it" as he wanted to be working with cattle like his father rather than working with words – although he always had a fine facility for the latter.

Fr Cyril Haran of Sligo was on the staff at that time, but Mickey stayed only three years.

He was picked at centre-field for the Sligo minors in 1960 and that began a 17-year career in the black and white.

He said: "We beat Mayo in the Connacht championship and we had Galway in the final and they beat us by two points, and they went on to win the All-Ireland."

Among Mickey's colleagues on that team were Peter James Brennan, Danny McHugh (RIP), Brendan McHugh (RIP), Tony Grey, and Joe Hannan.

In those days, Mickey's footballing heroes were Galway great Seán Purcell and Sligo's own Nace O'Dowd.

"Nace could play anywhere. He played full-back for Connacht, he played centre-field for Connacht and he played centre-back for Connacht, a big strong man who had great hands. He was fond of socialising."

In those days, Mickey's home club, St Pat's Dromard, were junior and Mickey made his debut for the adult team aged just 13 in 1956 when, he said, he "came in for an uncle of mine, Pat Kearins".

Mickey made his senior debut for Sligo in 1961 at 18 years of age, on Gabriel Kelly from Cavan, and Sligo won. Cathal Cawley, Brendan McCauley and Bill Shannon, who had transferred from Mayo, were on that team.

Mickey is adamant that the 1971 Sligo team were the best team he played on. They were beaten by Galway by a point after a replay, and Mickey did not train after Sligo won their first ever Connacht final in 1975. "I was busy at other things." he quipped.

MICKEY KEARINS IN CROKE PARK IN 1968 AFTER DRAWING WITH KILDARE

Swinging back to 1965 and All-Ireland champions Galway only beat Sligo by three points en route to retaining their All-Ireland title.

"We had Mickey Durkan, who played a great game, on Noel Tierney at full-forward and Gerry O'Connor was centre-back and Joe Hannan was in the corner. Danny McHugh was on that team and his father actually died the day before, but he still played."

Mickey played left-half forward but through the dint of practice, his left foot became as good as his right foot. He had some great battles with Galway's John Donnellan, who told the world as a Fine Gael TD that if it were raining soup the then party leader Alan Dukes would be out catching it with a spoon.

Mickey played Railway Cup with many of these Galway greats from 1963 to 1975 and is still very friendly with the great Séamus Leydon and John Keenan was "a great player and a very modest man".

Mickey won his first Sligo senior championship with St Pat's Dromard in 1968 along with his brother Peadar and Tommy Cummins who played in goals for Sligo also.

St Pat's won again in 1970 and 1971 and 1973 and 1974, and Mickey won two with an amalgamation with Ballisodare in 1962 and 1963, which makes seven county titles.

Mickey was player-manager of that great team from 1968 to 1974.

"There was great loyalty in that team and 10 or 11 of them would make today's Sligo county team – and that is no exaggeration."

That team was packed with Kearinses, Clarkes and Bolands, and they were physically powerful.

In those years, Mickey was player-manager of Sligo as well from 1968 to 1972, a few years before his toughest opponent Brian McEniff did something similar in Donegal.

Sligo reached the All-Ireland minor football final in 1968 powered by the late, great Aidan Richardson.

"Sligo senior teams in those years had 10 or 11 players that were as good as anyone anywhere, but we were always short four or five. Tommy

Cummins, John Brennan, Jimmy Kilgallon and Hughie Quinn also came through from that minor team to our senior team in 1971."

Tom Colleary, Pat Colleary, Jim Colleary and Aidan Colleary from Curry all played for Sligo in those years.

Mickey scored 0-14 in the drawn 1971 Connacht final against Galway and then scored 1-8 in the replay as Sligo lost in extra time.

Mickey recalls taking a side-line kick for Sligo in that replay and he was hand-tripped by John "Tull" Dunne, Galway county secretary, and he fell to the ground. The referee brought the ball on 10 yards and Mickey pointed so it was an expensive trip on Tull.

"Brendan McCauley was a great man to give a pass, as was the late Cathal Cawley. Liam and Aidan Caffrey, Mattie Brennan and Paddy Henry were also key figures on that team."

But success came in 1975 with James Kearins, Barnes Murphy, John Stenson, Robert Lipsett and John Brennan all featuring strongly as Sligo won their first title since 1928.

"It came too late for me, and Barnes Murphy was the player-manager and he was very dedicated and a very strong man."

Sligo beat Mayo after a replay, confounding many critics, and Mickey scored 1-6 in that replay and missed a penalty in the subsequent All-Ireland semi-final against Kerry, as he points out candidly.

"Sligo people went mad, but I did not get the same craic out of it as if we had won it a few years previously as I had not trained much for that final. Only for Barnes Murphy, I would not have been there at all as he kept at me. I was going to retire in 1974 and I should have retired in 1975 and Nace O'Dowd was over the team in 1978 and cajoled me back, but it was a mistake as I was not near the pace."

Elsewhere Mickey developed a friendship with Kerry legend Mick O'Connell, who he met through Railway Cup matches.

"A fellow called Hugh O'Flaherty, a judge, and Seán Purcell and I were invited out to Micko's house in Valentia Island. Seán Purcell said to me that we will have a few drinks when we were in Cahirsiveen before we went out to the island as there would be no drink in O'Connell's. There were about 40 mostly ex-players invited by Mick O'Connell to his home.

"There was everything you could need in the house, but he later invited our family, Frances, Adrian, Karl, Valerie and Evanna, and we were invited to go fishing with him. He was a gifted player and so elegant."

On the Sligo front, the "most intelligent player" was Brendan McCauley.

Mickey then took up the refereeing even before he quit playing. He wanted to be involved with the GAA, but had no interest in being involved in the county board.

"It is not the nicest job, but there were great times and I had a local team of officials with me."

Mickey quickly rose up the ranks, and was one of the first of the true greats to take up the whistle, and he refereed the Connacht final of 1979 between Roscommon and Mayo, which the Rossies won.

"Roscommon should have won the All-Ireland in 1980. It was their own fault that they didn't."

Mickey refereed the All-Ireland semi-final between Dublin and Cork in 1989, but did not get the final and feels that some of those in authority did him no favours.

And he recalls another incident when he was refereeing a Meath vs Armagh match in the late 1980s, when only for Meath full-back Mick Lyons he would have been nearly "lynched".

"It was a tough game and Colm O'Rourke caught a ball on his chest and Jim McKeer hit him a genuinely good tight shoulder and the ball fell out of O'Rourke's hand and into McKerr's hand.

"O'Rourke turned around and started f****** me out of it. Colm felt he should have got a free and did not react well to what was a genuine tackle and I sent him off. We had a fierce job to get out and I was surrounded by a crowd of angry Meath officials. Only for Mick Lyons – he came and took me by the arm and away. And I could hear one Meath voice saying, the f***** should be killed.

"I got a phone call that night from a Meath sponsor and asked me not to put in a bad report. I reported Colm O'Rourke, but I did not report the abuse I endured after the match."

When asked if he enjoyed the refereeing, he candidly replied: "Yes, for the simple reason that we would have a great time on the way home after matches. It was very sociable. You met players from all over the country and when the match was over, it was over."

"I never played in an All-Ireland final and it is a magical occasion so I would have loved to have refereed an All-Ireland final, because even if you were only in the stands, the hairs would be standing on the back of your neck when the two teams took the field."

Referees' expenses were not great in those days as only £7 was allocated for a meal and travelling expenses were 15p per mile.

"You could eat nowhere in those days for £7 so I phoned up Croke Park and told them if they would tell me where they were eating in Dublin for £7."

He was never tempted to go back and manage or become involved with Sligo – but he is a firm fan.

"That Sligo team of 2002 that beat Tyrone well and drew with reigning All-Ireland champions Armagh were a fine, well-balanced side and Eamon O'Hara was a great athlete and leader. He was all over the place and he was being taken out a lot off the ball in that match.

"They could play football as well, and it was a pity that Paul Taylor was just not a bit fitter, but he was a marvellous player."

But Mickey was a happy man when O'Hara's mighty left-footed goal brought another Connacht title to Yeats County.

Mickey said: "Tourlestrane are playing well but their style is quite defensive as everyone seems to be adopting Donegal's tactics.

"It is not attractive and the club final between Corofin and Kilcoo a few weeks ago was just terrible to watch. Corofin were well able to play but were backpedalling and I did not watch the second period of extra time. But I was hoping Kilcoo would win."

Mickey is looking forward to supporting Sligo and fondly recalls the last time he went to London when he left on the Friday and did not return to base until the following Tuesday as he met up with old friends.

"That is the great thing about the GAA as you meet with people from all over Ireland. I was one of 10 and got the chance to be educated but I was not interested. But I can drive into cattle yards in Cork, Clare and Kerry and I would not have to tell them who I was.

"The GAA did a lot for me. I don't think they meant to do it, but it helped me a lot in my business all over the country."

Apart from the GAA, Mickey's other great love is the cattle business. "I still like shuffling with cattle," he said.

When asked to name some of his other great Gaelic heroes, Mickey references an old friend from Muredach's called Liam Caffrey, who met his wife, who is sadly deceased, at Mickey's wedding to Frances.

And he paid a warm tribute to the late great Easkey and Sligo gael Willie Maloney, who sadly passed away in December 2019.

"I was at Willie's funeral and he was a great character. Willie was a great GAA man, he loved the GAA and he was never there for his own benefit. And he was a true Sea Blue and he wore them forever in his heart."

Mickey also recalls some tough battles with Easkey over the years.

"We had some very tough games with Easkey, but the minute the game was over, it was over, and you could meet any one of them afterwards and they were gentlemen off the field. Easkey won a county title in 1966, and we beat them in the final in 1968, which was our club's first senior county title."

So, what are his thoughts on the current state of the Sligo county side who are currently operating in Division 4 of the NFL?

"I think we just don't have the players and the manager can only do so much. And they are losing Niall Murphy and that lad from Tourlestrane also [Adrian McIntyre]. It is hard to know if the interest is still there."

He added that there is far too much emphasis on training as opposed to playing in the GAA generally.

"I read where up in Meath an under-16 team had 28 training sessions in one month. Now that is really crazy. Mick O'Dwyer of Kerry said no GAA man should be at a gym. He should be out running in the field and if he is able to run plenty and has any bit of skill, he will get the ball and know what to do with it.

"It is most important to have the stamina to run, but now they are all obsessed with building up muscles and looking good.

"And is anyone focusing on the high catch and kicking long range points? In the All-Ireland club finals there was far too much lateral play."

When asked who is going to win the All-Ireland this year, he reckons that Donegal will not be too far away.

"They are a fine squad and some good young lads, and if Michael Murphy is fit, he is as good as four men. But he has a lot played and I think that Paddy McBrearty is the best forward in Ireland at the moment."

So what about his neighbours, Mayo?

"They seem to have that little bit lacking and key moments seem to go against them."

And what about the amount of people who are on backroom teams?

"If I were in charge of a team, I would not have them there. When Mick O'Dwyer was successful with Kerry, everyone said he had the players and we know that. But look at Laois, Kildare and Wicklow, where he got some very good results. He had great control in Kerry and there was nobody else but him. Today they are bringing in all sorts of head doctors, dietitians and psychologists, and they are all getting paid."

Mickey was one of the first player-managers of them all and he had no big backroom team. But he never needed too many people around him.

He never needed them because he was unique – Sligo's greatest ever player with magic in his boots and courage in his big heart.

And a lovely ability to gently ruffle plumage, a man who tastes life through the teeth and loves to put a smile on the faces of those who are lucky enough to listen to him.

Sláinte, Mickey!

CARMEL GUNNING

The queen of ceol traidisiúnta in Sligo, Carmel Gunning, spoke to Gerry McLaughlin about a rich and varied career dedicated to music

PUBLISHED ON NOVEMBER 21, 2019

THE GREAT IRISH WRITER FRANK O'Connor said that "music was the breath of life." For Carmel Gunning, the Sligo queen of *ceol traidisiúnta na hÉireann*, it is something much more. It is life itself.

And for 50 years, she has lived that life to the full, in a rich and varied career that has run the entire gamut of music, from the pure drop on her peerless tin whistle/flute, to ballads of the people, to country and western, and searing songs of resistance and to teaching many hundreds of children and adults that rich gift of many forms of music and song.

But when she sings 'The Grave of Wolfe Tone', or 'Four Green Fields' or 'The Boys

LEFT: CARMEL GUNNING

of Barr na Sráide' you can hear all the anthems of the dispossessed, all the wounds of the oppressed and all the lost battles in the hills and glens of the land she clearly loves.

Carmel is from Geevagh or Gaobhach, a high and 'windy place' or 'the land of the Gael', a place where you could come across a few long-stepping mountainy men, high-fielding giants of the GAA, a place nestling near the Arigna coal mines, a place where memory is sacred and words are gifts to be given away, a place full of proud ancient songs and stories and a place where that same GAA is the glue that keeps the community together.

When the Irish language and culture was almost crucified in the 19th century by official Crown policy, it did not survive on the fat plains or the strong farms, but in the heathery hills of the west of Ireland, in thin rushy parishes and in the places burned by the black thumb of Cromwell.

And that is where the music and old songs remained, for both cost nothing, and folk memory is always best kept in song and that is where we have made many of the heroes and legends of our land.

Poetry and song remain the greatest gifts of the *gnáth-dhaoine*, the ordinary people who always tend to be footnotes in history.

On Saturday, November 30, 2019, Carmel launched a book in Paddy's Bar in her native Geevagh called 'Shamrocks From Geevagh' with some rare old poems and songs from the area.

Speaking to the *Sligo Weekender*, Carmel said: "The music of this land is central to who we are, our identity, and it is the language of our soul."

Growing up, Carmel had all of these songs and stories all around her and took the music from her Nangle people, an ancient French-Norman family, and her mother's Mulligan family.

Her grandparents were also noted musicians, as was her uncle Johnny, so in another arena she would be termed a real blue blood.

Music, song and story ran deep in her DNA and she was playing the tin whistle from a very young age, and picked up tunes from her father Tom Nangle, who would lilt them to her, and her mother Kathleen Mulligan was a fine singer also.

All of her family were very musical, and she was always a performer who really came to life on the stage.

She was born in 1950, and fronted her first country and Irish band called Carmel And The Chrystals at the age of 19 in 1969. She played in Geevagh, Keadue, Boyle and many surrounding areas along with her brother Tom Nangle (Jnr).

Carmel won an All-Ireland medal for a slow air on the tin whistle at the Fleadh Cheoil in 1976, and a senior Scór title later for various instruments.

But she was never a cultural one-trick pony, as she also played the pubs and halls of the north and west of Ireland in the early 1970s as a one-woman band. Carmel is acknowledged as a truly great tin whistle and flute player, with a rich deep ballad voice. She also plays the guitar and the button accordion and is the gifted composer of many haunting airs.

She has played on equal footing with some of Ireland's greatest traditional musicians including the late great Fred Finn and Peter Horan, Matt Molloy, Josie McDermott, Kevin O'Loughlin, Joe Burke, Séamus Tansey, and with Mick Shannon, Joe O'Dowd and P J Hernon in the Sligo Trades Club for many years in the 1970s and 1980s.

Her first solo recording was the 'Hills of Sligo' in 1995 and she went on to produce 'Around St James's Well' the same year followed by 'Carmel Sings Country' (2002), 'The Sligo Maid' (2004), 'Lament For The Birds', 'Jack Harte Featured Appearance' (2005), 'The Sound of Coleman Country' (2006) and 'Corran Hill' (2008).

And she launched another valuable collection of songs called 'The Sligo Maid' last September in Earley's Bar to great acclaim, along with a CD called 'Cathair Shligigh' that includes a poignant tribute to her much-loved Tommy Nangle.

In 1975 she was a founder member of Comhaltas Ceoltóirí Éireann in Sligo. But it is her long and distinguished teaching career and her own compositions that will possibly be her most enduring legacy.

She has tutored BA and MA music students at the University of Limerick. Past pupils from the Carmel Gunning School of Music, which she runs from her Sligo home, are Dervish whistle and flute player Liam

Kelly, Orlaith McAuliffe, Olivia McTernan and June McCormack, among many others.

She has played Irish music all around the world, from Norway to Australia and from the US to Japan.

In 2006, she led the St Patrick's Day parade and played a number of concerts in Perth, Australia, and her summer school festival attracts pupils from across Ireland, the UK, Europe and the US.

Carmel won her first medal at Feis Shligigh in 1960 on the tin whistle and that was the beginning of over 50 years of various accolades.

She said: "There was music all over the house, and I was born in Ceathrú d'Arigna, the Arigna Quarter, as we were very close to Arigna. And my father Tom played the tin whistle and we used to listen to Ceolta Tíre in the 1950s. I was only about seven and he would be whistling those tunes to me so that I'd get them off.

"That is how it all started and 'Job of Journey Work', 'Céilí House' and 'Din Joe' were all popular traditional music programmes on the radio. My brother John and Maura, who were older than me, were very musical and my brother Tom was a great singer."

And Carmel also picked up tunes at national school like 'The Dawning Of The Day', '40 Shades of Green' and 'Shanagolden'.

"I had a very broad education in St James's in Geevagh. I boarded at the Marist convent in Tubbercurry and I used to sneak in to the music room to play tunes on my tin whistle."

Carmel sang and was involved in musicals in the school and when she left, she and her brother Tom Nangle, Tony Mullaney, Kevin Conlon and his brother, formed a band called Carmel and the Chrystals. They sang all over the North West.

"We were a country and Irish band and I used to love singing '21 Years' and Margo had it out that time and folk was strong too and then I started work in Sligo Courthouse and that finished that particular gig.

"I was never nervous on the stage and I just love performing. Music is very therapeutic and great for the soul and it is even better when they like your music.

"I bought a guitar and my brother Tom taught me three chords and I sang in pubs on my own all over the place for many years in Donegal, Sligo, Leitrim, Roscommon and Mayo, just me and the guitar and the mic and I had the keyboards as drums".

Carmel's solo career lasted from the early 1970s to 1996, when she was in a car crash.

She played in the Irish House and McGettigan's in Sligo. She played in Joe O'Neill's in Bundoran in Donegal, where she came second in a singing contest when the jazz singer Cleo Laine was adjudicating.

Carmel said: "In 1976 I won the All-Ireland competition at the Fleadh Cheoil for a slow air on the whistle and the following year I won the all-Ireland Scór competition representing Coolera of Sligo.

DETTA CONLIN, CARMEL GUNNING, DENNIS Ó GALLACHÓIR AND LEO CONLON AT 'THE LAKES OF SLIGO' LAUNCH IN 1989

"The artist can evoke great emotion in slow airs, which are mostly sad, and for the last ten years I was grieving for my brother Tom and I isolated myself to a degree, but now I am coming out again into the big bad world.

"The whistle is a great instrument and a hard instrument to play and it is very important in a group as it can either make or break that group.

"It is the loudest instrument and if you are not a good whistle player and you are playing with great musicians it could ruin the whole thing."

So, who were the whistle players that influenced Carmel?

"My uncle Johnny Nangle was a great player and was so smooth and I wanted to be like him. I did hear Peter Horan from Killavil and my father was always talking about Packie Deignan from Leitrim and Josie McDermott and Fred Finn, who was a distant relation.

"I got heavily involved in CCÉ in Sligo in the mid 1970s. Mark Duffy and Vincey Fowley were teaching a bit of music but there was not much going and there were not too many sessions."

The old branch was reformed along with notables like public representative Declan Bree, and Carmel also formed a singing circle.

"We had sessions in the Trades Club with Ronan Ryan, Joe O'Dowd and Sheila O'Dowd, Seamie O'Dowd and P J Hernon. People like Peter Horan and Fred Finn would come and visit and play also and they were great times."

Carmel has been teaching Irish music since that fateful year in 1976 when she won the all-Ireland playing 'Sé Fath Mo Bhuartha' – a haunting tune – and 'Seán Ó Duibhir a' Ghleanna' and 'An Buachaillín Donn'.

Carmel got second in the all-Ireland in 1977 for the tin whistle and she was teaching her children when they were very small.

"Paul, John, Leonard, Finian and Ailbhe are all musical too but they are all doing different things. But my grandchildren Ciaran and Luke are shaping up well. And then people would come to me and ask to teach their children and they came from all over the place to my home and it went on to 1996 and kept teaching in Sligo, although I did not travel much."

Carmel has also worked as a researcher in Ceoláras Coleman in Gurteen, which recalls the late, great Sligo fiddler Michael Coleman. She spoke to various musicians in the 1980s and 1990s and "loved that".

"It was great for the history and I spoke to the late Johnny Giblin, Frank McGee, who was a mighty historian, Séamus Horan, and the Wynnes from Glangevlin. I really enjoyed that."

She added: "I was on the very first Comhaltas tour of Ireland in 1970 along with Ann Mulqueen, who does a great version of Roisin Dubh, Séamus Mac Mathuna and Eamon Coyne, among others. And it was very hard touring in those days as I had a small family. But I love teaching, and some think the whistle is just a toy and pick it up from the notes.

"A lot of what I do is in me and the best way to learn is by ear rather than a book, which is only a guide, and they are not concentrating on the actual music and they are not hearing the music."

"I like to have a student up and running after six months and you will not have a book with you when you are playing on the stage. I have taught in England, Scotland, France, the US, Australia and all over and I love the interaction and the communication with young people.

"Music can be funny at times and can be political, but I tend to stay away from the politics as it would bring you down and of course you are never a prophet in your own home town no matter what you do."

Carmel was excited about her book 'Shamrocks From Geevagh', which was launched in Johnny Mac's Bar on November 30, 2019

"It is to mark 50 years in the business, and I have been composing airs and songs since 1983. I have already brought out the 'Sligo Maid' and it was launched in Earley's of Sligo. It is 64 original compositions including a tribute to my later brother Tom Nangle, who passed away in 2008.

"There are also photographs of that long journey in traditional song and story. There are waltzes, slow airs and laments. I also released 'Cathair Shligigh', a CD of jigs reels and slow airs".

Geevagh is never too far away from Carmel's thoughts.

"We had a famous poet in Geevagh called Michael J Kearns, who was known as the Bard of Geevagh. He was born in 1886 and lived until 1967. He wrote many poems and I have put music to them. There are 40 songs in this book 'Shamrocks From Geevagh' and I have put the melody of the song with it.

"The book is dedicated to all singers, bards, poets, musicians and songwriters from in and around Geevagh. It is a tribute to the place that formed me. Michael wrote 'Shamrocks From Geevagh' and I will be singing some of the songs on the night in Paddy's Bar in Geevagh."

Carmel segues into anecdotes about the ever-cranky Van Morrison and about the late Peter Horan and Fred Finn, who used to play a lot in Ted McGowan's pub in Gurteen.

"We were asked to play at the Eurovision stars in Dublin in 1970. They put a big stage up in the grounds of Trinity College, so Joe Burke, myself, Patsy Hanley and Matt Molloy were asked to play. Van Morrison was there too, and he got up on the stage and he started to sing an Irish song in his own style, which the audience didn't like.

"They booed him off the stage and chanted 'we want Comhaltas'. He was fit to be tied and stormed off the stage, so we had to rush back to do our performance."

"Peter Horan used to play in Gurteen every Tuesday, and he was a lovely singer and a gentleman. Peter and Fred Finn went into Ted McGowan's in Gurteen and they started playing at 5pm in the evening and they played until 5am the next day. And they came out and Fred says to Peter: 'Jasus, there is a great stretch in the evenings.'

"There are very few people in traditional Irish music that I have not played with and Séamus Tansey, Matt Molloy, Joe Burke and Patsy Hanley were really top class."

What does traditional Irish music mean to Carmel?

"It is my life. I probably like it better than life itself. It has been my friend in the bad times. Whenever I am down, all I have to do is play an old tune and it lifts me."

The breath of life... indeed!

CULLEENS CARNIVAL

CO. SLIGO.
SUNDAY, JUNE 2nd TO SUNDAY, JUNE 16th.
(Proceeds in aid of Kilglass Church Building Fund).

THURS., JUNE 6th — Come with the Crowd to hear—
BIG TOM and the Mighty MAINLINERS
DANCING 9 P.M.   ADMISSION 8/-.

FRIDAY, JUNE 7th — CEILI
THE BLACKTHORN CEILI BAND
(Of Radio and Television fame)
DANCING 9 P.M.   ADMISSION 6/-.

SUNDAY, JUNE 9th.
THE BREAKAWAYS SHOWBAND
All the way from Co. Tyrone—Ireland's most versatile young band.
DANCING 9 P.M.   ADMISSION 8/-.

TUES., JUNE 11th—Just returned from England after making his latest record—
THE JACK RUANE SHOWBAND
Come and hear his latest release "Everybody Wants to Go ...to Heaven."...
DANCING 9 P.M.   ADMISSION 8/-.

WEDNESDAY, JUNE 12th.
GRAND VARIETY CONCERT
Including laughable Sketches, Choral Singing by the School Choir, Figure Dancing, Solo Items, etc.
Doors Open 9 p.m.   Admission 4/-; Children Half Price.

THURS., JUNE 13th—Irelands Jackpot of Entertainment—
THE MILLIONAIRES SHOWBAND
Stars of TV. Show "Hoedown," "Showband Show," "Round About Seven," "Go 2 Show," etc.
DANCING 9 P.M.   ADMISSION 8/-.

FRIDAY, JUNE 14th — ANOTHER CEILI NIGHT.
Music to suit all tastes.
THE ASSAROE CEILI BAND
DANCING 9 P.M.   ADMISSION 6/-.

SUNDAY, JUNE 16th—Last BIG SOUND of the Carnival.
THE ALL-STAR CLASSIC SHOWBAND
DANCING 9 P.M.   ADMISSION 8/-.

BUS SERVICE—Bus from Ballina at 8.30 via Bonniconlon, Corballa, Enniscrone, Rathlee, Easkey and Fortland on June 2nd, 3rd, 6th, 9th, 13th and 16th. BUS from Sligo at 8.15 via Ballisodare, Beltra, Skreen, Templeboy and Dromore West on June 2nd, 3rd, 6th, 9th, 13th and 16th. Bus and Dance 10/-.

CULLEENS SUMMER FESTIVAL

FRIDAY, MAY 23rd - JUNE 8th.

FRIDAY, 23rd:
7.30 p.m.: U-13 9-a-side Football. Kilglass v Enniscrone. Ref. M. Gordon. Dancing to: **FRANKIE McBRIDE and the POLKA DOTS.**
1st heat Old Time Waltzing Competition (open and confined).

SATURDAY, 24th:
Minor Football Tournament, sponsored by Ideal Aluminium Windows, 7.30 p.m.:
Enniscrone v Castleconnor.
Dancing to:
PAT ELY and the ROCKY TOPS

SUNDAY, 25th MAY:
2 p.m.: Open Sports for Boys, Girls, Men and Women (Sponsorship by First National Building Society). Kavanagh Cup S.F Tournament, 7.30 p.m.: Enniscrone v Castleconnor. Dancing to: **GERRY and the MERRYBOYS.**

FRIDAY, 30th MAY:
U-13 9-a-side football, 7.30 p.m.: Quigabar v Culleens. Ref. B. Varley. Dancing to: **MARK GEOGHEGAN.**
2nd heat of Old Time Waltzing Competition (Open and confined).

SATURDAY, 31st MAY:
m.: Pony Show and Sales. Sheep Dog Trials.

Minor Football Tournament, 7.30 p.m.: Easkey v Bonniconlon. Ref. Paul Cavanagh. SHOW DANCE: Dancing to: **PHIL MUNNELLY.**

SUNDAY, 1st JUNE:
Car Treasure Hunt at 3 p.m. (Sponsored by Jacobs Service Station). Kavanagh Cup Tournament, 7.30 p.m., Easkey v Bonniconlon. Dancing to: **BREEZY.**

WEDNESDAY, 4th JUNE:
Color/Kosangas Cookery Demonstration at 8 p.m., by Mrs. Eileen Keaney (Home Economics Adviser). Adm. £1 (Proceeds to N.S. Fund). Free Draw.

FRIDAY, 6th JUNE:
U-13 9-a-side Football Final at 7.30 p.m. Dancing to:
MICK WOODS BIG BAND
Final of Waltzing Competitions.

SATURDAY, 7th JUNE:
Minor Football Tournament Final at 7.30 p.m. Dancing to:
HENNIGAN BLOOZE BAND

SUNDAY, 8th JUNE:
Kavanagh Cup Tournament Final, 7.30 p.m. (Winners sponsored by Ulster Bank, Ballina). Dancing to
THE BLUE RIVER BOYS

● GAA President, Dr. Mick Loftus, will present all Cups. Trophies to all prizewinners
● The organising Committee wishes to express thanks to all sponsors of the various events.

THE HILLTOP

It's at the heart of a west Sligo community.
Gerry McLaughlin spoke to Shane Scott about
a new chapter at the Hilltop in Culleens

PUBLISHED ON SEPTEMBER 17, 2020

"THAT WILL BE ALL FOR NOW, folks – your next dance, please." Those were immortal words in the golden days of Irish showbands and they were uttered thousands of times over many years in one of Sligo's most iconic pub and dance halls.

And the Hilltop remains the beating heart of the community under the careful guidance of the Scott family who are well-known in construction and business circles all over Sligo.

The Hilltop in Culleens was west Sligo's greatest ballroom of romance for decades and hundreds of couples met under its storied roof as all the top bands played in this mecca for good music.

And they came in droves to dance to the likes of Big Tom McBride, Margo and Daniel

LEFT: ADVERTISEMENTS FOR EVENTS AT THE HILLTOP IN 1968, ABOVE, AND 1986, BELOW

O'Donnell in the 1960s, 1970s and 1980s when McBride was still the king. Susan McCann, Philomena Begley, Ray Lynam also were among the top artists to play there, and the place was packed to the rafters when it was owned by the legendary Tommy Joe Tuffy, who was in this famous pub for 70 years.

It was also the scene of some great carnivals in the 1960s in a field just across from the premises.

The hand of history is written large on the Hilltop, now owned by the eternally enterprising Liam and Mary Scott, who are about to write a brand-new chapter in its distinguished history.

There has been a pub in this location for over 100 years and the first owners were Gordons. And it is in an ideal location on the main Sligo to Ballina Road.

It is also the place where Daniel O'Donnell and Margo got their first gigs and they came from all over Sligo and Mayo to jive the night away.

But the Hilltop has been much more than a pub, as for generations it has been the beating heart of Culleens with its shop, petrol station and post office added on. It catered for the area's every need.

Next month the Scott family will open a major new extension to the premises, which will put life back into that lovely part of west Sligo.

Shane Scott was up to his neck in construction work when he spoke to the *Sligo Weekender* about plans for the new-look Hilltop to be opened next month.

He said: "There is a great sense of history here and the Hilltop was part of the big band scene back in its day. There was a major event here called the Culleens Carnival in the 1960s and 1970s which was held here every year. This was a huge part of the cultural life of the area.

"They came in scores from all over Sligo and parts of Mayo and there was a big marquee put up across the road. All the top bands came here and it was a mighty time."

He added: "The dance hall itself was the first place to play host to Margo and Daniel O'Donnell and that gives you an indication of just how popular it was and just how important it was all over Sligo and in and around Ballina as we are only a few miles from the Mayo border."

"In those years Tommy Joe Tuffy ran the place and he was in the place for 70 years. He was down today to take a look at the shop to see how we were getting on with the big renovations and he is a great character and so much part of the history of this special place."

"There has been a pub on this site for 111 years and it began in 1909 when it was Gordon's and it was a small cottage where the pub started out and the licence has been there since 1909.

Shane's family took over the business in 1998 and he was only 10 when the family moved up from Dromore West.

"We re-created some of those big nights when we came here first and we had Richie Kavanagh, T R Dallas and Séamus Moore, who was very popular. We have also hosted a few big bike rallies and we have the space on the forecourt to cater for them.

"The largest one was in 2007 when we had over 700 bikes which was quite a sight and the place was full of exotic-looking characters in black leather and wearing some cool shades. They came from all over Ireland and it was one of the biking clubs that organised it and we organised food to be brought in for them, which was quite an undertaking as you can imagine.

"There were big bands playing in the lounge at that time too and there was always a great tradition of music. We carried on the music for as long as we could, and we used to hold social dancing as well.

"This has always been a great community focal point and we had Easkey Community Bingo here every Friday night while they were getting their community centre built."

He continued: "We held a lot of fundraisers for the community, for national schools, football clubs and we also hosted some great 21st birthday parties which were very memorable, and we had the space for parking as well. It is in an ideal location and we get people coming from Ballina.

"We are at the heart of the community and when I am trying to explain Culleens to people, our place is kind of the village, the shop, the pub, the petrol station and the postal agency too".

But it is not just people in the locality that are attracted to the Hilltop.

These days it is all go as the Scott family are putting the final touches to a major redevelopment and it is handy that Shane's dad Liam Scott is a very well-known contractor and his mother Mary has great business acumen.

So it is only natural that Shane is a business consultant in England, but these days his and his family's firm focus is getting the new Hilltop off the ground.

"We intend to open in October. It is a brand new building with a brand new forecourt with 24-hour HGV fuel services as well as the usual fuel services. We will have a supermarket, an off-licence and a full deli area as well. We will keep the post office agency and these days we are getting there, and it is all go, and the floors are being tiled as we speak.

"My dad Liam is a contractor and it has been a real family effort. My mum Mary has been running the shop and the pub here for the past 20 years, so they are a very good team.

"It is a great advantage to have that background at home and we have been in the community for long enough now to know what is really needed."

It is a brave move to take in these Covid-19 times, but all the Scotts are very positive people.

"The bar is still there but the dance hall is knocked, and we will be opening the pub again as soon as the government lets us. It is hard to know what way it will go. The supermarket is going to be a big convenience store and we will have an off-licence."

Shane said he was delighted with the response of the community to the family venture: "Yes, there is a lot of excitement in the area and they are a proud people here and proud of their native place and are glad that Culleens will have this new place of their own. They are saying they can't wait until it is opened. At present the local area is under served for larger vehicles to pull in, but we will have vastly increased space for these big trucks to pull in and the 24-hour service will be of great benefit to the lorry drivers. There is no place really from Ballina to Sligo to properly pull in a truck and we are confident that we can cater for this need.

"And the deli is very important, and we will have breakfast, dinners and all sorts of food services."

This is undoubtedly a very brave venture in these uncertain times but they say that fortune favours the brave. And the Scott family certainly don't lack courage or business nous.

Shane said: "It is something that mum and dad have wanted to do for quite some time and they had momentum even before Covid-19 hit

THE HILLTOP

and they have got that momentum and drive still and we are all working hard with them to make sure that it will be a success."

On another level, Shane said it would be lovely to hear some people speak of their memories of the Hilltop in the era of big bands and carnivals.

"It would be great to hear other people's memories of the way they were, and I would like to record those stories. It would be great to capture some of those stories. I intend to get in touch with those people because their memories are priceless, and it would be a great social history as well.

"A few people have already contacted us about their memories on Facebook and that is an exciting project as well."

So the legend of the Hilltop lives on in the Scott family, who are writing yet another chapter in its famed story.

TOMMY KILCOYNE

Tommy Kilcoyne is a GAA legend – just like his father Tom before him. He talked to Gerry McLaughlin about his father and about his own remarkable time on Sligo's County Board

PUBLISHED ON AUGUST 13, 2020

IN THE NAME OF THE FATHER: long-serving Sligo GAA County Board secretary Tommy Kilcoyne from Achonry is part of a unique GAA double act that went on for 83 years.

His late father Tom Kilcoyne held the post for 45 years and was also County Board treasurer in the same period. It is a record that is unparalleled in the history of the GAA, and a testament to these men's love for the association.

Tom Kilcoyne was in office from 1924 to 1968, while his son Tommy took over in 1970 and retired in 2007 after 38 years at the helm. During that time, he saw his beloved Sligo win Connacht Senior Championship

LEFT: TOMMY KILCOYNE

titles in 1975 and in his final year in 2007, which was the perfect send off for this soft-spoken gentleman who is always measured, balanced, courteous and learned, and is always able to see both sides of an argument.

Tommy also has an encyclopaedic mind and a forensic memory on all matters GAA.

To survive in the GAA you need backbone, and Tommy Kilcoyne has that also, as well as great diplomatic skills. That is stitched in his DNA from his father Tom, who fostered a deep love for the GAA in Tommy, who was then perfectly qualified to take over as County Board secretary in 1970.

And his family are real Sligo GAA blue bloods. His father Tom taught in a local national school and once travelled to New York for the famous 1947 Polo Grounds All-Ireland final between Kerry and Cavan – he was an umpire on that momentous day when Cavan triumphed.

Tommy's uncle Mick Kilcoyne was a noted Gaelic footballer in his day. Kilcoyne Park in Tubbercurry, which was opened in 1964, is named after him. Mick's grandson Brendan Kilcoyne captained Sligo in the 1997 Connacht final, where they were only beaten by a point by Mayo.

Tommy is rightly proud that he was in office when Sligo took those Connacht titles and he was also a member of the backroom of the Irish Compromise Rules team in 2006 and 2008.

But his involvement with the GAA did not end in 2007 as he became Sligo GAA's Central Council delegate from 2010 to 2016 and played a key part in overcoming a choppy start for the outstanding development of the Centre of Excellence in Scarden.

It is now a facility that is the envy of many counties and former Sligo GAA County Board chairman John Murphy from Tubbercurry was a driving force in getting the project started.

Tommy has been president of Sligo GAA since 2016.

But he is not a man who is naturally comfortable talking about himself, preferring to reference his late father and others.

He was also editor the highly successful Sligo 125 book published in 2009 which covered the 25 years after John McTiernan's GAA history, published in 1984.

This is a priceless record of matches, results and interesting snippets about Sligo GAA and will be a real bible in years to come.

Tommy was also involved with the establishment and development of Cummann na mBunscoil, which has been a major boost to the GAA in Sligo.

Listening to his quiet eloquence, the history of the GAA in Sligo unfolds in front of your eyes, from the cloth-capped era from the 1920s to the 1950s to the modern era of multi-coloured football boots, loads of hydration and social media.

Tommy and his father Tom are a huge part of that history and Tommy could certainly write a great book on the story of Sligo GAA and the Kilcoyne family.

He said: "My uncle Mick Kilcoyne and was one of Sligo's most prominent footballers in the 1920s and he was on the Sligo team that won the 1928 Connacht title. He was also a noted athlete, won a Sigerson Cup medal with UCD and he died at a relatively young age in 1963. He was actually 63 that year – he was born in 1900.

"The pitch in Tubbercurry is named after my uncle Michael. His son Fr Paddy Kilcoyne died a few weeks ago –he was a priest of the Achonry diocese. He had played on the Sligo team on the day the pitch was opened in memory of his father Mick in 1964.

"Luke and Mickey were also sons of Mick and they also played for Sligo. Brendan Kilcoyne is Mick's grandson and he captained Sligo in the 1997 Connacht final and they lost by just one point to Mayo and they were a very young team and Mayo went to the All-Ireland final."

Meanwhile, Tom Kilcoyne Senior was principal of a national school in Achonry for many years and had been a student in St Pat's in Drumcondra in 1918 when the Spanish flu hit.

Tommy said: "He actually contracted it but thankfully recovered. Sadly some of his friends did not survive it. My father was only 21 but his hair turned white after the illness. He taught in different schools in this parish – in Carrowrile and in Carniara – and then he became principal of Achonry School in 1928 and he was there until he retired in 1965.

"The Kilcoyne family were always interested in the GAA much more than politics and my father had a great grá for the GAA. He and my mother Kathleen, née Carney, instilled a great love for the GAA in me."

Tommy was born in 1945 and his earliest memories are of going to matches with his father, who was also secretary of the Connacht GAA Council.

Tommy said: "He was Connacht Council secretary from 1934 until his death, which occurred in 1968."

That was a tremendously exciting period in Connacht football as in the 35 years that he was secretary, teams from this province won 11 All-Ireland titles.

Tommy said: "Galway won six, Mayo won three and Roscommon won two. Those were the halcyon days of Connacht football as you had Seán Purcell in Galway, Packie McGarty in Leitrim, Nace O'Dowd in Sligo, Gerry O'Malley in Leitrim, while Mayo had Tom Langan and Pauric Carney.

"In the last 50 years since 1970 only two titles have come west and both were won by Galway. I went to many of those Connacht finals with my dad as a child in the 1950s and early 1960s. Tuam Stadium was like Croke Park in those days. I remember an National Football League game between Sligo and Offaly in the 1950s at O'Connor's Field in Tubbercurry."

Elsewhere, 1958 was a wonderful year for Tommy's home club Mullinabreena as they won their first and only Sligo county title by beating Sooey in the final on a score of 1-12 to 1-8 in Corran Park, Ballymote.

They were captained by the legendary Nace O'Dowd. Tommy was in his 13th year and was at that final.

He said: "That was a wonderful win for Mullinbreena and Padraig Gorman, who went on to be Sligo GAA County Board chairman, was on that team and quite a number of them are still alive. It was a huge thing and it remains the only county title the club has won, and it certainly inspired me.

Tommy then recounted those players from that great side that are still alive: Liam Marren, Jerry McManus, Eamon McGuinness, Padraig Gorman, Peter Gallagher, Pauric Gallagher, Tom Johnston, Harry McGowan.

Twelve years later, in 1970, Mullinabreena reached another county final and Tommy played at left-half forward, but they were beaten by the Mickey Kearins-inspired St Patrick's.

"Mickey Kearins was the star of that side that beat us," he recalled.

Meanwhile, from an early age Tommy was helping his father Tom with a huge amount of correspondence that had to be dealt with on a daily basis, long before faxes or emails.

Tommy said: "I did a lot of that in my early days. It was nearly all by post and there was only a limited amount of phone activity. It is remarkable the way the GAA was able to run at that particular time – there were very few full-time officials and it was all done on a voluntary basis. Even up in Croke Park there were only three people for a considerable number of years. And there was 80,000 at the Down and Offaly All-Ireland final in 1961.

"I did a lot of the correspondence for my father as did other members of my family. As well as being secretary, my father was also treasurer of Sligo

TOMMY JNR, TOMMY AND GERALDINE KILCOYNE IN 2015

County Board from 1924 up to his death in 1968 and only missed out on one year in the late 1940s when someone else was treasurer.

"He represented Sligo on the Central Council from 1947 to 1968. And he was secretary of the Connacht Colleges Council for many years, so he was a busy man."

Tommy remembers his father as a gentle man who "did not have a temper and was a very pleasant man".

"We have very good memories of a very happy childhood with him. He was also very caring."

Tom Kilcoyne served with quite a number of county chairmen: John A Dockry from Ballymote, Patrick Brennan from Curry, Michael Jennings from Collooney, Jack Brennan from Cloonacool, Joe McMorrow from Sligo, Luke Colleran from Curry and Peter Laffey, an All-Ireland winner with Mayo in 1936 and father of ex-Sligo star Mick Laffey.

Tom Kilcoyne was 71 when he passed away and had been in a number of GAA positions when he died.

Tommy went to Achonry National School, where he was taught by his father, and then to Coláiste Muire, Ballymote.

He then went to UCG (now NUI Galway) from 1963-66 for "three great years", where he got to know the late great Enda Colleran and Pat Donnellan. Martin Newell was also a contemporary as Galway won three All-Ireland Senior titles from 1964 to 1966. Tommy played for UCG in the Galway Senior Championship in the summer and he graduated in Irish, English and economics. He then went to St Patrick's in Drumcondra to train to be a primary school teacher.

Tommy played for Erin's Hope in a Dublin Senior Championship match against a St Vincent's team that included Kevin Heffernan and Jimmy Keaveny. He played along with Mick Gleeson, who went on to win two All-Ireland titles with Kerry, and John Gibbons of Mayo.

Tommy first taught at St Patrick's National School in Nun's Island in Galway before coming back as principal in 1969 in Lisaneena National School just outside Collooney. He was also playing with Mullinabreena.

After his father's death in 1968, Pauric Keane from Tubbercurry was appointed County Board secretary. Tommy was assistant secretary and a year later, in 1970, he was appointed County Board secretary.

He said: "I had an idea of what the job entailed from my father and Joe McMorrow stood down as chairman and Brendan McCauley took over, so it was a bit of a fresh start. Joey Murphy was the new treasurer."

In 1968 Sligo Minors had reached an All-Ireland final and Mullinabreena's Robert Lipsett and John Brennan were on that team. Tommy's brother Francis was a sub on that team and Walter Kivlehan was a selector, to complete a strong Mullinabreena connection.

"We are a small parish, but we have had quite a few well-known figures like Padraig Gorman who went on to be chairman of the County Board and also Connacht Council chairman. Paddy Kearins was a member of the Connacht Council for a number of years as well."

Benny Wilkinson was a member of the Sligo squad that won a long-awaited Connacht Senior title in 1975, and he came on as a sub against Kerry in the All-Ireland semi-final.

When Tommy took over as County Board secretary, the clear objective was to win a Connacht title. They almost did a year later only to lose by a point to Galway in 1971 after a replay, when they had an arguably stronger team than that which triumphed in 1975.

"Sligo had only won one Connacht title in 1928 but had a very good team in the late 1960s, contesting a National Football League semi-final. The 1968 Minor team was coming along and we had a great leader in Mickey Kearins. In 1971 we had a great chance to win a Connacht title with a big, powerful team. That team was stronger than the 1975 team and we had lost a few of them by the time 1975 came along.

"Cathal Cawley, the late Peter James Brennan, who passed away recently, Jimmy Kilgallon, Sean Davey from Ballymote, John Gilmartin from Grange and Jim Colleary from Curry were all gone.

"We drew with Galway in Castlebar, that was the day Mickey Kearins scored 0-13 and we lost the replay and we lost by a point.

"That was very disappointing and there was a feeling that the chance had gone, but young players like Robert Lipsett, John Brennan, Tommy Cummins and James Kearins blended well with the older players."

Off the field, Tommy's first major engagement was the emotional 1971 GAA Congress in Belfast, where GAA president Pat Fanning showed great courage and leadership by ending the ban on GAA members playing or attending foreign games.

Bearing in mind the location of Congress with the Troubles in full flight, this could have been a very divisive issue had it gone to a vote.

But there had been soundings taken in every county in Ireland and there was a big move for change, so Fannin simply announced that the ban was no more. And while Tommy felt it was the right decision it was a bit ironic that Sligo, as a County Board, were opposed to the removal of the ban.

Happily, Sligo immediately benefited from this change as it enabled the great David Pugh and Gerry Mitchell to line out for Sligo later that year.

Tommy said: "That was my first Congress in the Whitla Hall in Queen's University and it was very dramatic. Pat Fanning handled the matter very well because he realised that there was a mood for change and that the GAA was moving forward so he didn't allow a divisive vote to take place.

"He just ruled that it could be deleted, and I thought as a young man that he handled it very well. I understood its significance, but it just did not have any place in a progressive organisation like the GAA. Sligo and Antrim had voted to keep the ban, but the mood was for change and we accepted that. We had a tangible benefit in that both David Pugh and Gerry Mitchell of Sligo Rovers later played in the Connacht final of 1971."

But things got better in 1975 and Sligo beat Galway well in the first round in Markievicz Park.

Tommy said: "We played Mayo in Markievicz in the final and it ended in a draw. Sligo then went to Castlebar and had a narrow win over Mayo with goals from Dessie and Mickey Kearins. That was a mighty day and 47 years since the previous win. That was a wonderful team and it would have been heartbreaking if Mickey Kearins had finished his career without winning a Connacht medal, given the huge contribution he had made to Sligo football over many years. He was such an iconic player, and everybody was delighted for the county and for Mickey in particular."

Sligo then ran into the greatest team of all time in Kerry a few short weeks late and lost heavily in the end.

Tommy said: "We competed with them fairly well for the first 40 minutes and John Brennan at full-back was holding the line fairly well. But he was moved outfield and Sligo attacked and it was only then that Kerry got through for their three goals and they won by 17 points eventually."

Playing apart, there were huge developments in clubs getting their own properties with the support of the county board and the Connacht Council.

Tommy said: "A lot of that started in the 1970s and there were really only three really good pitches in the county at the start of the 1970s, Markievicz Park, Kilcoyne Park and Corran Park, Ballymote. Easkey had a fine facility also. But all clubs started work, the economy was fairly good in the 1970s and there was some money around and a lot of clubs got their pitches developed."

A deep recession in the 1980s presented huge challenges for the GAA and Tommy was interviewed by Sligo's Tommie Gorman of RTÉ in an iconic piece from 1986 about the ravages caused by severe emigration. The Easkey club was especially affected by this deep crisis.

"I did that interview with Tommie Gorman and it comes up in 'Reeling In The Years'. Clubs were struggling to field teams because a lot of young men had emigrated. Easkey were badly hit and lost almost 15 players, a whole team, but the Easkey club kept going and is a very vibrant club."

Sligo did struggle in the 1980s although they reached a Connacht final in 1981 spearheaded by the great John Kent from St Mary's.

"Mayo beat us in that final, but the county team was struggling in that decade because the club teams were struggling. It was only into the 1990s that things improved."

St Mary's were head and shoulders above the rest, winning eight county titles in a golden period from 1977 to 1987. And they won three Connacht club titles in 1977, 1980 and 1983.

They were powered by great local talent like John and Jim Kent, Tommy Carroll and Gerry Monaghan, Mick Laffey and Castleconnor's Barnes Murphy, Mayo stars like Eddie MacHale and Mick Barrett, Joey Bird and Donegal native Cathal O'Donnell.

Tommy does not accept that they were a bit like 'The League of Nations' as they attracted so many talented players who came into Sligo.

"St Mary's were and are a great club and are the only Sligo team to have won three Connacht titles. They had loads of leaders and a lot of good players who wanted to play for them. They were an exceptional side indeed. The Kent brothers and Mick Laffey were the backbone of Sligo teams around that time."

In the 1990s, coaching came to the fore and coaching officers were appointed in county boards and in clubs.

"The County Board put a lot of work into development squads and it paid off in 1996 when we had very good Minor teams, a team managed by Leo Boland and they lost after a replay through a late goal to Mayo. Noel McGuire, Dara McGarty, Philip Gallagher, Tommy Brennan John McPartland and captain Sean Davey were all on that team. They went on to form the basis of the county Senior teams in 2002 and 2007."

Around this time, Sligo started to bring in outside managers. PJ Carroll from Cavan came first and got a few promotions for the county, but things really took off under Mickey Moran in 1997 when he led a very young team to a Connacht final.

"During PJ's two years Sligo drew with Galway in the Connacht Senior Championship. Mickey Moran arrived in 1997. He was a brilliant coach and did great work and got on well with the players and they were playing well. We lost narrowly to Mayo in the Connacht final by a point and we were in Division One of the National Football League and we actually managed to beat both Dublin and Kerry which was quite a feat in 1997."

Sligo had a good win over Mayo in Markievicz Park in 2000 but the great Galway team came and beat Sligo fairly heavily and Mickey Moran moved on. Peter Ford came in and brought a bit of extra edge and had the team "playing great football".

2001 was a seminal year for Sligo as they lost narrowly to Mayo in the Connacht Senior Championship and then went to Croke Park for the first time since 1975 and had a great victory over Kildare in the Qualifiers – "a wonderful win", says Tommy.

Sligo built on this and a year later had an exceptional season. They lost the Connacht final narrowly to Galway but stormed back with a brilliant victory in the Qualifiers over Tyrone, a team that won the All-Ireland title the following year.

It got even better against Armagh in the quarter-final as Sligo came back from a six-point deficit, and 14 men, and drew with that year's All-Ireland champions Armagh. Dara McGarty had a half chance of a goal for glory but fisted over the equaliser and it went to a replay in Navan.

These are Tommy's first- hand recollections of that truly special year.

"Sligo went to New York and it was a great bonding exercise. Peter (Ford) re-jigged the team that had lost the Connacht final. He brought in Nigel Clancy, Noel McGuire, David Durkin, Dara McGarty, Kieran Quinn and John McPartland for the Tyrone match.

"That was a very good team and just like Mickey Kearins in 1975, we had a great on-field leader in Eamonn O'Hara. Eamonn was fantastic – his attitude, commitment and the way he could lift the crowd and the team every time he got the ball was just wonderful. I could not speak highly enough about Eamonn.

"We had a very good defence midfield and a powerful attack. Eamonn O'Hara and Paul Durcan were great at midfield. We were trailing by six points and down to 14 men late in the game, but we came back and Dara McGarty got the equaliser at the end. That was one of the great days for Sligo football."

Sligo just came up short in the quarter-final replay in Navan. There were strong claims that Seán Davey was pulled down in the square but the penalty was not given.

"I was in the stand that day and did not have a great view, but I watched it again on video. Looking at it again I think it was penalty and it was a harsh decision not to award the penalty. Eamonn O'Hara and all the lads did everything they could that day, but it was just not to be and Armagh went on to win the All-Ireland final later that year. But that shows the quality that was in that Sligo side."

The following year, things did not happen, and Peter Ford resigned. Tommy Breheny of St Mary's came in as manager for 2007 and he brought a "new dimension to the game".

Tommy said: "His thoroughness and attention to detail were phenomenal, and he was very organized, and he got everybody on board and we still had a great panel of players.

"Again, we went to New York and it brought the team together and came back and beat Roscommon at Hyde Park. That result gave us great hope for the final, which was also in Hyde Park against Galway, who were ironically managed by Peter Ford.

"Eamonn O'Hara's goal with the left foot was one of the greatest goals ever scored in a Connacht final. It was a close finish and Galway had a great chance to level it near the end, but Jarlath Fallon's shot just drifted wide. And I think the photograph of Noel McGuire near the end and the look on his face when he gets the cup says it all about just how important it was for Sligo. It was a wonderful occasion to win. They got great support and it was a tremendous occasion for all of the county.

"I feel very fortunate that I was County Secretary for those two great years 1975 and 2007, which was my last year as secretary. I was delighted to go out on a high note."

Elsewhere, Tommy cites the success of Sligo at secondary schools level as being very important for the development of football in the county.

"Banada Abbey won an All-Ireland in 1992 and St Attracta's won an All-Ireland in 2006 and David Kelly was on that team. And Summerhill College got to an All-Ireland final in 1985 and all of those things helped along the way. The other thing that was very important was the founding of Cumann na mBunscoil which really improved Primary Schools football. And it played a big role in developing the game in the county"

Tommy highlighted the growth and importance of Ladies Gaelic Football.

He said: "My own club, St Nathy's, is probably the most successful club in the county. Noelle Gormley and Angela Doohan, who captained Sligo to an All-Ireland Junior title in 2006, were from this club and they were managed by Paddy Henry from Tourlestrane. Ladies' football has helped the men's game immensely and women are playing an increasingly important role in clubs all over the country.

Meanwhile, Tommy was also involved in the International Rules Series with the Irish team in 2006 and 2008.

He said: "The then GAA president Nickey Brennan appointed me assistant tour manager in those years. Ireland played Australia in Pearse Stadium and in Croke Park in 2006 and the latter turned into a rough and tumble affair. It nearly brought about the end of the series.

"Two years later we went to Australia and it was a great opportunity for me to get to work with the likes of Seán Boylan, who was the team manager. Anthony Tohill, Padraig Joyce Seán Walsh and Eoin Liston were also involved and that is a great personal memory and we had a wonderful time. Seán Cavanagh was captain and we won the series".

"It was a totally different culture and it was very hot, but we got a great welcome from all the Irish people over there. A lot of people came to the games and there was a great atmosphere. We met the Australian ambassador, who was actually a son of ex-GAA president Pat Fanning."

Elsewhere Tommy still had and has a strong role in Sligo GAA as he was Central Council delegate from 2010-2014 and is – in 2020 – president of the County Board. During that time Tommy represented Sligo's interests during an initial choppy start of their excellent facilities at Scarden, on the outskirts of the town.

"That was very interesting as I met with many others from different counties and there was a great camaraderie. The biggest development in Sligo at that time was the Sligo GAA Centre of Excellence at Scarden. That was a wonderful achievement and is a great credit to all concerned.

"While these things are always about money, great credit is due to the then president of the Connacht Council, Lauri Quinn from the Shamrock Gaels club. He was a big help to us.

"John Murphy, the then County Board chairman, also did great work and it is a great facility now. It is also great to see Liam Óg Gormley, our Games Manager, doing such great work around the county.

"In a few years' time, you will see Sligo bouncing back as a major force. We have had very good Minor teams and I am very confident that we will be challenging for Connacht titles in the near future."

Tommy's role was to present Sligo's case for Scarden and he did so with his customary great attention to detail and diplomacy.

"It was a case of putting our case and we always got great support from successive GAA director generals like Liam Mulvihill, Paraic Duffy and Tom Ryan. I have nothing but the best to say for them and we were always pushing an open door. Especially when we had a viable project and a reasonable way of financing it, you were always given a good hearing.

"Scarden is now a base for county teams and it was always difficult in my times to be impinging on clubs to get their pitches for county teams to train especially in wet times of the year. You would hate going in and ruining a pitch whereas we now have three fine pitches in Scarden. It is also located close to where a lot of people are living and almost half the population of the county lives in Sligo town."

After Tommy left Central Council, he was invited to become president of the Sligo GAA County Board in 2016, a life-time honorary appointment which he regards as a "great honour".

He said: "It is great to be following in the footsteps of John Higgins, Paddy Clifford, John Joe Lavin, Dr Tommy Lavin and all those illustrious people who held it before me."

Any even though he is no longer involved as extensively in GAA matters, he has a wise listening ear but stresses that life changes and "things move on and we now have good energetic young people running the GAA in Sligo".

"Things are looking good, but the pandemic has been a complete nightmare for county boards, the way it has developed. And I hope that we will be looking forward to better times next year."

In a literary sphere Tommy was editor of a valuable book which celebrated 125 years of the association in the county back in 2009.

"John McTiernan edited a history of the GAA in our centenary year in 1984, a great piece of work and it was compiled by Christina Murphy, Seán Denson, Seán McGoldrick and John McTiernan, who edited it. So when the 125 came up 25 years later in 2009 I was asked by the county board to update the history and add in the extra 25 years. I edited it and I had great help from John McTiernan, Rory O'Beirne, Jonathan Davey and Gerry O'Connor. I am happy with the way it turned out and it got good reviews and there is a great record of games played in times gone past – Jonathan Davey played a key role in this respect."

Tommy is still involved in his own club and has no wish to go back as a county board delegate as he has done his time.

"My family is very important to me and I still have a big interest in the GAA. I taught in and was principal in Ballinacarrow from 1971 to 2007 which was in the parish of Collooney. I retired from the county board and the teaching at the same time."

So what does the GAA mean to Tommy?

He said: "The love of the GAA was passed on to me by my parents, particularly my father. I am always aware of the important contribution it makes to society in Ireland and especially in every parish. And that was emphasised even more this year by the work the clubs did all over the country to help older people and vulnerable people in their areas when the lockdown came.

"That was very obvious here in my own area in Achonry-Mullinabreena where the club made a very big effort to help out everybody. I think that's the main thing about the GAA. It is in the community, of the community and it helps the community and it gives us great entertainment. A summer without the GAA to me seems very bare really."

But he sounds a note of caution when asked if he has been at any of the resumed matches. "No, I have not been at any matches yet. I would be very careful of what matches I would go to. I think we all need to be careful and the fact that this pandemic has gone from New Zealand to Sligo to San

Francisco to Brazil in less than a month or two makes us all very wary of it. I am being very careful at the moment.

"My hopes for Sligo GAA are that all the work that is going on will pay off and we will be contesting Connacht finals in the very near future with a realistic chance of success".

"I know we are up against two giants in this province in Galway and Mayo and we would have won a lot more but for that fact. We have always competed well, and I have no doubt but that we will continue to compete well."

One thing is certain. Sligo was lucky to have such a wise, eloquent and genuine leader over many years.

But Tommy was just following in the footsteps of his father and the whole of Sligo GAA should be grateful for the remarkable contribution of this exceptional family.

TOM KILCOYNE